THE GLOBALIZATION OF SURVEILLANCE

ONE WEEK LOAN

THE GLOBALIZATION OF SURVEILLANCE

THE ORIGIN OF THE SECURITARIAN ORDER

ARMAND MATTELART

Translated by Susan Gruenheck Taponier
and James A. Cohen

polity

First published in French as *La globalisation de la surveillance* © Editions La Découverte, Paris, France, 2007.

This English edition © Polity Press, 2010

Polity Press
65 Bridge Street
Cambridge CB2 1UR, UK

Polity Press
350 Main Street
Malden, MA 02148, USA

Ouvrage publié avec le concours du Ministère français de la culture – Centre national du livre

Published with the assistance of the French Ministry of Culture – National Centre for the Book

ISBN-13: 978-0-7456-4510-0
ISBN-13: 978-0-7456-4511-7(pb)

A catalogue record for this book is available from the British Library.

Typeset in 10.5 on 12 pt Sabon
by Servis Filmsetting Ltd, Stockport, Cheshire
Printed and bound by MPG Books Group, UK

The publisher has used its best endeavours to ensure that the URLs for external websites referred to in this book are correct and active at the time of going to press. However, the publisher has no responsibility for the websites and can make no guarantee that a site will remain live or that the content is or will remain appropriate.

Every effort has been made to trace all copyright holders, but if any have been inadvertently overlooked the publishers will be pleased to include any necessary credits in any subsequent reprint or edition.

For further information on Polity, visit our website: www.politybooks.com.

CONTENTS

INTRODUCTION

Since September 11, 2001, the increase in measures of exception adopted by democratic governments in the 'global war on terror' has been accompanied by growing interference from systems of surveillance in the everyday lives of their citizens. Mounting security concerns have met with a mounting technological response. In a situation of escalating military and police repression, one must not forget that the tensions between security and freedom, secrecy and transparency, constraint and consent, and subjection and resistance are part of a less easily discernible, long-term trend. In other words, the fragile balance between the exception and the rule has its own history. Each policy of exception has been added on to previously existing measures and doctrines to form a legacy that has obstinately remained in place. From total wars to colonial or neo-colonial expeditions, low-intensity conflicts and the quelling of riots and popular uprisings by the established authorities – all these destabilizations of apparent democratic tranquillity have ended by diminishing the protection of fundamental liberties. It has taken the temerity of rebellious individuals and groups to resist this process.

Every break with the rule of law has been accompanied by a brutalization of democracy and a regression of the values underpinning it. In the face of great 'evil', there are no limits to the extraordinary means used to stop it. In every instance, the logic of suspicion has reaped immediate dividends from fear and left a lasting punitive stamp on 'normal' procedure. All these abuses of authority for reasons of state provide an extraordinary means of analysing the darker aspects of democratic societies. Their recurrence over time makes it all the more relevant to adopt an historical view so that we can understand and think critically about current events. A perspective informed

1

by history also offers a new way of seeing the inextricable ties that have gradually developed between states of emergency or exception, surveillance and security, crises and the means of social control, with special emphasis on the means for influencing opinion. For exceptions go hand in hand with persuasion, dissuasion, campaigns and propaganda. Controlling and registering bodies implies 'control over hearts and minds' and 'wills', to use the terminology forged by experts in psychological warfare. This categorical imperative is one of the common themes running through all of our analyses and thinking in these pages

This book opens at the end of the nineteenth century, when the first plans were made to extend fingerprinting as a method of forgery-proof identification to society as a whole and mass movements were stigmatized by crowd psychology. It ends in the age of global information technology networks, with the rise of a worldwide identification and tracking system that is transforming citizens into socio-political suspects as well as individualized targets of the market and business order.

In this genealogy, three questions are intertwined. First, alongside regimes of emergency or exception, how have concepts and doctrines been forged in order to 'put security into action' or, using the preferred expression of moral statistics with its actuarial techniques, to 'ensure' social order 'against disruptive forces'? The purpose of such concepts and doctrines is to designate the profile of an enemy, whether supposed or real, domestic or foreign, transnational, total or global; the born criminal or modern savage, the crowd, the insurgent, the subversive, the protester, the foreigner, the terrorist. All these highly elastic categories draw their performative force from the vagueness surrounding their definition. Second, how were socio-technical systems introduced, which enlarged the scope of techniques derived from the police and the military to exercise inquisitorial power over individual and collective freedoms? Finally, from which geopolitical centres, via what networks and channels, and through what struggles has the internationalization of practices and doctrines of so-called national security come about, under the cover of defending democracy?

Failing or refusing to have one's personal data recorded is the crime today. The tracking grid now provides meaning on a planetary scale, even though it takes on the contours of each particular reality. Many other great fears besides those engendered by manifestations of extreme political violence are eliciting inquisitorial gazes and producing scapegoats as a consequence. Powerless to combine aspirations for freedom with the aspiration for security, the heads of the world-system network resort to strong-armed management of inequalities instead of declaring war on the mechanisms that reproduce them and reconstructing damaged systems of solidarity. These realities are intelligible only when examined in relation to the combined effects of unbridled capitalism's project to control every facet of life and the revolts this project stirs up against itself.

Part I

Disciplining/Managing

— 1 —

SURVEILLANCE: DELINQUENCY AS A POLITICAL OBSERVATORY

What is surveillance? It is 'a new mode of obtaining power of mind over mind, in a quantity hitherto without example,' replied Jeremy Bentham (1748–1832) in a book entitled *Panopticon*, published in London in 1791, which the French revolutionary National Assembly hastened to publish that same year in Paris.[1] The English philosopher, the founder of legal utilitarianism and author of several penitentiary reform Bills, formalized the concept of the panopticon in developing his pragmatic theory of criminal law as the right to punish. A panopticon is an architectural device featuring a central point – a tower – that gives the prison warden a full view of the entire circle of the building's honeycomb structure, whereas those under surveillance, who are housed in separate, individual cells, are seen without seeing the person who observes them. This mode of spatial organization underlay an overall project for society, a sort of utopia. Moreover, Bentham thought that this ideal model was 'applicable to any sort of establishment, in which persons of any description are to be kept under inspection; and in particular to penitentiary-houses, prisons, houses of industry, work-houses, poor-houses, lazarettos, manufactories, hospitals, mad-houses, and schools'. 'Morals reformed – health preserved – industry invigorated – instruction diffused – public burdens lightened – economy seated, as it were, upon a rock – the Gordian knot of the poor-law not cut, but untied – all by a simple idea in Architecture!' he argues from the outset in his book. He claimed it was less costly for the state, insofar as it required fewer wardens and those that were indispensable could be hired under contract management. In fact, none of Bentham's projects were to come into being – at least not as he had imagined.[2]

The genesis of the surveillance society was brought to light by

7

Michel Foucault in 1975 in his book *Surveiller et punir. Naissance de la prison*, translated into English under the title *Discipline and Punish: The Birth of the Prison*. The panopticon, he said, constituted the paradigm of disciplinary society, the 'deep, solid substratum that continues to exert its power over society today'.[3] Earlier society, under the sign of sovereignty, exercised its authority within the boundaries of a territory. Discipline, on the other hand, is exercised over the bodies of individuals with their complicity, since those who are subject to it are 'caught in a situation of power which they themselves support'. They are just one of the gears in the disciplinary machine. The technological unleashing of the productivity of power, which internalizes social norms within the individual, was prepared behind the scenes starting in the seventeenth and eighteenth centuries. Norbert Elias demonstrates this process by tracing the evolution of 'the civilizing process of Western civilization', beginning not with prisons but with changes in sexual behaviour, table manners and violence. The 'ebb and flow of outer and inner constraints' gradually resulted in 'reinforcing dependence and constraint which regulate and fix affective life through a form of self-control, in short by self-restraint'.[4] Rationalization, he writes, 'is only one of the aspects of a transformation encompassing the whole psychic economy of man, the control of drives no less than the control of the Ego and the Super-ego'. The driving force behind the transformation of psychic self-restraint is none 'other than the set of interdependent constraints, of groupings of human interrelations, of the social fabric, with changes always working in a definite direction'.[5]

Surveillance – security: two concepts, one society

From the panoptic vision centred on surveillance as taming the body in order to educate the soul, Foucault shifts to another paradigm, 'biopolitics' and its project for a 'security society'.[6] This project coincided with that of liberalism, a doctrine based on the work of Adam Smith, an upholder of the Scottish Enlightenment, and François Quesnay, the leader of the Physiocrat School, in the second half of the eighteenth century. Smith developed a theory of the market as the mainspring of a future 'universal mercantile Republic', while Quesnay contributed a theory of *laisser faire, laisser passer* within the context of enlightened despotism. Along with the project for a liberal society, there appeared a new art of governing, a new governmental rationality that took into account the masses, the human

8

species, the multiplicity, the 'public', in other words, the 'population viewed from the standpoint of its opinions, its ways of doing things, its behaviours, its habits, its fears, its prejudices, its demands, whatever can be affected by education, campaigns or convictions'.[7] Unlike a disciplinary society which exercises its authority over the body, a security society exerts its power over society as a whole, over the 'the lives of human beings' (as opposed to the power of death which characterized the prerogative of the sovereign). A disciplinary society is centripetal; the individual, locked in his cell, who is seen but does not see, is the 'object of information but never the subject of communication', Foucault emphasizes in *Surveiller et punir*. A security society is centrifugal; it opens up; its mode of communication broadens the physical and moral horizon.[8] Indeed, the principle of laissez-faire is perfectly in line with the utopia of a mode of communication of goods, bodies and messages dominated by fluidity and transparency. It is utopian, for the paradox of a security society is that, as technological generations go by, it is destined to liberate the virtual forces of communication flows while ceaselessly restraining their emancipating virtues on the pretext of reasons of state or market requirements. A security society does not erase the disciplinary society; it incorporates it and complements it without eliminating it, such that they are intimately joined together. Each in its own way foments the production of a new knowledge of individuals as targets of an anatomy and economy of the forms of power. Each has its own 'arrangements', a heterogeneous set of mechanisms that naturalize it: discourses, institutions, architectures, techniques, regulatory decisions, laws and administrative measures, scientific statements as well as philosophical, moral and philanthropic propositions.

The history of industrial society can be seen as alternating and combining these two forms or models of social organization. A disciplinary society inspires biotypes. It leads to classification, distinguishing the species of 'criminal or delinquent bodies' from other human beings. It thereby creates a *Genera sceleratorum*, just as the naturalists ordered and classified plant and animal species by finding the principle of a *Systema naturae* or *Genera planetarium*. A security society, on the other hand, engenders positive knowledge about the reorganization of the political body. On principle, this knowledge does the exact opposite of the 'negative', oppositional philosophy of the 'jurists', 'literati' and 'metaphysicians' who helped undermine the foundations of the Old Regime and overthrow it but were unable to build the foundations of a new one. Indeed, in the first quarter of the nineteenth century, Claude Henri de Saint-Simon, the precursor

9

of positivism, openly opposed this philosophy of intellectual revolt by formulating his plan for the scientific reform of society and the planet. He viewed society and the world as a large organism structured by material and spiritual networks and, above all, managed like a large industry through an alliance between scientists and the 'industrial class' (manufacturers, farmers and merchants) – a sort of forerunner to technocracy. At a 1948 conference chaired by Georges Gurvitch, bringing together historians, philosophers, economists and sociologists to discuss the genesis of technocracy, sociologist Georges Friedmann explained:

> It was through industrialization that technocracy asserted itself and began to express itself through various doctrines. It was not referred to explicitly in Saint-Simon and his followers, but it was there in substance and has been ever since. It is the effort to 'substitute the administration of things for the government of persons'. [. . .] 'Everything for industry, and for it alone'. For Saint-Simon, industry was an idealistic, humanistic category of technocracy. I call it idealistic and humanistic in order to nuance the matter, but it was nevertheless undeniably a form of technocracy. [. . .] By 'things' they meant the means of production, the factories, etc. In their view, Progress lay in things and not in human relationships in the strict sense, although they often used the noble term 'association'. But association itself – the association on which coordinated, creative science depended – was in their minds linked to the organization of industrial matter.[9]

Throughout the nineteenth century, one can see emerging the outlines of the march towards doctrines prefiguring technocracy, in the sense that they insist on organization as the construction of reality in accordance with scientific and technical rationality. These doctrines took mathematics as their model and paved the way to the 'scientization' of the economy as well as the management of the population as a whole.

On the art of biotypes

Taking the body as a clue, phrenology aimed to reveal the isomorphism between somatic shapes and moral predispositions and to deduce personality from bodily measurements and make this object of study a positive science.[10] The initial hypothesis, formulated by the Viennese physiologist of Italian ancestry, Franz Josef Gall (1758–1828), was that human faculties and tendencies are innate and have their seat in the brain. As the cranium is merely a faithful imprint of

10

the outer surface of the brain, Gall asserted, one can use cranioscopy to determine the cerebral functions in general and those of its varied parts in particular. He therefore inspected and palpated skulls, made moulds of them and collected others in the form of dried specimens. He drew up a topography of their protuberances (bumps or bulges) and hollows. He performed dissections, removed organs and carried out autopsies on brains. He retraced the biographies of their owners. Prisons, together with asylums, hospices, orphanages and barracks, supplied him with a natural experimental pool to identify predispositions and inclinations. The fact that he had begun his career in Vienna under the aegis of two high civil servants, one the prefect of police and the other the head of censorship, opened the doors to numerous penitentiaries for him. In 1807, he brought his collection of skulls to Paris, where he settled and taught for twenty years until his death.

From his cranioscopic investigations, Gall deduced the existence of twenty-seven faculties or fundamental organs in human beings, all of them localizable. They included, among others, the propensity for marriage, the propensity for murder, the proprietary feeling, or the propensity for stocking supplies which was associated with a propensity for theft, the organ of the metaphysical mind and of mental depth, the sense of justice and injustice, the protuberance of goodness and of poetry, the faculty of devotion and the innate predisposition to receive revelation, the function of 'firmness, constancy, perseverance, stubbornness', and so on. Gall was convinced that the new discipline he had founded would have repercussions not only for the knowledge of human beings as such but for medical research, morals, education and lawmaking. When the time came for penal reform, his disciples were called upon for their close cooperation.

Prior to phrenology, physiognomony enjoyed success in sophisticated social circles during the second half of the eighteenth century. Johann Kaspar Lavater (1741–1801), a minister from Zurich and a theologian fascinated by the occult, sought to probe, unencumbered by scientific procedures, 'the interiority of the individual though the exterior', the 'soul through the body', the 'content through the surface', the 'invisible through the visible'. This was to be done, in particular, by closely observing faces and listing their shapes and expressions, which he considered to be intangible data. These codifications were to delight writers and artists in the following century. Balzac drew inspiration from them for La Comédie humaine. The inventors of the language of lines, cartoons and story engravings, the ancestors of the comic strip, saw them as a way of capturing a social type in a few lines and features as well as proof of the comic power

11

of pictures. Among them was the Swiss Rodolphe Töpffer, author of his own treatise on physiognomony, published in 1845, in which he argued against Lavater's theses on the 'intangibility' of the face.[11]

Phrenological work ensured the transition from physiognomony to anthropometry. But, as Georges Lanteri-Laura notes in his history of the movement of thought and research on the brain and the skull, the excesses of Gall's poorly grounded and premature prototype project, basing knowledge about the moral human being on the physical human being, meant that 'any attempt to establish a knowledge of man exposed the mind to dangers, among them that of finding itself stymied'.[12] In this initial attempt to develop knowledge of the totality of the human being from a particular part of the body looms the future aim of all 'biotypology'.

Anthropometry: from the measured body to the political body

What the nineteenth century grouped together under the name 'anthropometry' was the product of the first formalizations of demographics or the science of the state of the population and its flows. The approach was invented by the Belgian astronomer and mathematician Adolphe Quételet (1796–1874), an apostle and artisan of the institutionalized use of censuses and national and international statistical systems. His methods of analysing and predicting flows as well as his techniques for measuring the body were part of a knowledge that prefigured a new art of governing and a new type of state. His seminal work appeared in 1835 under the title *Sur l'homme et le développement de ses facultés ou essai de physique sociale*.[13] His earlier research was mainly concerned with the 'laws of births and mortality'. Georges Canguilhem notes that the first attested use of the word 'normalized' in the French language was in 1834: 'Between 1759, the date when the word "normal" first appeared and 1834, the date when the word "normalized" was first used, a normative class appropriated the power to identify the function of social norms with the way they used those norms whose content it determined – a splendid example of ideological illusion.'[14] In other words, it derived the social from the biological, and vice versa. At the epistemological level, the appropriation of the concepts of 'normal' and 'pathological' by projects of social observation indicates the important role played by the medical approach in thinking about the social body. Canguilhem wrote:

'Normal' is the term by which the nineteenth century was to designate the prototype of schools and the state of organic health. [. . .] Both hospital reform and pedagogical reform expressed a demand for rationalization that also appeared in politics, just as it appeared in economics under the effect of the early use of machines in industry and finally resulted in what has since been called 'normalization'.[15]

Oriented by a 'normative intention', the project led the inseparable trilogy of delinquency, police and prison to serve as a political observatory from which to monitor the entire social field. As Foucault pointed out, the first system of police files and reports on individuals in order to locate and identify criminals appeared in France in 1833. In the period from 1830 to 1860, industrial societies showed considerable interest in national and regional studies on crime and the mapping of any phenomena falling outside the norm.[16]

Quételet introduced the idea that only the objectification of society, that is, taking individuals into account *en masse*, united in a whole, could provide a principle of action and give rise to a new type of social bond. By applying probability calculus to social facts, he turned risk technology into a political technology that was first used in the seventeenth century in the area of private insurance (fire, shipping, floods, etc.). Studying the diversity of easily measurable physical traits among large numbers of individuals, he sought a unity underlying these variations, beginning with height. He drew a histogram or chart of the frequencies of these heights broken down into sections. He went on to look at other physical attributes: arms and legs, skulls, weight. From them, he deduced a mathematical law that crystallized the notion of the 'average man': there was, according to Quételet, a central tendency, a 'type', a 'module' relative to which variations can only be explained by an accident, thus verifying the laws of chance. The existence of a mean around which individual measurements can be divided is the sign of regularity embedded in the laws of nature which, in his view, had the validity of a divine norm. This regularity, which held true for physical characteristics, could be extrapolated to moral characteristics. As Alain Desrosières, a historian of statistical reasoning applied to the 'politics of large numbers', notes:

The drawing of connections between these two types of regularities found *en masse* rather than individually, the first pertaining to physical attributes and the second to moral traits, makes it possible to complete the reasoning: moral decisions are manifestations of tendencies randomly distributed around average types, the reunion of which constitutes the moral attributes of the average man, the ideal desired by the Creator and symbol of perfection.[17]

13

From the science of human body measurement, the specialist in moral statistics derived knowledge that was useful for the body politic: a mode of government based on the existence of general laws of probability governing 'social facts'. The average human being was established as a 'pivotal value' of the social system, and the 'perturbing forces' that threatened its stability were identified in relation to it. Quételet listed and mapped court cases, compared them with demographic movements and drew up tables of criminality. He calculated the tendency towards crime or suicide, the greater or lesser probability of crimes being committed according to season, climate, sex, age, region and social group. From this vital accounting, he derived a 'crime budget' to help lawmakers take the measures required to reestablish the equilibrium of the whole.

'The social contract must be converted into an insurance contract and the state into a company for collective savings and mutual insurance.'[18] As each individual contracts a social debt, they bind each other and receive as much as they give. It was in these terms that Émile de Girardin, founder of La Presse (1836), presented probability reasoning as a tool for 'universal politics'. To ensure that each citizen fulfilled his or her obligations of a new type, Girardin – the first to ask advertisers to 'finance the newspaper' and to publish novels in instalments to achieve higher newspaper sales – proposed that all citizens, from birth, would be given an account book or 'life record' which would include their 'individual balance sheet'. It would be a means of tracking to judge the degree of each person's involvement as an individual belonging to a whole. This lifelong identification document would play at once the role of an insurance policy, birth certificate, passport, voter registration card and official family record book.

The projects to construct an 'insurance society' implicitly foreshadow the idea of a welfare state with its system of comprehensive social insurance, which was not to come into being until the end of the nineteenth century, as François Ewald clearly demonstrated in tracing its genealogy in a Foucauldian perspective.[19] They also prefigure the project of structuring international relations through the constitution of a 'great community of nations'. If the principle of mutual security is the foundation of social peace at the national level, the same holds true at the worldwide level since this principle is also seen as serving to ensure the retreat of 'armed peace' and the institutionalization of general and sustainable disarmament.

Legal photography

Girardin's plan for an individual life register was shelved among the forgotten social utopias. Other forms of identification suggested by research on risk technology would come to the fore. In 1871, Quételet published his *Anthropométrie ou mesure des différentes facultés de l'homme*.[20] This treatise on the morphological norms of the individual paved the way for the positive science of individual identification. The junction between the Belgian demographer's theory and its possible practical applications was supplied by Alphonse Bertillon, the artisan of scientific police work. As a magistrate from the crown prosecutor's office explained to participants at the third International Conference on Criminal Anthropology held in Brussels in 1892:

> Quételet was the first to demonstrate that mathematical rules governed the mysterious distribution of dimensions in nature. [. . .] The highly ingenious and eminently useful application of the scientific principles of anthropometry to the search for and reconstruction of the identity of criminals is the work of a French scientist, as modest as he is praiseworthy, Mr. Alphonse Bertillon, the chief of criminal identification at the prefecture of police and son of the regretted professor of demography of l'École d'anthropologie.[21]

It should be noted that the topic of Alphonse Bertillon's first study was 'savage races', a central issue for the school of physical anthropology founded by Paul Broca. Bertillon set up his bureau of identification in 1882, but he had been thinking about it since 1879, when he introduced the practice of doing both full-face and profile (right-side) portraits of delinquents.[22] At the time, many scientists resorted to photography to conduct their experiments. Albert Londe applied it to the insane at Salpêtrière Hospital to record the symptoms of mental illness, while Étienne Jules Marey used it for his experimental subjects in his physiology laboratory, the 'Physiological Station', to record the cadences of human movement, in an early version of animated pictures.

The use of photography to identify prisoners was authorized by the Ministry of the Interior only in 1872. Until then, it had been prohibited even inside prisons on the grounds that such a measure would cause prisoners 'an aggravation of their punishment not provided for by law and further prevent them from resuming good behaviour'. The wave of repression that followed the Paris Commune (1871) signalled a turning point. A circular from the penitentiary administration decreed that 'all civil prisoners', especially individuals sentenced for

15

insurrectional acts, should be photographed. Thousands of prisoners, men and women, were put on file. Bertillon turned this filing process to his advantage by creating a meticulous codification system. The excessive cost and unwieldy technical procedures nevertheless caused him to abandon systematic photography around 1885. According to the manual he wrote for police technicians entitled *Anthropometric Identification. Identification Instructions*, in order to guarantee reliable results, the photographs had to be taken at the same studio, by the same photographers, using the same camera and lighting, and, as far as possible, at the same time in the morning. But, in 1885, he admitted to colleagues attending the second penitentiary conference in Rome: 'Photography is of limited help. One has to be thoroughly familiar with human physiognomy to identify the same subject at different arrests from among many photographs. [. . .] Photography is hardly useful anymore and now serves only as a means of verification.'[23] On the other hand, Bertillon believed in using the 'spoken portrait', a kind of identikit picture he had invented from his investigation on statistical frequencies, consisting of a description of the individual using conventional, abbreviated symbols to facilitate remote transmission.

The method, known as 'bertillonage', later used internationally under that name, was above all the anthropometric description sheet or so-called 'Parisian file', where the measurements of certain parts of the body were recorded. At first there were seven measurements and later eleven: the length and breadth of the head, the bizygomatic diameter (between the cheekbones), the height of the right ear, the length of the left foot, the left middle finger, little finger and elbow; finally, the waist and the height of the subject seated and standing. All these measurements were taken with specially designed callipers. The colorimetry of the iris, using a chart of seven categories detailing the 'degrees of intensity of pigmentation', rounded out the list of measurement operations. The files were centralized at the Ministry of the Interior in two sets, one according to prisoner height and the other to prisoners' names in alphabetical order.

The inventors of physiognomic and phrenological biotypes had some fixed ideas, which were a cause of many blunders, but Bertillon, the inventor of scientific police work, had his share as well. In his major work, *La photographie judiciaire*, he speaks of creating an infallible identification method based on the 'valleys and hills that crisscross the ear' and of incorporating this sign of recognition in the registry of civil status from birth. Bertillon was also a graphology expert, a role he played as a prosecution witness in the Dreyfus trial. He authenticated the forged document that allowed the court to condemn the French captain for high treason.

Fingerprints or the invention of the mathematical ideal of identity

The task of finding the 'absolute, mathematical individual name' to replace the incomplete name received at birth monopolized the time and energy of Juan Vucetich, a twenty-four-year-old émigré to Argentina from the Croatian part of the Austro-Hungarian Empire and head of police statistics in the city of La Plata. In 1891, he experimented with the dactyloscopic system. The Bertillon system had been in operation for some ten years, and Argentina was the first country to have adopted it by decree. The official use of anthropometric identification raised questions about its reliability, however, because the recorded measurements were valid only after the individual was fully grown, which was not the case for dactyloscopy. Individual fingerprint patterns, which are infinite in their variety, never change after birth, a fact of which anatomists were well aware, thanks in particular to the research of Jan Evangelista Purkinje, a Czech, who had succeeded in classifying and categorizing them in 1823. In short, he had discovered the key to their graphic diversity. Yet fingerprints did not emerge as a legal question until the late 1880s, prompted by two essays by Francis Galton appearing between 1889 and 1891 on a method for indexing fingerprints he had developed. They contained an initial analysis and a classification of fingerprints based on a sample provided by J. W. Herschell, a high civil servant in the British administration in Bengal, who had been systematically using natives' thumbprints for some forty years to authenticate public documents. However, Galton's work on the legal aspect of research on fingerprint patterns was just a side interest for him, for he was essentially an anthropologist, though of a very particular sort: he had initiated eugenics in 1860. His writings on 'hereditary genius' made extensive use of Quételet's anthropometric procedures to demonstrate, through correlations, that the aristocracy is the logical fruit of natural selection. He maintained archives on the families of 'eminent men'. Similar investigation on the possibilities for controlling the racial, physical and mental traits of individuals led him to produce the first composite photographs, images of enlarged or shrunken faces, deformed through the arbitrary combination of cranial and facial characteristics. He owes his place in the history of the modernization of the

17

judiciary police to the system of fingerprint classification he invented. He nevertheless failed to solve the problem of filing the infinite number of identification sheets necessary for identifying subjects. His fingerprinting method proved to be so complicated that the British government commission in charge of evaluating it concluded that it was 'fit for a small collection of identification sheets'.[24] Scotland Yard ultimately chose another method.

To systemize fingerprint patterns and build up a genuine *casillero* or filing system, Vucetich created a criminal record office with two cabinets, each comprising 160 compartments, in which to store the prints. To do this, he simplified the classification by reducing the number of fundamental types. In a report on the value of his method to the Minister of Justice, the Paris Academy of Sciences described it as follows:

> The process takes into consideration only four shapes (compared to Galton's forty-one) which are very easy to distinguish, and within each of the fingerprint patterns, six varieties of particular features or characteristic points. The primary division into a series is formed by the patterns of the right hand, the secondary divisions or sections by those of the left hand. The first subdivision in the series is determined by the thumb and the rest by the other fingers in succession, from the index to the little finger. The secondary groups are just as easily formed.

The commission's verdict was final: 'In every country where the Vucetich system has been adopted, it has proved to be superior to the anthropometric method; initially subordinated to it, then used concurrently, it soon supplanted it.'[25] At first, Bertillon was reluctant to admit that the papillary lines of the fingers present sufficient variability to serve as a base for a repertory of hundreds of thousands of cases. While he agreed to incorporate this datum into his own system, he considered it solely as an element of verification of anthropometric measurement, which remained the keystone of his approach to delinquents.

Social defence: security and early biometric identification

Finding a forgery-proof bodily signature was the common goal of the anthropometric and dactyloscopic projects. The aim was to prevent fraud, as in cases where repeat offenders take on another identity or an identical name, which results in sending an innocent person to prison. In addition to the discourse for legal purposes, a further

18

discourse was geared to the public as a whole. From the very first use of biometric techniques for police purposes, the idea arose of extending them to the masses. In 1885, at the International Penitentiary Congress in Rome, the director of prison institutions at the French Ministry of Justice argued in favour of introducing an 'individual card' or 'life certificate' containing personal anthropometric data for all inhabitants. The proposal was reinforced by the argument that such an identification document would guarantee the security of administrative procedures, life insurance policies or banking operations.[26] Seven years later, the participants at the International Criminal Anthropology Congress in Brussels expressed the desire 'to see the system of anthropometric identification adopted and extended to all countries, not only to identify repeat offenders but also to certify individual identity reliably and quickly'.[27] The learned assembly of scientists approved the recommendation unanimously, but none of the proposals were to take effect. For more than a century, the democracies in the industrialized countries refused plans for widespread biometric identification for fear of violating the privacy and rights of citizens. Many went so far as to object to the very principle of the ID card. In France, between 1913 and 1969, only foreigners and migrants were required to yield anthropometric data, in the form of two photographs and prints of all ten fingers.

In contrast, as soon as the criminal identification office was set up in La Plata, Juan Vucetich worked to have the process extended to 'everyone without distinction' in the name of protecting the 'right to identity', which guaranteed respect for the dignity of each and every individual.[28] The application of this principle turned not only Argentina, but also Brazil, Chile, Uruguay, Bolivia, Paraguay and Peru into experimental laboratories for the use of the identity card (*cédula de identidad*) coupled with fingerprints. Paradoxically, the plans to introduce this forerunner of the biometric identity card in the name of respect for individuality were negotiated at large congresses held by regional police authorities, where the construction of a common policing zone was discussed. Resounding speeches were given at these congresses about 'social defence which presupposes an enemy', the emblematic figure of the enemy being the European immigrant – not the one who worked for an honest living but the 'destructive terrorist, more fearsome and savage than the legendary Furies; the blind fanatic; the bold seditionist; the trade-union agitator who generally takes advantage of the worker's innocence and ignorance'.[29] They denounced the 'cohort of highway robbers landing on the freest beaches of beautiful, young, rich America to bring crime to a peak and disturb the order of life'.[30] 'Dactyloscopian prevention' of this 'new plague' went outside the penitentiary walls in order to control this social category. The violent image associated with such agitators in the discourse of 'social defence' was the main argument used to justify extending the measure to society as a whole. Vucetich's disciples persistently repeated that dactyloscopy was a 'mathematical component of the law', a 'component of social peace and freedom' and an 'international bond'. In the face of abundant criticism, they replied: 'Dactyloscopic individuality is not an ignominious label but a safeguard.'[31]

Yet the laws on individual identification carry with them an infamous memory. For the local population in colonial empires and apartheid regimes, the obligation to have an official identification document on one's person at all times or a pass to move about on one's own territory was a 'humiliating badge, a sign of inferior status'. Such a measure, introduced in South Africa at the beginning of the eighteenth century and gradually reinforced during the nineteenth century, gave rise to intense anti-pass campaigns in the twentieth century. These included a demonstration in Pretoria in 1956 instigated by the Federation of South African Women and the action organized four years later by the Pan-African Congress, which ended in tragedy when Albert John Luthuli, the head of the African National Congress (ANC), who received the Nobel Peace Prize that same year, and his companions, burned their passes in public. As a result of this movement, the pass laws were suspended for a few weeks, only to be enforced again with even greater vigour to prevent the black population from migrating to urban areas.[32]

— 2 —

PUNISHING: THE APPREHENDED MULTITUDE

What is 'punishment'? What is the difference between individual crime and crime emanating from 'plebeian violence'? What can be done to repress and prevent it? These questions mobilized a network of criminologists – scientists, forensic experts, magistrates and police officers – who, beginning in the 1880s, periodically met for discussions and debates at international criminal anthropology congresses, for example, in Rome in 1885 and at the 1889 Paris World's Fair.

At the centre of the controversies was the Italian school of criminology which answered the above questions with a project to redefine the foundations of the right to punish. Among the major figures in this movement were Cesare Lombroso, former military doctor and professor of forensic medicine at the University of Turin, and Enrico Ferri, a professor of penal theory at the University of Sienna, a left-wing Member of Parliament and the founder of the journal *Avanti*. They were the originators of the Criminal Anthropology Congress. The title of the review they published suggests the scope of the school's intellectual project: *Archivio di psichiatria, antropologia criminale e scienze penali per servire allo studio dell'Uomo alienato e delinquente*. The question of the connection between 'alienated man' and 'delinquent man' runs through the research of the precursors of psychiatry such as Henry Maudsley in Great Britain and Rudolph Virchow in Germany. Unlike the Italian school, however, none of them used it as the basis for a theory of punishment.

By correlating madness and crime, the *Scuola positiva* raised the question of the negation of free will, for this twofold form of organic degeneration, mental and cerebral, meant the classical theory of responsibility and imputability for crimes was inapplicable. In this new view of crime, the right to punish acquired a positive, scientific

21

foundation. The aim of punishment was not to avenge society – the essence of criminal law and a faint echo of the old 'eye-for-an-eye' approach. Rather, the 'delinquent man' had to be rendered harmless in the name of 'social defence', a principle founded on a Social Darwinist theory according to which law originates in the struggle for existence. Thus, there was nothing absolute about the enforcement of punishment; it became a question of fact. There could be no single, fixed, inflexible and invariable punishment for all individuals guilty of the same crime; punishment must vary according to the danger each type of delinquent represented for society. The sole yardstick was the interest of society. The more 'anti-social' and 'dangerous' the delinquent, the more rigorous the treatment should be. The degree of dangerousness – a fuzzy notion at best – would be determined by a battery of tests and indicators.

More than a century later, in 2008, the controversy over this doctrine of 'social defence' would start up again with renewed vigour when the French government drafted a Bill on 'security detention'. Once again, the same fuzziness surrounded the criteria for 'dangerousness'. Indeed, the law authorizes the detention of criminals sentenced to more than fifteen years in prison once they have completed their sentences, which means that people may be kept in prison, not for crimes they have committed, but for crimes they *might* commit. Such an indefinite extension of imprisonment is contrary to the fundamental principles of a free society since, according to criminal law, people go to prison because they are responsible for their actions, not for what they might do.

Controversies over the biotype of the modern savage

In 1876, the Italian school of criminology published its seminal work *L'Uomo delinquente* by Lombroso, with the subtitle 'Studied in relation to the disciplines of anthropology, jurisprudence and economics'. To construct the biotype of the 'criminal', it borrowed from phrenology the characterization of the innate penchant for crime as a 'carnivorous instinct' linked to an overdeveloped brain, and the technique of cranioscopic examination. It combined this method with the use of recording devices to measure reactions or different types of sensitivity (to fragrances, metals, obscene photographs, sounds, weapons, etc.). Like Gall, Lombroso recruited most of his subjects for observation in prisons and asylums. He considered these imprisoned delinquents to be representative of all delinquents, both known and unknown, apprehended or not. The photographs used to illustrate his experiments constitute a portrait gallery of the Quasimodos of crime. Their long, asymmetrical faces, projecting jaws, sloping foreheads, pointed heads, prominent eyebrows, wide eyes, prominent cheekbones, average occipital recess, crossed eyes reinforcing a fierce gaze, irregular teeth, detached ears resembling handles, black or brown hair rather than blond and similar 'stigmata of degeneration' in both sexes were said to reveal physical and moral insensitivity, excessive vanity, vengefulness, sensuality and a tendency to frequent 'places of ill repute'. To those who thought they recognized in this portrait of the typical criminal someone they knew – a friend, a colleague or a loved one, Lombroso retorted: 'It should be remembered that it is not the existence of one or two of these traits but indeed the presence of all of them that can reveal criminal tendencies.'[1] Of the hundred criminals he observed, only forty presented all of the characteristics, and yet he claimed that the sixty others were also 'born criminals'. His colleagues thus objected that he had made a disparate set of anatomical, pathological and physiological characteristics and birth defects into 'the famous harlequin known as the typical born criminal'.[2]

Beyond the debates over the comparative biotypes of the 'dishonest man' and the 'honest man', and through the very fluctuations of the author's thinking from one edition and translation to the next, what stands out in Lombroso's investigations is the triangle of criminal-madman-savage. Gabriel Tarde, an examining magistrate who was soon to be put in charge of criminal statistics at the French Ministry of Justice, put his finger on the problem posed by this triple assimilation:

There are two, superimposed theses in your work. The first, which is the former one, assimilated the criminal to the primitive savage and explained crime as an atavism; at that time you rejected the hypothesis of crime as madness. But since then, you say you have yielded to powerful reasons and adopted the latter explanation, without abandoning the earlier one by the way. They alternate in your work and one might say they mutually reinforce each other. However, do they not partially contradict each other? Madness is a fruit of civilization and up to a point develops in line with its progress; it is almost unknown in the illiterate classes, and even less among the tribes of the inferior races. If the criminal is thus a savage, he cannot be mad and if he is mad, he cannot be a savage. Between these two theses you must choose, or if you make a compromise between them by speaking of quasi-madness (but why not also of quasi-atavism?), you should know that you are blunting and mutilating one with the other.[3]

23

Tarde insisted that criminals had no particular stigmata. There were no clear-cut, indisputable anatomical characteristics; there were only organic and physiological predispositions to crime, which develop more or less easily depending on the social milieu. Societies have only the criminals they deserve. Tarde also spoke of 'molecular movement', noting that one should keep in mind the passing states that affect all individuals in the various circumstances of life, for there is an infinite scale between the first stumble and the most atrocious crime. Crime is a sort of polyhedron, which each person views from a particular angle: biological, social, legal or physiological. No doubt the milieu makes the criminal but, like a broth that contains no germs, it is powerless to give rise to crime. Thus, the broth and the germ, the social and the biological sides, are both fundamental aspects of criminality.[4]

L'Uomo deliquente was judged fit for translation into French in 1887, eleven years after its original publication. However, the first French edition was based on the fourth Italian edition, which explains why Lombroso smoothed over certain rough spots. When it crossed the Alps, the title L'Uomo deliquente turned into L'Homme criminel, and the subtitle was changed to 'An anthropological and medical study' before being transformed again later on into 'The born criminal, the moral madman, the epileptic'. By the time of the congress in Rome, the school had already traded its original name of School of Positive Criminology for School of Criminal Anthropology, and the journal had replaced 'psychiatry' in its title with 'criminal anthropology'. The new title, Archivio di anthropologia criminale e scienze penali was taken up by the French criminologists who launched the Archives de l'anthropologie criminelle et des sciences pénales in 1886. The Scuola positiva thus continued to expand under the sign of criminal anthropology. Its upholders were present at the congresses on this scientific discipline, held every four years in major European capitals until the eve of the First World War.

Outside this geographical sphere, they especially marked the Argentine judicial landscape, where theories of 'social defence' were to be adopted and assimilated by the disciples of Juan Vucetich and the police school of the city of Mar del Plata bearing his name. Lombroso's book was translated into Spanish and published in Buenos Aires, Argentina, where the best fingerprint identification system had been invented. It was all the more influential as the Argentine police had made 'the European immigrant' the emblematic figure of anarchism and social disruption, and the works of the Italian criminologist – unlike those of Enrico Ferri – gave particular attention to 'political criminals' and the preventive and repressive systems that the 'science of government' should apply to them. The main objects of study were those categories of individuals who 'take pleasure in satisfying their innate criminal tendencies, or those who, attracted by their own abnormal nature to the most foolhardy innovations, see those who govern them as the cause of all their ills and turn their perverse instincts against them'.[5]

From the born criminal to crimes of the crowd

In 1892, at the third International Congress of Criminal Anthropology, which took place in Brussels, Tarde presented a substantial report in which he examined 'crimes of the crowd'. He began by noting that the problem had been overlooked by criminology:

> In the new as well as the old schools, with very few exceptions, crimi-nologists have been too exclusively concerned with individual crimes and not sufficiently with collective crimes, and are hence deprived of the light that the study of the latter could shed on the true explanation of the former. [. . .] Up to now the criminality referred to as collective has been seen only as a sum total of individual criminalities. To a certain extent, such a viewpoint is admissible when the individuals have acted only in a dispersed fashion, despite ties of association uniting them; it is manifestly false when they have acted in common and *en masse*, driven by impulses they all shared, from which virtual forces emerge that, in isolation, would otherwise remain dormant.[6]

His text should be read in counterpoint to *La Folla delinquente* (*The Delinquent Crowd*), published the previous year by the Italian Scipio Sighele and immediately translated into French. A professor at the Free University of Brussels close to the *Scuola positiva*, Sighele defined himself as a 'psycho-physiologist' while claiming affinity to the 'criminal sociology' of Enrico Ferri, who had the project of developing a 'collective psychology'. Thus, he recommended the study of 'abnormal and transitory relationships among human beings, i.e. meetings, collective events, due to opportunity or chance and which are not stable and organic but rather inorganic and ephemeral, such as theatre audiences, assemblies, crowds, etc'.[7]

Throughout the 1890s, criminal anthropology and the nascent social sciences invested too much energy in studies – and polemics – about crowds as 'non-homogeneous, inorganic aggregates'. Summarizing the change that occurred during those years, Sighele noted in the preface to the second edition of his book:

Despite the opinion of certain individualistic aristocrats, the crowd has gained a degree of power that can no longer be denied. Indeed, at present the most characteristic phenomenon, perhaps the only one that allows us to define our waning century, is the importance that the collectivity has assumed with respect to individuals. In the past, the individual was all-important in politics and in science. Today, the individual is declining in politics before the collective being that is public opinion; in psychological science, before the collective being that is the crowd . . . Group psychology has turned it into a stormy sea, a terrible power that surprises with tempests and its waves that can submerge everything.[8]

What was looming in this discussion of the crowd was a debate over a new being – *society* – endowed with autonomous laws in relation to individuals. The concept of the 'crowd' thus took on key importance in defining the orientations of the human sciences: 'There are mysterious psychic reactions in human collectivities, just as there are unforeseeable chemical reactions in any organism – which is a collectivity of cells. Group psychology should study these strange psychological fermentations which, until now, sociology has not even deigned to honour with so much as a glance.'[9]

The debate that commenced over the multitude in motion revealed the exercise of new forms of democratic expression opened up by the freedoms of the press, association and assembly. It also revealed the fears raised by the sudden emergence of the masses in public life. Finally, it brought into focus the relationship between the much-debated memory of revolts, riots and popular movements and prejudices regarding the 'violence of the plebs' in the course of past and recent history. This was all the more true as the definition of the criminal crowd stood at the intersection of different disciplinary perspectives and political positions, as illustrated by the debate on the 'nature' of multitudes involving Gustave Le Bon, Scipio Sighele and Gabriel Tarde.

Gustave Le Bon: the psychology of crowds and the 'populace'

The version of 'crowd psychology' professed by the psychopathologist physician Gustave Le Bon grew out of an earlier line of research that had led him in the early 1870s to combine the 'criminal question' with the hierarchization of civilizations, classes and the sexes. His studies, based on laboratory experiments, were related to the anatomical and

mathematical research conducted by the school of physical anthropology founded by Paul Broca. This framework, which emphasized
'human races' as an object of study, attracted many military doctors
and administrators serving in the colonial empire. Le Bon measured
the volume of skulls and brains of persons – men and women, adults
and children – belonging to 'superior' and 'inferior' races and classes.
His idea was to demonstrate the unequal distribution of intelligence
and reason. At equal ages, heights and weights, the skull size of men
and women varied according to the degree of civilization.

> The differences, while low in inferior races, become enormous in supe-
> rior races. In this case, women's skulls are often hardly more developed
> than those of women from very inferior races. Whereas the average
> skull size of male Parisians ranks among the largest known skulls, the
> average skull size of female Parisians ranks them among the smallest
> skulls observed, at about the level of Chinese women, and barely above
> female skulls in New Caledonia.[10]

Whence Le Bon's ferocious opposition to immigration (of 'inferior'
categories, naturally): 'The worst disasters on the battlefields are
infinitely less fearsome than such invasions. The instinct of ancient
peoples to fear foreigners offers us very sure lessons.'[11]

Le Bon denounced racial mixture in especially harsh terms. He
viewed it as the reason for the 'frightful decadence' of the Latin
American countries and the domination of the British Empire over
the economy of the continent's southern cone. He made a scathing
attack on the 'invasion' of France by Italian immigrants. It was at
this time that ideological proponents of 'integral nationalism' borrowed from Greek history the term *metic* (*métèque* in French) to
denounce the 'foreigner' as a 'parasite' from which it was necessary
to 'protect the nationals'. It was also the period when xenophobic
campaigns were unleashed against immigrants reputed 'incapable of
being assimilated', which were usually combined with virulent anti-
Semitism. Le Bon was in the anti-Dreyfus camp, by the way, and his
book on the crowd became bedside reading for teachers at the French
War College.[12] Le Bon's notion of the 'soul of the crowd' cannot be
dissociated from that of the 'soul of the race'. Both are characterized
by the inhibition of thought and by exalted emotion. In the case of
the cataleptic subject, 'the crowd', it was conjunctural; in the case of
inferior categories (races but also women and children), it was structural. 'By the mere fact that he is part of a crowd, the human being
thus descends several degrees on the scale of civilization. In isolation,
he may be a cultivated person; in a crowd, he becomes instinctive, and

hence a barbarian.'[13] The crowd resembles 'inferior forms of evolution, such as the savage and the woman'.[14] Under the sway of mutual suggestion and of an agitator transformed into a hypnotist, the crowd turns into an irrational, changeable, impulsive, emotional, irritable, mobile, intolerant, conservative and authoritarian 'being', moving with extreme swiftness from idea to action, led almost exclusively by the unconscious.

Whereas the spectre of the Paris Commune haunted the inventors of scientific police methods, it was the spectre of the events of 1789 that drove crowd psychology, at least as Le Bon conceived it. In his view, the crowd was the product of the triumph of egalitarian illusions that began with the Revolution. His view of the irrationality of crowds was closely related to that of Hippolyte Taine, who stigmatized the 'revolutionary crowd' in his *Origines de la France contemporaine*, published between 1875 and 1893. This thesis, which treated the Revolution with violent anathema, holding it to be the cause of the decline of modern France, can be interpreted as a psycho-historical fresco of the dictatorship of the crowd and the pathology of its leaders. This is one of the reasons why historians of crowd psychology consider Taine to be the real precursor of this movement of thought.[15] For Le Bon, the era of crowds was the apocalyptic horizon on which the future was taking shape. Collective logic, whether ephemeral or not – parliamentary assemblies, trade unions, associations, public meetings – had taken power. The people-as-populace had become sovereign. From the populace to the rabble, crowd psychology was to furnish an endless supply of characterizations of the protagonists of 'social unrest'. As for the press, 'once the director of opinion, it has been forced, like governments, to take a back seat to crowds'.

Scipio Sighele was undoubtedly the thinker who did the most to apply the postulates of crowd psychology to examining the role of the press in producing criminals. Nevertheless, he was not living in conservative nostalgia. Unlike Gustave Le Bon, he accepted as a given the advent of multitudes, but he called on journalists and writers to act responsibly, since he was convinced that the press had a criminogenic effect. Starting in 1892, with the first edition of *La Folla delinquente*, he maintained that the press was 'the form of suggestion in which all the others are concentrated'. It gave rise to 'certain impulses and certain violent, criminal, senseless acts that no human force can moderate'. He ceaselessly repeated that behind every readership, there were 'journalists that influence it by suggestion and provoke it, just as behind every crowd there is always a sect that is almost its leaven'.[16]

For the journalist 'is nothing more than an agitator of his readership; created by it, he can lead it well beyond the point he himself wanted to go'. He was particularly harsh on news reportage of criminal trials.

Sighele transposed this same interpretation on to literature. He evaluated the effects of the 'incendiary power' of certain novels, plays and phrases 'on the dry straw that is the reading public, especially the modern public, so nervous and excitable'.[17] In the works of writer Gabriele D'Annunzio, he hunted down the 'degenerates' (the neurasthenic assassin, the child-murderer, the incestuous brother, the madwoman, etc.). In Zola, he ferreted out 'the prostitutes and alcoholics of the worst *faubourgs* of Paris; the cynical wealthy classes; the lively, quivering crowds of workers, soldiers and mystics – crowds that were different in composition and goals but which all acted out the frightfully obscure problem of the collective soul'. In Eugène Sue's *Mystères de Paris*, which he saw as a direct precursor of Italian criminal anthropology, he tracked down 'the other barbarians, as remote from our civilization as the savage populations described by Fenimore Cooper: delinquents'. Above all, he lamented the fact that the writers at the turn of the century 'present a diagnosis but propose no cure', even though the modern world sorely needed one, for it was 'unquestionably sick and degenerate'.

Gabriel Tarde: modernity and public opinion

Gabriel Tarde, for his part, refuted the postulates of crowd psychology on the basis of his project for an 'inter-psychology' or 'inter-mental psychology' hinging on what he called the laws of imitation. He presented these laws in 1890 in an eponymous book that made him known to a wider audience than the one to which he was accustomed through his writings on criminology, law and criminal philosophy.[18] Once again, his report on 'crimes of the crowd' is essential to understanding his overall approach:

> How does a crowd form? By virtue of what miracle do so many people, previously dispersed and indifferent to each other, find themselves in solidarity, aggregated into a magnetic chain, shouting in unison, running together and acting in concert? By virtue of sympathy, the source of imitation and the vital principle of social bodies. A handful of leaders awakens this slumbering power and directs it to a determinate point. However, for this initial impulse to be followed up and for the embryonic crowd to swell quickly, some prior work, basically quite similar in nature, must take place beforehand in people's brains.

> A slow contagion from one mind to the next, a calm, silent imitation, has always preceded and prepared these rapid contagions, these noisy, rousing imitations that characterize popular movements . . . A common faith, a common passion, a common goal; thanks to the twofold contagion involved, this is the vital energy of this animated being we call a crowd.[19]

From the Hundred Years War to the French Revolution, including the *Fronde* and the *enragés*, there is a family resemblance in the expressions of riots and revolts in history:

> Rashes, all essentially the same, breaking out from the same fever – a moral epidemic, sometimes salutary, sometimes disastrous, which consists in the conversion of an entire people over an entire continent to a new religion, a new political dogma, and which imprints on all the churches of a common religion, and all the clubs of a single party . . . a fundamentally identical character in spite of their superficial diversity.[20]

The magistrate's lapidary judgment was unequivocal: 'No matter what the goal, even a noble and legitimate one, that stirs up a crowd, its formation is always, in a significant way, a genuine regression on the scale of social evolution.'[21]

These analyses infuriated many of Tarde's foreign colleagues who attended the criminal anthropology congress in Brussels where he presented his text. They reproached him for giving the impression that 'association turns men into riff-raff'. As Professor Moritz Benedikt of the University of Vienna pointed out, 'to understand the psychology of revolutions and revolts, one must consider this: what breaks out on those occasions is not merely a momentary emotion but an accumulation, a real capital of hate and passion for which the milieu is generally just as responsible as the rebels.'[22] Tarde replied:

> I have been accused of showing only the ugly side of the crowd; I am sensitive to this critique and I readily acknowledge that my report goes too far in this respect. I would complete my thinking by saying that the crowd, when it is stirred up by a generous idea, sometimes becomes not inferior but superior in nobility of collective soul and intrepidity, though not, I would say, in reason or intelligence [. . .] I distrust unanimity, for, while in union there is strength, in unison there is no harmony.[23]

As a matter of principle, the creator of inter-psychology denied the sudden ruptures that appear in the history of 'human inventions', of which imitation is one of the motivating factors.

In 1901, Tarde, who in the meantime had been appointed to the prestigious Collège de France, returned to the question of the crowd in his book *L'Opinion et la foule*. He reiterated that he did not believe in the crowd, because its future lay in the past. The future would be made neither by crowds nor by classes, for:

> class struggle which comes into being and gathers strength during crisis periods engenders class spirit, the broadened modern form of clan spirit: and wherever class spirit is reinforced, there is growing scorn for the rights of individuals belonging to a foreign class. [. . .] It gives rise to collective attacks, i.e. on the one hand, oppressive laws, crimes of exaction, and on the other, riots, peasant revolts, bloody revolts.[24]

The social figure of the future would be the public, one of the most striking manifestations of the new forms of sociability. Tarde thus took the opposite view from the belief that disorder was inevitable, the price to pay for access by the masses to the exercise of citizenship. By forming audiences, the press and all remote means of communication become the social sphere of this 'modern world' that the psychology of crowds dreads. 'We have the psychology of crowds,' he wrote. 'What remains to be done is a psychology of the public, understood in this other sense, that is, as a purely spiritual collectivity, as a dissemination of physically separate individuals whose cohesion is entirely mental.'[25]

The first total war was to bare the hidden face of this new vector of democratic modernity: action upon public opinion.

— 3 —

MANAGING MASS SOCIETY:
THE LESSONS OF TOTAL WAR

The year 1914 was 'the great turning point prior to which liberal democracies were becoming freer, but after which the necessary security measures cost them all the ground they had gained', wrote Bertrand Russell.[1] Throughout his life, the British philosopher and logician, whose commitment alongside conscientious objectors opposed him to his Cambridge colleagues, continually maintained this position.

If there was one pitfall that thwarted the high standards of the rule of law, it was indeed the First World War. The concept had barely come into existence when it was threatened by the suspension of the freedom of movement, assembly and expression, and the reversibility of political and social gains. The principle had appeared at the end of the nineteenth century, first in German legal thought and then in French legal thought. It affirmed that the state, in its relationship with its subjects, was subject to the rule of law and the recognition of juridical avenues open to citizens against abuses committed by the state.

The Great War, a total war and the first so-called modern war, marked the advent of the new forms of reason embodied by the engineer and the manager – in short, the spirit of organization. It was a war of equipment or a war of machines. In the words of Ernst Jünger, it 'plugged the network of modern life, already complex and considerably ramified through multiple connections, into the high-tension power line of military activity'.[2] The theatre of operations was closely linked to the systematic organization of industrial resources and reserve labour supplies, just as the morale of the army was linked to the morale of the people. To cement the alliance between civilians and the military, the front and rear lines, but also to demoralize the enemy and rally the support of the neutral countries, the belligerents equipped themselves with a censorship apparatus and organized propaganda services. Each country joined in the conflict on the basis of its method of mobilizing society and the economy, as well as the nature of its army, its way of organizing the use of force, and the oppositions and resistances encountered within the nation itself

Acting upon public opinion: American democracy revisited

'During the war, it came to be recognized that the mobilization of men and means was not sufficient; there must be a mobilization of opinion. Power over opinion as over life and property, passed into official hands, because the danger of licence was greater than the danger of abuse', wrote the American political scientist Harold D. Lasswell in 1927 in *Propaganda Technique in the World War*, a seminal work in the functionalist sociology of the media.[3] During the immediate post-war period, propaganda was ennobled in the United States under the title of 'governmental management of opinion'. The evaluations drawn up by those who had led the campaigns of persuasion during the conflict consolidated the myth of the omnipotence of the press in influencing public opinion in peacetime. As these operations were also the testing grounds for the modern industry of advertising and public relations, the same image of efficiency worked to their advantage. What predominated was a behaviourist representation of the recipients, whose reactions obeyed the stimulus-response schema, with no choice but to follow 'the master's voice'.

On the other hand, the post-war balance sheet wrote off as a loss the strict control over information exercised by the Committee on Public Information or Creel Committee, named for its head, set up in 1917, which included representatives of three major departments – state, army and navy – as well as professionals from the advertising and press industries. Yet the Committee had been denounced many times during the war by organizations for the defence of individual freedoms, including the American Civil Liberties Union (ACLU), which was founded in this period. The ACLU constantly criticized the deviations from democratic practice made possible as much by the confusion between propaganda and 'public information' as by violations of human rights resulting from the Espionage Act (1917) and the Sedition Act (1918), a pair of laws which criminalized criticism of the federal government and authorized the deportation of 'undesirable' foreigners. Through these acts, the executive branch gave itself

33

the authority to hold 'foreign enemies' from a country at war with the United States and imprison them in an internment camp, without any legal mandate.

These measures continued a classic state practice that began in 1798 with the Alien and Sedition Acts. During the First World War, these laws caused a thousand US citizens to be imprisoned for expressing pacifist views, while preventing German nationals from entering Washington, DC, and prohibiting them from coming within 3 miles of either coastline. Such restrictions proved recurrent. During the Second World War, 40,000 Japanese nationals and 70,000 Japanese-Americans were interned in camps. Defenders of civil liberties who brought suit against the George W. Bush administration and the US armed forces for abuse of power were quite right in seeing in the detention camp in Guantánamo Bay the stamp of this tradition of extra-judicial measures.

During the interwar period, American theoreticians were discreet, to say the least, regarding the tension between measures of exception and freedom of expression, as Lasswell's book testifies.[4] What the dominant thinking did note, on the other hand, were the ways in which the regime of suspended freedom of information in wartime revealed deficiencies in the management of media in times of normal democratic government. It should be recalled that the 'Great War' and the 'Great Society' (i.e., mass society) were expressions that appeared simultaneously and shed light on each other. This is clearly demonstrated in Walter Lippmann's *Public Opinion* (1922), which soon became a classic in American journalism schools and political science departments. The author set out in this book to combat the 'original dogma of democracy'. From his experience as a captain in charge of propaganda in the expeditionary corps on the French front, Lippmann had learned three lessons. First, 'without some form of censorship, propaganda in the strict sense of the word is impossible. In order to conduct a propaganda, there must be some barrier between the public and the event.' Next, it is necessary to do away with the widely shared illusion of free expression: 'The ideal of the omnipotent, sovereign citizen is, in my opinion, a false ideal. It is unattainable. The pursuit of it is misleading. The failure to produce it has produced the current disenchantment.'[5] That is why, ultimately, the means of mass communication must be adapted to the complexity of the Great Society, the multidimensional nature of information and advances in technical knowledge. This entails taking into account 'the need for interposing some kind of expertise between the private citizen and the vast environment in which he is entangled'.[6]

Not to be outdone, Harold D. Lasswell justified strategies of persuasion as a legitimate mode of government in peacetime. He argued that the Great Society was fragmented and giving too much room to individual liberties might prove to be contrary to the collective interest, which the state must guarantee. 'If the mass will be free of chains of iron, it must accept chains of silver.'[7] The role of the media is to warn of anything that could threaten or otherwise affect the system of values of a community or of the parts that make it up. In his later works, Lasswell theorized the function of the media under the concept of 'surveillance of the social environment'. Two other functions flow in large part from this function of consensus: connecting the components of society to produce a response to the environment and transmitting social heritage.[8]

The lesson that Edward Bernays, a nephew of Freud and founder of the American public relations industry, drew in 1928 from his participation in the Creel Committee could not be blunter:

> If we understand the mechanism and motives of the group mind, is it not possible to control and regiment the masses according to our will without their knowing about it? [. . .] The conscious and intelligent manipulation of the organized habits and opinions of the masses is an important element in democratic society. Those who manipulate this unseen mechanism of society constitute an invisible government which is the true ruling power of our country. [. . .] It is the intelligent minorities which need to make use of propaganda continuously and systematically. [. . .] They govern us by their qualities of natural leadership, their ability to supply needed ideas and by their key position in the social structure. Whatever attitude one chooses toward this condition, it remains a fact that in almost every act of our daily lives, whether in the sphere of politics or business, in our social conduct or our ethical thinking, we are dominated by the relatively small number of persons – a trifling fraction of our 120 million – who understand the mental processes and social patterns of the masses. It is they who pull the wires which control the public mind, who harness old social forces and contrive new ways to bind and guide the world.[9]

Bernays goes on to note:

> Trotter and Le Bon concluded that the group mind does not think in the strict sense of the word. It has impulses, habits, and emotions instead of thoughts. In making up its mind, its first impulse is usually to follow the example of a trusted leader. This is one of the most firmly established principles of mass psychology.[10]

The contrast could not be greater with the argument made in favour of the use of intelligence by the philosopher John Dewey who, during the same period, saw education as the key to responsible participation of the citizenry in managing public affairs and public negotiations. For Dewey, education provided indispensable support for a democracy formed by a multiplicity of self-managed groups – local, cultural or industrial – to solve the political and social issues not only of the United States but of the whole world:

> Society is many associations not a single organization. Society means association [. . .] Universalization means socialization, the extension of the area and range of those who share in a good. The increasing acknowledgement that goods exist and endure only through being communicated and that association is the means of conjoint sharing lies back of the modern sense of humanity and democracy.[11]

The 'genuinely modern civilization' Dewey sought was, of course, yet to be created.

The one space of expression that the new 'engineering of assent' left to ordinary citizens was the sphere of consumption – the place where, for lack of power to participate as actors in the public sphere, they could legitimately demand and exercise their sovereignty and freedom of choice. This belief underpinned the Fordian project that governed the mode of social regulation during the interwar period and assured the mass integration of workers into the world of merchandise. In his aptly titled book *Captains of Consciousness*, the historian Stuart Ewen calls this 'mass participation in the values of the mass industrial market'. He summed up this ideal in a quotation from a famous work published by Christine Frederick in 1929, entitled *Selling Mrs. Consumer*: 'Consumptionism is the name given to the new doctrine, and it is admitted today to be the greatest idea that America has to give to the world – the idea that workmen and masses be looked upon not simply as workers and producers, but as *consumers* . . . Pay them more, sell them more, prosper more is the equation.'[12] Ewen demonstrates quite well how the captain of industry was transformed into a manager during this period and how, with the support of the advertising apparatus and audience-measuring techniques, consumption began to establish itself as the 'natural expression of democracy'.

The armistice had hardly been signed when the 'witch hunt' against the 'Reds' (including actual communists and socialists but also many people with liberal ideas) gave an inkling of the role that would be played by campaigns to stigmatize the 'enemy of the nation' in times of crisis. In January 1919, Seattle shipyard workers went on strike, demanding higher wages after wartime decreases and a reduction in the workweek. They were soon followed by miners and steel-workers. From the outset, the Justice Department and the Federal Bureau of Investigation brandished the thesis of a plot hatched by the 'radical movement' to overthrow the government, which they linked to the 'Bolshevik threat'. The police staged hundreds of raids and had foreign-born strikers expelled from the country. The Sacco and Vanzetti episode was only one of the most well-known instances of this police operation when public opinion rose to a fever pitch of conservative patriotism. Major newspapers such as the *New York Times* and the *Chicago Tribune* either turned a deaf ear to protests or simply supported the government's manipulations.[13] The film industry did not lag behind. In 1921, the film-maker David Wark Griffith undertook production of a melodrama by Adolphe d'Enéry entitled *Les Deux Orphelines* (*The Two Orphan Girls*), which recounted the misfortunes of two young women in Paris during the French Revolution. Above all, the film conveys a political vision: the revolutionary Reign of Terror was presented as a manifestation of what the silent film's intertitles referred to as 'Bolshevism'. As one critic noted:

> In a more subtle way, Griffith was already elevating to the highest degree of narrative effectiveness an aesthetic that enhanced the individual from the point of view of form and incorporated him into a community while distrusting the crowd perceived and presented as a dangerous, uncontrollable organic entity. Griffith thus depicted some American political myths in a highly personal, lyrical style.[14]

The First World War also prompted the US government to establish a permanent link between business interests and the armed forces. As soon as the war had ended, a project took shape to bring industrial production in line with strategic imperatives. On the initiative of the US Navy, then the dominant branch of the military, three large corporations in the long-distance communications sector formed an oligopoly that divided up the various segments of telephone and radio-telephone production and national and international service, and placed government representatives on their boards of directors. The plan aimed to counter the supremacy, clearly demonstrated during the war, of the United Kingdom and its fleet in the area of radio communication, and to build technologies allowing for the control of communication networks as a basis of strategic power. It also inaugurated a mode of cooperation between the industrial complex and national defence requirements that was to intensify during the Second World War and become institutionalized during the Cold War.

The birth of technocracy

The war paved the way for policies of rationalized production by refining the technologies of 'economy of motion', that is, sets of procedures to observe and measure the human body at work. Of course, this quest for economy of motion had been developing since the late nineteenth century, with studies carefully breaking down the movements of athletes, soldiers and workers initiated by Étienne Jules Marey and his team of physiological researchers, as well as factory experiments launched by F. W. Taylor and continued by his disciples such as Frank Gilbreth, the first to combine a camera with a chronometer to measure the successive positions of workers manufacturing a part. But the war effort gave high priority to physiological and psychological understanding of the 'human motor'. Ergonomic calculation of 'optimal' energy expenditure was used to test the response time and aptitude of artillerymen in combat, as well as workers in munitions factories. Psycho-technical tests were useful in the hiring of aviators, lorry drivers and radio operators. Psychologists of emotions examined pathological battle fatigue and neurasthenia in combatants. The degree of exhaustion and loss of the mental ability to react and make decisions was measured using a 'fatigability index', detected with a pneumograph and a sphygmograph.[15]

The notion of 'opinion management' was consistent with the principles of 'scientific management' of companies, which had been become naturalized, in spite of sporadic resistance, through the holy alliance between trade unions and employers during the First World War, in a context marked by a 'state of emergency' and the suspension of the right to strike or protest.

During the interwar period, technocracy emerged as the new 'economy' of power. This was the period in the United States when standards and objectives of effectiveness and efficiency were exported from the private sector to public administration protocols. Effectiveness refers to 'employee output and the rapidity with which projects and operations are successfully completed', whereas efficiency means 'the use of resources such that, with a given set of inputs, maximum outputs are produced, or such that a given output is produced with a minimum set of inputs'.[16] Political science in its nascent phase, seeking to emancipate itself from the discipline of history where it was confined by the university's traditional mode of organization, adopted these standards as the criteria for a 'science of democracy' and a 'science of government' whose performance could be measured and whose results could be evaluated. The technocratic configuration inspired a vast, voluntarist programme built on the threefold conviction that it could eliminate the economic and social crisis, expand productivity through science and re-enchant technology.[17]

Although the term 'technocracy' first appeared in 1919 in the magazine *Industrial Management* under the pen of William Henry Smith, an engineer and investor from Berkeley, California, it did not become widespread until the 1929 crisis, when technocracy had a utopian flavour for some. Thus, the great idea of Howard Scott, who popularized the word, was to use the physical sciences directly to solve social problems. To do this, a monumental survey of the energy resources of the United States was required to define 'continental areas' to be placed under the all-powerful control of technicians. The following excerpt from Scott's short book *Introduction to Technocracy* (1933), a bible for 'technocrats', including economists, engineers and physicists, provides a sample of the 'newspeak' which presented the control of energy resources as a panacea: 'The physical revenue within a technologically controlled continental area would be the net amount of energy available in ergs, converted into use value and services, minus operating costs and the expense of maintaining the physical plant and machinery of the area in question.'[18] According to Scott, this calculation of energy resources should enable society to content itself with a four-day workweek and a four-hour workday.

The philosopher Antonio Gramsci wrote in the early 1930s: 'Hegemony is born in the factory', meaning that Fordism, which he equated with 'Americanism', carried with it not only a new mode of producing goods through rational organization of the production system, but also a type of society, a certain lifestyle, a certain way of thinking and feeling about life[19] whose vocation was to become universal. That is precisely the meaning it was given in the dystopias of the interwar period, those fictional accounts of imaginary societies in which the worst conditions of life reign, which extrapolated the anthropological effects of a global plan for the programmed control of individuals. One such anti-utopia, *The Islanders*,[20] written by the Russian author Yevgeny Zamyatin (1884–1937), was published in St Petersburg in 1918. Conceived after a long stay in industrial England to supervise the construction of icebreakers, the book depicts the production of the serial individual, the fetish of high speeds, a dehumanized world, an air-conditioned hell, in a society dominated by great machines – Technology, the State or Religion. 'All of them [were] identical, like buttons, like Ford automobiles, like ten thousand copies of the *Times*.' Wisdom lay in figures, clocks and rails in a society aligned with the 'precepts of mandatory Salvation'.

In 1920, Zamyatin completed a second anti-utopia, *We*, at the very moment when the Soviet authorities were thinking of adopting Taylor's principles of the scientific organization of labour to set up a planned economy.[21] Published in Czech in 1927, on the initiative of the semiotician Roman Jakobson, and in French and English shortly thereafter, the original Russian edition was not published until the fall of the Berlin Wall. The author depicted a world organization called 'OneState', where harmony was a duty. Between freedom without happiness and happiness without freedom, its builders chose the latter. The only way to deliver humankind from crime was to deliver it from freedom. 'We' is a body with a thousand heads, as no one has a name. Each person is represented by a number and finds satisfaction in being merely a molecule, an atom, a phagocyte. There is an invisible metronome, an automaton and a phonograph in each component of 'We'. In this urban planetary society, emptied of its countryside and peasants, the pace of life is determined by the 'Timetable'. Its literary heritage is summed up by the railway schedule and by F. W. Taylor's veritable bible, *Principles of Scientific Management* (1911). The only thing lacking in Taylor's book, its failure to control time throughout the twenty-four hours in a day, is achieved in the new society. To eliminate the real disease – the imagination – the enemies of happiness must undergo the 'great operation', a lobotomy that turns the brain into a chronometer. No more desire or pity or love. Noble sentiments are nothing but a prejudice from feudal times. However, as in *The Islanders*, an 'alien body' could always find its way into the 'cogs' of the machinery. In *We*, the 'Mephis' (an abbreviation of Mephistopheles) were those who resisted. Headed by a liberated woman named 'I-330', they lived naked and in direct contact with nature, outside the high-tension walls that protected the world of artefacts inside which the cells of *We* were confined. Between the two forces that governed the world, entropy and energy, the Mephis opted for the second because it destroyed the happy tranquillity of equilibrium and tended towards painful perpetual motion. They were convinced that the 'final revolution' existed only in the minds of philosopher-mathematicians, because there is no life without difference: 'Difference of temperature, difference of potential. And if the same heat or cold reigns everywhere in the universe, it has to be shaken up to produce fire, explosion, Gehenna. We will help them.'

Zamyatin's writings proved to be an archetype for the anti-utopias that followed. They imagined a eugenics of human happiness, embodied a few years later by the incubation and conditioning centre of the Fordian or Taylorian society in Aldous Huxley's *Brave New World* (1932), and technologies for training the body and mind, like the truth drug in *Kallocain* (1940), a story by the Swedish writer Karin Boye. In all of Zamyatin's works, there prevailed the seamless order of the world state or 'OneState', founded on mutual surveillance and the civic obligation to inform on others, a vision which reached its peak with 'Big Brother' in George Orwell's *1984*, published in 1948.[22]

The lost war: an early laboratory for permanent exception

The question of propaganda figured prominently in the inventory of causes for the German imperial army's defeat drawn up by Nazi ideologues during the interwar period. In one of the first Nazi works on this issue, Eugen Hadamovsky wrote:

> The German people were not beaten on the battlefield, but in the war of words and because their spirit was broken. The Germans were sent into this mighty battle with not so much as a single slogan while the enemy nations took up arms 'against the Hun', 'for world peace', and 'for the League of Nations' [. . .] Today, every school child knows that we did not merely have to fight a military war, but were also exposed to economic warfare, and that the latter, coupled with the weapons of propaganda (psychological warfare) finally caused our downfall.[23]

When the troops retreated from the Marne Front in July 1918, the German High Command spoke of the 'generalized depression', but could not find a way to counter it: 'Germany is hypnotized by enemy propaganda as a rabbit is by a snake.'[24] The Nazi Party's fixation on propaganda operations was thus all the more significant as its theoreticians bore this earlier failure in mind. Already in 1925, Adolf Hitler presented his conception of the symbolic weapon in *Mein Kampf*. It was a way of ensuring the government's hold over the citizens' entire existence by creating a 'community of sacrifice' (*Opfergemeinschaft*) in which the civilian and military spheres were merged. To do so, he borrowed extensively from crowd psychology, even plagiarizing from it the stereotypes of the feminine nature of the great masses subjugated by their feelings.[25] At the international level, it was the strategic instrument of 'psychological warfare', paving the way for military intervention. This notion was indeed an invention of Nazi

41

Germany too, which explains why the expression was suppressed by ad hoc Allied services during the Second World War in favour of notions such as 'political warfare', 'propaganda war', 'war to win the minds of the enemy', 'war of nerves', 'indirect aggression' or simply 'international communication'. The expression was not used again until the advent of the Cold War. But the conception of psychological warfare as a springboard for total mobilization can only be explained from within a theory of the state.

'Silent dictatorship' was the name used by one historian to describe how the German Empire organized its society of total mobilization during the hostilities.[26] In the interwar period, military strategists and legal theoreticians strove to draw lessons from it for peacetime application. The idea of the omniscient grip of power runs through their writings. 'As war is the ultimate test of a country to safeguard its existence, a totalitarian politics must therefore develop in peacetime the necessary preparatory plans required for the struggle for life of a nation at war, and fortify the foundations of this struggle for life to such a degree that they cannot be destabilized in the heat of war,' wrote General Erich Ludendorff in *Nation at War* (1936). It was Ludendorff's firm conviction that 'all the theories of Clausewitz have to be thrown overboard'.[27] In Clausewitz's view, war can have its own 'grammar' but not its own 'logic'. The logic is determined by the political aim. War 'cannot follow its own laws but has to be treated as a part of some other whole, the name of which is policy . . . Policy is the guiding intelligence and war only the instrument, not vice-versa. No other possibility exists, then, than to subordinate the military point of view to the political.' Clausewitz insists in a 'Note':

> War can be of two kinds, in the sense that either the objective is to *overthrow the enemy* – to render him politically helpless or militarily impotent, thus forcing him to sign whatever peace we please; or *merely to occupy some of his frontier-districts* so that we can annex them or use them for bargaining at the peace negotiations . . . The distinction between the two kinds of war is an actual fact. But no less practical is the importance of another point that must be made absolutely clear, namely that *war is nothing but the continuation of policy with other means*.[28]

However, the character of politics changed with the changing nature of war, in particular with the rise of 'machine warfare'. Total war and its strategy of general mobilization of the nation as a whole understood only antagonism and the murderous clash of armies. This notion was echoed in the thought of political scientist and philosopher

Carl Schmitt, a Nazi Party sympathizer, who conceived of politics as a merciless confrontation between 'friends' and 'enemies'.

German writers on strategy spoke obsessively between the wars about how 'the state must tame war'. The philosopher Walter Benjamin, a severe critic of the 'eternal war' these authors were calling for, remarked in 1930 that if the question kept coming up, it was because there was 'something peculiar' about the war that had just ended: it was not only a 'mechanized material war, it was also a lost war. And in addition, it was, in a very specific sense, a German war.'[29] It was the failure of state power in the face of war that underlay their 'mystical theory of war'. War was a cult and an apotheosis. This theory required the state to 'adapt its structure and attitudes to the magical forces that it is compelled to mobilize in wartime, and to show itself worthy of them. Otherwise, it will not succeed in exploiting war for its own ends.'[30] This 'mystique of universal death teeming with miserable conceptions like a thousand-legged monster' made war synonymous with the rejection of international law. The first total war, a war without mercy, indeed marked the denial of international law of war, the foundations of which had been laid by the jurists and peace activists starting in the last decades of the nineteenth century. The use of mustard gas, which made no distinction between military and civilian populations, was an illustration of this.

> When there is no longer any distinction between the civilian population and the combatants – a distinction thoroughly eliminated by gas warfare – the most important foundation of international law also disappears. [. . .] Every future war will at once be a slave rebellion and be fomented by technology. [. . .] It suffices to see the impassiveness with which they [German war theoreticians] evoke the notion of the war of the future, without attaching to it the slightest concrete notion. Those who thereby paved the way for the Wehrmacht would almost make us think that their supreme goal was the uniform, the goal to which they aspired with every fibre of their being. In relation to this goal, the circumstances in which war might later impose itself were much less important.[31]

A prophetic text if ever there was one, when one thinks of the use made in later wars of the atomic bomb, the new generation of chemical weapons (white phosphorus, napalm, etc.), cluster bombs and anti-personnel mines.

The idea of the structural necessity of restricting 'individual freedom' to allow the 'universal state' to deploy its potential energy is at the core of the analyses of Ernst Jünger, a writer fascinated by war, who volunteered on the German side and thought the Warfare State should henceforth serve as the paradigm for the whole organization of society. Indeed, he believed he could detect signs of its emergence in the evolution of international power relations, writing in the 1930s:

> Thus, in many countries after the war, we will be able to observe just how far the new methods of organization already conform to the model of total mobilization. Let us take, for example, certain phenomena such as the growing restrictions on 'individual freedom', although to tell the truth, this demand was problematic from the beginning. And it is possible to imagine that all countries, as soon as they claim to play a role on the international stage, will be forced to radicalize those restrictions if they want to be able to unleash forces of a new kind.[32]

Already in the 1920s, in an essay entitled *Die Diktatur*, Carl Schmitt defined state sovereignty as the ability to decide to make exceptions, to suspend the usual standards of conduct in order to set in motion the forces and instruments needed to escape from crisis in a way that ensures the state's very survival.[33] This theory of the state of exception anticipated the way the Third Reich was to stay in power by continually suspending the legal constitutional order. The Constitution of the Weimar Republic, the regime that had preceded it, was in fact never abrogated. The *Führer* put it in parentheses for a period of four years when he came to power in February 1933, after which the suspension of the law as the guarantee of citizens' rights to oppose abuses of power was systematically renewed by decree every four years, so that the regime became a state of exception or of permanent emergency. The perversion and degradation of the rule of law (*Rechtstaat*) lay in assimilating the law, as a matter of necessity, to existing legality. In accordance with the logic of that assimilation, Hitler's jurists considered the Nazi regime to be respecting the rule of law, not only because the Constitution had never been repealed, but also because the *Führerprinzip*, the 'Leader Principle', had become the new legality of the state – the 'master state' (*Herrenstaat*).

The aftermath of 11 September, 2001, and the situation of exception created by the global war on terror made Carl Schmitt's work relevant once again. His theory was to be used by political philosophy, on the left as well as the right, without achieving unanimous acceptance.[34] Yet, by focusing too much on this theory, we may lose sight of the fact that US strategists too had plenty of time to develop their own doctrine of war without mercy, thanks to the war against the Axis powers formed by Nazi Germany, fascist Italy and Japan, and later the Cold War.

44

'National struggles inevitably become conflicts between good and evil, crusades against sin and the devil. Modern wars can be fought successfully only in an atmosphere of unreality and make-believe,' observed Nicholas John Spykman following the disaster of Pearl Harbor, in one of the first American treatises on geopolitics to examine in a prospective manner the strategy to be adopted by the United States as a world power.[35] This fundamentalism, verging on the religious, would confer on the Cold War its character as an 'ideological' or 'psychological' war.

Part II

Hegemonizing/Pacifying

— 4 —

THE COLD WAR AND THE RELIGION OF NATIONAL SECURITY

What is national security? In *The Imperial Presidency*, published in 1973, Arthur M. Schlesinger, a former advisor to John F. Kennedy, explains that this notion, with its 'incantatory power', was used for the first time on the eve of the Cold War and reached a culminating point with the presidency of Richard Nixon. The expression was so incantatory that it succeeded in 'blocking any critical analysis', for it appeared 'at the very least presumptuous, if not antipatriotic, to ask what "national security" meant exactly'.[1] It was the 'proper language for everything connected with Empire' and a 'symbol' carrying all the 'mystical values of the Empire itself', added Joseph Comblin in his history of national security and its effects on Latin America, published three years later. National security is 'that value we talk about all the time, which never needs to be explained or justified; it is prior to any reflection and discussion, the presupposition of which everyone is presumably quite conscious'.[2]

Finally, for historian David Reynolds, whose study of the origins of the Cold War was published shortly after the fall of the Berlin Wall, national security should be understood as a 'gospel' that reactivated President Wilson's messianic project to remodel the world order, formulated at the end of the First World War, in which the United States 'could and should use its enhanced power to export liberal, capitalist, democratic, and anti-colonial values'.[3]

The 'global enemy', first edition of the crusade against evil

National security became the infallible criterion used to separate friends from enemies, good from evil, virtue from sin. Cold War

strategies of dissuasion and persuasion were led to state this dichot-
omy in every possible form, continually confusing particular interests
with universal values, security with freedom, lies with truth, secrecy
with transparency, turning words around and diverting them from
their ordinary meanings. The function of George Orwell's 'newspeak'
in *1984* immediately comes to mind: 'The Newspeak vocabulary
was tiny, and new ways of reducing it were constantly being devised.
Newspeak, indeed, differed from almost all other languages in that its
vocabulary grew smaller instead of larger every year. Each reduction
was a gain, since the smaller the area of choice, the smaller the temptation to take thought.'[4]

Whoever is not with me is against me. Pondering this equation,
Schlesinger made the connection between the hegemonic practices of
the 'imperial presidency' and those attributed to the Roman Empire by
the Austrian economist and economic historian Joseph Schumpeter:

> There was no corner of the known world where some interest was not
> alleged to be in danger or under actual attack. If the interests were not
> Roman, they were those of Rome's allies, and if Rome had no allies,
> then allies would be invented. When it was utterly impossible to con-
> trive such an interest – why, then it was the nation's honour that had
> been insulted. Rome was always being attacked by evil-minded neigh-
> bours, always fighting for a breathing-space. The whole world was per-
> vaded by a host of enemies, and it was manifestly Rome's duty to guard
> against their indubitably aggressive designs.[5]

Through the dogma of national security, references to glo-
balism became an established feature of the rhetoric of geopolitics.
Henceforth, it was used to designate and denounce the enemies of the
'free world', as seen in the following excerpt from an appeal to the
nation by President Eisenhower in 1953:

> The struggle in which freedom today is engaged is quite literally a total
> and universal struggle . . . It is a political struggle . . . It is a scientific
> struggle . . . It is an intellectual struggle . . . It is a spiritual struggle . . .
> For this whole struggle, in the deepest sense, is waged neither for land
> or food – but for the soul of man himself.[6]

The importance of this struggle for the future of the world blurred
the ethical dividing line. The end justified any means. The Hoover
Commission Report on state reorganization openly stated as much
three years later:

> It is now clear that we are facing an implacable enemy whose avowed
> objective is world domination by whatever means and at whatever cost.

There are no rules in such a game. Hitherto acceptable norms of human conduct dot not apply. If the US is to survive, long standing American concepts of 'fair play' must be reconsidered. We must develop effective espionage and counterespionage services. We must learn to subvert, sabotage and destroy our enemies with cleverer, more sophisticated and more effective methods than those used against us. It may become necessary that the American people will be made acquainted with, understand and support this fundamentally repugnant philosophy.[7]

Thus, a form of permanent government of exception was legitimated. For beneath the rhetoric of the new gospel, a vast institutional system linking civilians and military was being deployed.

By 1946, national security already had its 'propaganda machine', in the words of Senator J. William Fulbright, who assailed the simplistic anti-communism of the new crusaders and the 'self-evident truths' conveyed by the 'national vocabulary' throughout the Cold War. These 'truths' concerned not only 'life, liberty and happiness', but also 'a vast number of personal and public issues, including the Cold War'.[8] At the core of the propaganda machine lay the National War College – the intellectual centre of US global strategy, equivalent to the NATO Defence College in Rome or the Imperial Defence College in London – along with the Industrial College of the Armed Forces, a school of applied knowledge. Both were postgraduate-level institutions that trained civilians as well as officers. Indeed the schools had been designed to stimulate this alliance, as their task was to implement national security by coordinating their activities. There was an oversized public relations apparatus that invested massively in commercial advertising targeted at the general public, as well as educational programmes organized in cities with the logistical support of the network of local chambers of commerce. They offered seminars in national security, so-called 'warning' programmes, lectures on 'survival strategy', 'freedom forums' and the like, where teams of officers spoke alongside representatives of the radical right.

The system of military bases, the new strategic frontier

In 1947, national security was enshrined in a law of its own: the National Security Act. As James Forrestal, Secretary of the Navy, explained to Congress, 'The bill provides . . . for the coordination of the three armed services, but what is to me even more important . . . it provides for the integration of foreign policy with national policy, of our civilian economy with military requirements; it provides for . . .

51

continual advances in the field of research and applied science.'⁹ The first order of business, if not the top priority, was obviously to unite the armed forces. In fact, it was with this goal in mind that military planners took up the reference to national security as early as 1945, thanks to the efforts of George C. Marshall, chairman of the Joint Chiefs of Staff, future Secretary of State under President Truman and the initiator of the Marshall Plan to aid European reconstruction. This singular genesis of the National Security Act meant that it was long referred to, especially by top military officers, as the *Unification Act* – the founding decree of inter-army coordination. The debate on coordination of the navy, air force and army was all the more vital as the war had established the hegemony of air power in major strategy choices. Indeed, the fact that the Secretary of the Navy defended the law before Congress shows that by the end of the war the organizational chart of the government departments in charge of military affairs was at odds with this new reality: the Navy had its own Secretary whereas the other armed forces came under the authority of the War Department.

A debate over the central role of aviation implied discussing the overall issue of the United States' global system of defence against acts of foreign aggression. This was where the foundations for a new geopolitics were laid. The previous era, in which hegemony was based on fleets, had seen US naval bases multiply on foreign territory, creating veritable enclaves that escaped the sovereign control of host countries. These takeovers had begun in 1898 with the landing of the expeditionary corps in Cuba and Puerto Rico, at a time when a new type of imperial expansionism was taking shape that differed from the model embodied by the European colonial powers. Between that date and the end of the First World War, the United States had created a sphere of influence that turned the Caribbean Sea into an 'American lake'. It was an 'American Mediterranean', to use the expression of Admiral Alfred Thayer Mahan, the father of modern American 'navalism', the 'evangelist of sea power' who justified this policy of imperial expansion by claiming it was the 'manifestation of the Divine Will' and was convinced that the empire would give the United States new Christian obligations towards the world.[10] Puerto Rico was annexed, the Virgin Islands were purchased, and Cuba, the Dominican Republic, Nicaragua and Haiti were reduced to the status of protectorates – not to mention the Panama Canal Zone, which was snatched from Colombia by organizing the secession of one of its provinces. As a result, even today, naval bases may be found at various strategic points across the Caribbean; Guantánamo Bay, Cuba, is one example among others.

By changing its scale, the air force redefined the strategic frontier of national defence. The strategic option of 'in-depth defence' of national territory obliged the United States to weave a tight network of air force and naval bases across the world to be close to theatres of operation, whether real or virtual. They were established in Greenland and Iceland to control the Arctic zone; in the Azore Islands to control the Atlantic; in the Philippines and the Marianne Islands to control the Pacific; but also in Germany, Italy, Spain, the United Kingdom, Turkey, and many other places. These relays were especially important in view of the delayed development of the B-36 intercontinental bomber. The mission of the outposts of national security strategy was clear: 'From these bases on America's "strategic frontier", the United States could preserve its access to vital raw materials, deny these resources to a prospective enemy, help preserve peace and stability in troubled areas, safeguard critical sea lanes; and, if necessary, conduct an air offensive against the industrial infrastructure of any power, including the Soviet Union.'[11] Parallel to these installations, in areas where it had no bases, Washington staked claims to permanent transit and landing rights. The establishment, extension and renewal of the bases would in most cases become the subject of secret quid pro quo negotiations. In exchange for bases in Franco's Spain, for example, the United States pledged to help the regime in the event of an internal uprising.

The network of air and naval platforms expanded continually during the Cold War until it formed the physical foundation for the superpower's military hegemony. It was no accident that, in March 2007, civilian activist movements against world militarization staged a mass protest against the extension of the base in Vicenza, Italy, and the continuation of the one in Manta, Ecuador. The Italian base was a powerful symbol, dating back to the beginning of the Cold War and NATO, in a country that the White House considered to be on the verge of turning communist. The Ecuadorian base was established after the Cold War, ostensibly to fight against drug trafficking, even though it performed other functions more in line with the original purpose of foreign bases.

A techno-military matrix

The Pentagon was established in 1947 and the Departments of War and the Navy were eliminated. A sign of the hegemony of aerospace power, the Strategic Air Command (SAC) was created around the

53

same time, grouping together long-range nuclear bombers. The new Department of Defence not only unified the three armed forces under its authority but was also in charge of the other major objective of the national security law: pursuing synergies between the military and researchers in the civilian, industrial and university sectors. Liaison committees were set up to oversee the interlinking of military demand and civilian supply that had brilliantly demonstrated its effectiveness in the war effort. For, unlike the First World War, which mobilized and extended already acquired scientific and technical knowledge, the Second World War and the Cold War were techno-scientific conflicts, in which operational research and innovation were constantly used to transform the tactical, strategic and logistical balance of forces. Whereas the demobilization in 1918–19 resulted in complete disengagement of the civilian sectors, during the immediate post-Second World War period, the close relationship between military authorities and civilian research was – despite some hesitation – maintained.

Investments in defence research climbed with the institutionalization of what was to become the military-industrial complex. In 1950, a teacher at the Industrial College of the Armed Forces made the following observation:

> The revolutionary change in attitude toward research and development in governmental and military circles, and the greatly increased understanding of the importance of these activities to national security, may be shown by a few budgetary facts. In 1930, only 14% of the public and private budget for research and development in this country was spent by the government. In 1947, the governmental portion of the national bill was 56%. This increase was largely due to the motive of national security. . . The 1941–1945 annual average was 500 million dollars, not counting the greatest scientific–technological project in history, the development of the atomic bomb. This was a war period. But in 1947, a year of peace, the government expended 625 million dollars, again not counting the cost of atomic energy projects. In 17 years, the amounts in the national budget were multiplied more than 27 times.[12]

With the Korean War (1950–3), the Soviet launching of the Sputnik satellite in 1957, which set off the space race, and the installation of intercontinental missiles in the same year, budgets skyrocketed.

The influx of funds enabled the Strategic Air Command to inaugurate in 1955 the first defence system prefiguring the large system of real-time connection between computers: the Semi-Automatic Ground Environment (SAGE) network, the touchstone of the future Worldwide Military Command and Control System (WWMCCS). This gigantic spider web, aimed at controlling the environment of an entire continent, became a metaphor – and myth – of 'total defence' of the Homeland. Its civilian counterpart was a techno-utopian belief in a new society and a new world order made transparent and fluid solely thanks to the free flow of that new raw material known as information. This notion, originating in a mathematical theory of communication, was limited from the start to a strictly physical, quantitative definition, reduced to data. By emphasizing the technical aspect of things, it obliterated the political moment of communication because it stemmed from a conception of communication proper to telecommunications engineering, according to which the main problem was finding the most efficient (i.e., fastest and least expensive) method of coding to send a message from a transmitter to a receiver; it was thus interested solely in the channel and chose to ignore the production of meaning, culture and memory.

So it was that a purely technical vision of the communication process, stamped with determinism, came into being, in symbiosis with the idea of history as a linear representation of ever-extending progress, in which innovation and modernity circulated from top to bottom, from the centre to the peripheries, and from those who know to those who are presumed not to know. Beginning in the 1950s, the theoretical premises of 'post-industrial society' were sketched out within the US sociological establishment. It was also referred to as 'post-historical', 'post-capitalist', 'technetronic' (a contraction intended to convey the convergence between communication and information technologies, the telephone, radio and television and the computer) and, finally, starting in the 1970s, the 'information society'. It adopted as self-evident a combative discourse about society, oriented by the primacy of science and artificial intelligence and based on the announced 'end' of ideology, politics, class struggle, intellectual protest and hence political involvement, and the legitimation of the figure of the positive intellectual, oriented towards decision-making. This thesis matched that of the 'managerial society' as the ultimate horizon.[13]

All the same, it was through military contracts that the data-processing industry took off as a strategic sector – in particular its flagship corporation, IBM. As a 1975 report by the Organization of Economic Cooperation and Development (OECD) pointed out:

> In 1959, research and development contracts worth almost a billion dollars were allocated to computer manufacturers (in the United States). This figure is comparable to the total sales figure for computers in the civilian market in the same period, and it certainly exceeds considerably the support given to the computer industry in other countries.

Coinciding with these years during which the new and important industry was established, this policy has without doubt had more effect than
any other national policy pursued at the time or since.[14]

Sanctuary for the secret services

At that time, the cult of information was far from extolling the transparency per se of new intelligence technologies. It was synonymous
with secrecy, espionage and surveillance – in a word, entropy. The
National Security Act brought about a complete reorganization of
intelligence services. It set up the National Security Council (NSC)
and the Central Intelligence Agency (CIA), and created the position of Director of Central Intelligence (DCI), who supervised and
coordinated all the secret agencies. Three events precipitated this
redistribution of areas of competence: the dismantling of the Office
of Strategic Services (OSS), the agency in charge of military intelligence during the war; the US Army's coopting of General Reinhard
Gehlen, former intelligence chief of the Wehrmacht on the Eastern
Front; and a new awareness of the extent of the new enemy's networks and the sophistication of its espionage methods, following the
defection to the West of a cryptographer in the Soviet Embassy in
Washington.

The role of the National Security Council was 'to advise the
President with respect to the integration of domestic, foreign, and
military policies relating to national security'.[15] Conceived as an
extremely flexible instrument, it comprised only four statutory
members: the President, the Vice-President, the Secretary of State and
the Secretary of Defence, with the inclusion of other members left
to the president's discretion. The vagueness surrounding the definition of the CIA's functions left the door open to an excessive cult
of secrecy. The 'services of common concern' assigned to it at the
outset were never specified; nor were 'such other functions and obligations' that the Council might attribute to it.[16] What is clear is that
the authority of the executive branch markedly overrode that of the
legislative branch. Although the espionage apparatus was officially
set up not to control US citizens but rather the actions of worldwide
communism, the invocation of national security was so broad as to
blur the borderline between the national and foreign domains. A final
piece was added to the system by the president: the National Security
Agency (NSA). Initially called the Armed Forces Security Agency,
it did not acquire its definitive name until 1952. As it was the most

secret agency of US espionage, its existence remained unknown until 1957. It was originally assigned to put an end to the compartmentalizing of army, navy and air force cryptology activities; this unification was essential for the security of the communication networks, its primary function.

A series of legislative provisions further contributed to the emerging national security state. In 1947, a presidential order authorized loyalty reviews of government employees and called for their dismissal if necessary 'in the interests of national security'. This order was reinforced by another in 1953. The witch-hunt launched by Senator Joseph McCarthy from 1950 to 1954 resulted in stiffening these so-called anti-communist laws. The scope of the Smith Act of 1940 was broadened to repress 'propaganda that consciously and deliberately advocates the overthrow of the federal government by violence and force'. The Internal Security Act of 1950 restricted the freedom of association enjoyed by organizations of 'communists and communist sympathizers' and gave the executive branch the authority to imprison 'any person that may reasonably be suspected of committing acts of espionage or sabotage'. The Communist Control Act of 1954 outlawed the party. The enemy was already clearly identified in the preamble of the Internal Security Act: 'There is a world-wide revolutionary communist movement which is trying to set up a totalitarian communist dictatorship in the world and it is no longer up to Congress to establish the appropriate measures for recognizing the existence of this world conspiracy and to try and prevent it from achieving its aims.'[17] By this yardstick, a liberal became a progressive and a progressive became a communist. It was not until the anti-communist campaign attacked the army that its excesses became apparent and the Senate voted to censure McCarthy, marking the end of McCarthyism, at least in its most virulent forms.

Senate hearings: the great outpouring

In the 1970s, the Senate succeeded in lifting the veil on the 'fundamentally repugnant philosophy', in the words of the Hoover Commission, used to justify the excesses of the covert actions undertaken by the CIA and other intelligence agencies by unilateral decision of the executive branch. The revelations about the destabilization campaign against the regime of the Chilean president Salvador Allende (1970–3) and the Watergate affair played a significant role in the senators' initiative. In 1976, a commission headed by Senator Frank Church investigated the activities of the CIA, military intelligence agencies and the National Security Agency from their inception. The FBI was not spared. Witnesses testified to the long series of governmental overthrows and plots fomented throughout the world during the previous two decades against constitutionally elected regimes or opposition groups. The targets included not just Chile's Popular Unity government, but also, to cite only a few, Mohammad Mossadegh's Iran in August 1953, Jacobo Arbenz's Guatemala in 1954, and the Greek and Italian communist parties in the immediate post-war period.

The hearings revealed violations of the rule of law, committed in the name of 'national security', 'national defence needs', or the 'confidentiality required by the sensitive nature of the negotiations or operations under way'. The Commission's conclusions were uncompromising:

> Since World War II, with steadily escalating consequences, many decisions of national importance have been made in secrecy, often by the executive branch alone. These decisions are frequently based on information obtained by clandestine means and available only to the executive branch. Until very recently, the Congress has not shared in this process. The cautions expressed by the Founding Fathers and the constitutional checks designed to assure that policymaking not become the province of one man or a few men have been avoided on notable recent occasions through the use of secrecy . . . What is a valid national secret? What can properly be concealed from the scrutiny of the American people, from various segments of the executive branch or from a duly constituted oversight body of their elected representatives? Assassination plots? The overthrow of an elected democratic government? Drug testing on unwitting American citizens? Obtaining millions of private cables? Massive domestic spying by the CIA and the military? The illegal opening of mail? Attempts by an agency of the government to blackmail a civil rights leader? These have occurred and each has been withheld from scrutiny by the public and the Congress by the label 'secret intelligence'.[18]

The report went on to say:

> The imprecision and manipulation of labels such as 'national security', 'domestic activity', 'subversive activity', and 'foreign intelligence', have led to unjustified use of these techniques [of surveillance]. Using labels such as 'national security' and 'foreign intelligence', intelligence agencies have directed their highly intrusive techniques against individuals and organizations who were suspected of no criminal activity and

who posed no genuine threat to the national security. In the absence of precise standards and effective outside control, the selection of American citizens as targets has at times been predicated on grounds no more substantial than their lawful protests or their non-conformist philosophies.

Examples of these so-called 'counter-intelligence' or 'Cointelpro' operations included the 'Shamrock' operation to intercept telegrammes sent by Western Union, the Radio Corporation of America (RCA) or International Telephone and Telegraph (ITT) in the 1950s and 1960s; the 'Minaret' operation to wiretap the conversations of 6,000 foreigners and nearly 2,000 American organizations and private individuals, including Martin Luther King and Jane Fonda, between 1967 and 1973; the 'Chaos' operation that tracked down students opposed to the Vietnam War.

Beyond these cases of government interference, what was revealed in the 1970s was the systematic practice of secrecy, resulting in the executive branch's affirmation of the sovereign right to engage in new military activities outside the country without the consent of Congress or the public and without their knowledge. This was the case of the intervention in Vietnam. The transparency demonstrated by the investigation into what Senator Church called 'the dilemma of secrecy and open constitutional government' stood in stark contrast to the opacity then cloaking the other major Western democracies, where classifying clandestine operations against a government, community or individual as 'defence secrets' made it possible to shield them from scrutiny.

The intrusive practices denounced on this occasion did not cease, however, despite the recurrent warnings of Congress and the grievances expressed by the American Civil Liberties Union regarding violations of the people's right, recognized by the Fourth Amendment to the Constitution, 'to be secure in their persons, houses, papers, and effects, against unreasonable searches and seizures'. In 1999, Congress once again decided to open an investigation following accusations that the National Security Agency was intercepting the electronic messages of private individuals. Two years later, anti-terrorist measures were to prevent this new, in-depth review. The terrorist surveillance programme was to authorize the spy agency to intercept telephone communications and e-mail messages to foreign countries without prior approval from the special court set up by the Foreign Intelligence Surveillance Act in 1978 in the wake of the Senate investigations. The court, which meets behind closed doors, was not to recover its prerogatives until January 2007, under the pressure of the newly elected Democratic majority in Congress.

Echelon: prototype for a planetary wiretapping system

A programme to monitor communication flows, also secretly managed, was introduced at the international level during the immediate post-war period. The code name for this powerful electronic espionage network was 'Echelon'. The war had enabled a leap forward in interception techniques (Comint or Communications Intelligence) and decryption of the enemy's strategic correspondence. The British Secret Intelligence Service had mobilized Alan Turing, the inventor of the concept of 'programme', to break the code of the Enigma electromechanical number-generating machines developed by the Germans. In the United States, the future inventor of the mathematical theory of communication, Claude Elwood Shannon, a researcher at Bell Telecommunications Laboratories, had also worked on coding for the US National Defense Research Committee. This joint control of efficient electronic spying tools linked the United States to the United Kingdom in 1943, in the form of a secret pact to collaborate in an intelligence network named 'Brusa Comint'.

In 1948, the network was renamed 'Ukusa', referring to the initials of the two countries; the American side of its management was entrusted to the NSA and the British side to the Government Communications Headquarters (GCHQ). Initially, the priority objective consisted in eavesdropping on military and diplomatic transmissions from Eastern bloc countries and gathering intelligence on their military systems. But with the help of the satellite system, the Echelon mission was considerably expanded along with the number of partners. Three other countries became affiliated: Australia, Canada and New Zealand, and relays were installed in countries considered 'friendly', Germany and Japan. Each partner in the network was in charge of an area of the globe. But the founders retained the upper hand over the network, which made up the armature of the eavesdropping system. With this system it was possible to intercept, decode and use transmissions and data transfers sent by submarine cables and communication satellites, by sorting them with an artificial intelligence system. The key role of the United Kingdom put most of its European partners in an uncomfortable position, to say the least, in view of that country's close alignment with US foreign policy.

Thanks to information leaked by a former NSA employee, the

existence of Echelon was revealed for the first time in 1972 by the US magazine *Ramparts*, a forum for opponents of the military-industrial complex and the Vietnam War. The story was confirmed that same year with the revelations of eavesdropping on the telephone conversations of the Popular Unity government in Chile, headed by Salvador Allende, from a station located on a US military base in Puerto Rico.[19] The general public in Europe would learn of this spy network only in 1998 in a report ordered by the European Parliament's Committee on Civil Liberties.

Psychological warfare in times of 'declared emergency'

The notion of 'psychological warfare', originally coined by the ideologues of national socialism, did not appear officially in US propaganda services, either military or civilian, until the time of the Korean War. In 1950, the three armed forces created a bureau or division of psychological warfare. In 1951, President Truman set up a committee on 'psychological strategy'. In 1952, the Psychological Warfare Center opened at Fort Bragg, North Carolina, only to change its name four years later to Special Warfare Center. In 1953, President Eisenhower appointed an advisor on psychological warfare. The first definition of this notion in the dictionary of the military forces is: 'Psychological warfare – the planned use by a nation *in time of war or declared emergency of propaganda measures* designed to influence the opinion, emotions, attitudes and behavior of *enemy, neutral, or friendly foreign groups* in such a way as to support the accomplishment of its national policies and aims.'[20]

A number of sociologists of the media who had served in propaganda agencies during the Second World War were again enrolled during the Korean War, a decisive turning point in the Cold War. Among them was Wilbur Schramm, the future founder of the Institute for Communication Research of the University of Stanford, who had written one of his first studies about the role of communication during the siege of Seoul by communist troops.[21] During the same 1950s period, eminent theoreticians in the discipline played an advisory role in the writing of psychological warfare manuals under the aegis of the Operations Research Office (ORO), one of the oldest military research organizations, based at Johns Hopkins University and funded by contracts from the Pentagon. Others worked with the US Information Agency (USIA), established in 1953 for the purpose of coordinating governmental propaganda actions abroad. The USIA is an independent agency with a director who reports to the president through the National Security Council.

The academic community called for 'professionalizing psychological warfare'. As Schramm noted: 'The world has progressed to a state in which self-preservation alone demands the most intense psywar pressure that a large body of trained professionals commanding immense resources can bring to bear.'[22] The new academic discipline of 'international communication' appeared in 1952 in this political environment under the auspices of the American Association for Public Opinion Research (AAPOR), and its language was that of political combat. Paul Lazarsfeld, one of the founders of the field, wrote:

> The relationship between practical policy and social science should be a two-way relationship. It is not only that we should contribute to the social sciences. It is imperative not merely for academic reasons but because, to a considerable extent, the national and international welfare of the country, as Lasswell points out, is tied up with the techniques of social research. The policy-makers should be joined by social scientists, not only because we can help them, but because the exclusion of social sciences from the social events of the day impoverishes the social scientists who are themselves an important resource in a country. It is very much to be hoped that, in this sense, international communications research, because it is working in an exposed area, will contribute to the improvement of the relation between social sciences and those groups and institutions who are the actors on the social scene.[23]

In principle, like the missions assigned to intelligence agencies, psychological warfare was for use abroad. The national territory was excluded. Yet the Senate commission on USIA activities, presided over in 1972 by J. William Fulbright, revealed, like the aforementioned Church commission, that this sort of covert action also targeted US citizens. The Fulbright commission trained its spotlight on the 'pollution' of the US media (Church's own term) by news items put into circulation by intelligence and information services, and on the danger posed by disinformation campaigns to 'the very credibility and independence of journalists'. The example the Senators had in mind were the campaigns organized to overthrow the Chilean president Salvador Allende from the moment he was elected in September 1970 and throughout the three years of his government, when the major US newspapers and news agencies broadly disseminated information fabricated and released by the secret services. Beyond merely inquiring about these previously undisclosed actions, the congressional investigations examined the very nature of information. They showed, on the basis of this case study, how difficult it is to discern the borderline between information and propaganda.[24] This was not a new problem, to be sure, as evidenced by a lawsuit brought by civil liberties advocacy groups during the First World War against the Committee on Public Information. By creating an Office of War Information (OWI) in 1942, President Roosevelt had only perpetuated the ambiguity.

Communication – development – security: a strategic equation

The issue of information, propaganda and psychological warfare in state policies focusing on national security cannot, however, be reduced solely to strategies of manipulation. In addition, communication and its techniques were called upon to play a pioneering role in strategies to foster growth in so-called underdeveloped nations, another dimension of the Cold War. The performative notion of development set forth in 1947 in the Truman Doctrine on US aid was at the core of a vast programme to mobilize energy and public opinion against the great socioeconomic imbalances perceived as likely to play into the hands of 'worldwide communism'.

The notion of development became inseparable from that of security. The third term of the equation was communication. The behaviourist belief in the ability of the stimulus-response schema to manage social change was reinvested in the strategic thinking of an establishment that counted on information and communication technologies to act as an agent of development.

One of the first theoreticians of the security-development-communication triangle was a sociologist at the Massachusetts Institute of Technology (MIT), Daniel Lerner, a former OSS officer and specialist in psychological warfare.[25] Lerner's field of observation was the Middle East, a region identified by Washington as combining every major element at stake in the Cold War. His study was sponsored by the government radio station Voice of America, which was seeking to assess not just its own impact in the region but also that of competing stations, in order to adapt its broadcasts to local populations. The selected countries were Turkey, Lebanon, Egypt, Syria, Jordan and Iran (a seventh country, Iraq, had been chosen, but for political reasons the survey could not be carried out). The subtitle of Lerner's work, published in 1958, clearly indicates the aim and philosophy of this operationally oriented study: *Modernizing the*

Middle East.[26] He mechanically transposed to these populations what he had learned from his experience in fighting Nazism. The category of 'anti-Nazis' was turned into that of 'moderns', who combined the three forms of mobility (physical, social and psychic) characteristic of modernity. The 'Nazi' category fell to the 'traditionals', the group most reluctant to change. The last category was designated as the 'transitionals' or 'apoliticals', a neutral group forming the core target; it was made up of those most likely to respond to the messages of psychological operations and hence to switch camps and join the first category, those most ready for a change of attitude and behaviour and most disposed to shift from a culture locked in tradition to a so-called modern culture with its attendant 'cosmopolitan tastes'. The notion of modernization was explicitly assimilated to 'Westernization'. Its ultimate phase or promised land was none other than 'consumer society', the expression of progress conceived as a linear process.

For more than a quarter of a century, these strategies of persuasive communication, which were supposed to disseminate the desire for innovation among the least developed nations, were to govern sociological thinking about development and were applied to extremely diverse geographical areas. They continued to dominate until the univocal model for transition from the traditional to the modern as a stimulus to development proved incapable of extending the privileges of the few to the population as a whole. The Truman Doctrine had made development a prerequisite for security. In reality, as power relationships changed between the countries targeted for development and US power, security came to override development, especially as Washington called upon local military forces to achieve its ends. It is quite telling that Daniel Lerner had barely completed his research on the role of international radio broadcasting in the modernization of six countries, including Turkey, when he embarked on another entitled 'Swords and Ploughshares: the Turkish Army as a Modernizing Force'![27] Its thesis was closely akin to the theories, emerging at the time, of civic action and the central role of military elites in national development.

— 5 —

'CIVIC ACTION' OR THE REAPPROPRIATION OF THE NATIONAL SECURITY DOCTRINE

During the Cold War, from South Korea to Indonesia, from Pakistan to the Philippines, in Iran under the Shah, as well as Guatemala, El Salvador and the countries of Latin America's Southern Cone, military regimes drew on the doctrine of national security as a source of legitimacy. They were accomplice regimes, turned into pawns on the geopolitical chessboard, which the White House refused to call dictatorships and preferred to describe as 'authoritarian regimes', reserving the term 'dictatorship' solely for governments supposedly manipulated by 'international communism'.[1]

The armed forces in third world countries did not establish national security states all at once. Before these forces were transformed into occupying forces in their own countries, the Pentagon first proposed another form of participation in national development – 'civic action' – through numerous technical and ideological assistance plans. The military glossary defines this concept as 'the use of preponderantly indigenous military forces on projects useful to the local population at all levels in such fields as education, training, public works, agriculture, transportation, communication, health, sanitation and others contributing to economic and social development, which would also serve to improve the relations of the military forces with the population'.[2]

The mobilization of the armed forces in the service of development strategies has played a role in shaping preventive struggles against the sources of subversion. It made its first appearance in war colleges in 1961 in response to the rise of national liberation struggles across the world.

The army as an agent of modernization

The theory of military nation-building developed along with the concept of civic action. It was born in academic circles and think tanks such as the Rand Corporation, at the request of the Pentagon, which largely funded prospective studies on 'the role of military elites' conducted in Latin America, Africa, the Middle East and Asia, especially in Indonesia. These studies envisioned the army as the 'decisive group in determining the nation's destiny' because it combined national consciousness, professional expertise, knowledge of advanced technology, a proven system of authority and punishment, and a system of emulation. This belief in the predestination of the military elite underpinned the hope of seeing it become a privileged agent of modernization, which had not yet taken place because of demagogic, politicized civilian elites.[3]

In reality, these two concepts laid the groundwork for the military to take complete power. The theory of the army as the agent for forging national consciousness, thereby building a bridge between a society and its armed forces in a context of social peace, turned out in practice to justify the worst criminal behaviour; its strategists were like pyromaniac fire-fighters. The long series of putsches in Latin America and Asia during the 1960s and 1970s soon quashed the idealistic belief in the possibility of an alliance between the technocrats in uniform and society. Indeed, the putschist generals in Brazil never believed in the pedagogical virtues of the civic expedient. At the conference of American armies in Buenos Aires in 1966, Colonel Octávio Costa admitted to his Latin American and US colleagues who still feigned belief in this strategy of 'improving the relationship of the armed forces with the population' that:

> indoctrination regarding the supposed uselessness of the armies is so persuasive that it has shaken our confidence in our destiny and many of us are starting to justify our role as if we were no longer indispensable to our nations' security. That is one of the reasons, I believe, why we emphasize what is commonly called 'civic action', which is not always sincere and very often used to disguise or compensate for what we really have to do.[4]

Although at the outset the Pentagon had intended the concept of civic action for the armies of all developing countries, it was in Latin America that the notion gave rise to considerable debate within the military, together with the concept of national security. The United States had always considered the subcontinent as its geopolitical backyard. First, it was the original training ground for 'imperialist' doctrine and 'expeditionary culture without conquest' in the nineteenth century. As Alain Joxe explains:

> the expeditions to maintain order in Latin America, which were extremely brutal in some cases, were made to protect the interests of private American companies. In these recurrent expeditions, no distinction was made between the defence of private interests and defence of national interests. [. . .] The practice of the military expedition was often undertaken in the name of defending democracy and even human rights, without this assertion in any way preventing uninhibited recourse to war crimes and support for regimes that practiced torture and political assassination. [. . .] The Americans sought to introduce in Asia and the Middle East the model they had tested in Latin America.[5]

The prototype of the expeditionary adventures was thus developed well before the advent of the imperial strategies of George W. Bush's hawks. Second, in the wake of the Second World War, strategic alliances were forged between the two Americas. In 1942, the Inter-American Defense Board (*Junta Interamericana de Defensa*) sealed the rapprochement between the armies. US war colleges opened their doors to Latin American military and paramilitary personnel. The Inter-American Treaty of Reciprocal Assistance (IATRA, or Treaty of Rio) in 1947 and the Charter of the Organization of American States (OAS) in 1948 laid the foundations for an inter-American security system. One sign of the umbilical cord that tied North America to South America: the virtual US monopoly over arms supplies resulted in such total dependence that the US president had sole authority to assess the requesting country's needs for equipment and the use to which it should be put. This situation continued until the end of the 1960s.

Brazil: the formalization of a hybrid doctrine

The declaration of the Brazilian officer quoted above suggests nonetheless that armies have not always behaved as the passive recipients of the doctrines prescribed by their US teachers. A doctrinal graft or transfer always takes place in a concrete socio-historical context. As Joseph Comblin remarked in reference to the institutionalization of the principle of national security in Latin America: 'The new state naturally does not destroy the entire previous institutional edifice.

But it introduces radical changes: it creates new institutions; it scales down, eliminates or develops old institutions. In each country, the legacy of the past restricts freedom of action to a greater or lesser extent.'[6] Few strategists theorized the concept of national security to the same degree as the Brazilian generals who overthrew the constitutionally elected president João Goulart in April 1964 and remained in power for twenty-one years, following an interminable transition period. Indeed, a civilian president was not elected until 1985. To be sure, the architecture of the permanent state of exception installed by the Brazilian dictatorship responded to the original idea of national security. Yet in a significant departure from the US matrix, and in the absence of any judicial or legislative counterweight, it pushed this logic to its limits and radicalized it.

At the centre of the system stood the national security council, made up of a handful of generals, presided over by one of its members and flanked by an intelligence service. This supreme body had the power to intervene at any time in the life of the constitutional bodies, suspend them or impose its veto. As a result, although the parliament was maintained, it could be dissolved at any moment. The judicial branch was only allowed to handle cases of no importance, since exceptional jurisdictions oversaw the national security order. Habeas corpus was denied to any individual accused of violating the new institutional order. Since every citizen was considered a potential internal enemy, the list of subversive acts was limitless. The wording of a few Articles in the national security decree known as 'AI5' or Institutional Act No. 5 gives an idea of the system's scope. Promulgated in 1969, AI5 was the Brazilian dictatorship's basic law concerning exceptional instruments of control; other military regimes in the subcontinent were to draw inspiration from it.

Article 1: Every physical or moral person is responsible for national security.
Article 2: National security guarantees the realization of national objectives against opposing factors, both internal and external.
Article 3: National security includes in essence all means intended to preserve external and internal security, including the prevention and repression of adverse psychological warfare and revolutionary or subversive warfare.

§1: Internal security, an integral part of national security, is aimed at any adverse threats and pressures, regardless of their source, form or nature, that manifest themselves or produce an effect within the country.

§2: Adverse psychological warfare is the use of propaganda and counter-propaganda or any political, economic, psycho-social or military activity to influence or provoke opinions, emotions, attitudes and behaviours of foreign, enemy, neutral or friendly groups contrary to the realization of national objectives.

§3: Revolutionary war is internal conflict, usually inspired by an ideology or supported from outside, which aims at the subversive conquest of power through gradual control over the nation.

The decree goes on to enumerate a set of crimes against national security. Article 16 defines the crime of illegal propaganda: 'Disclosure by any means of social communication of a false or tendentious piece of news, or a fact that is real but truncated or distorted in such a way as to generate or attempt to generate unrest against the people or the government.' Article 34 declares an act of subversion to be the act of 'morally offending an authority by a factional attitude and social non-conformity'. Article 45 defines subversive propaganda as 'the use of any form of social communication – newspapers, revues, periodicals, books, bulletins, leaflets, radio, television, cinema, theatre or any other similar means as a vehicle of adverse psychological warfare propaganda, or of revolutionary or subversive warfare'. The list includes '"Workplace meetings. [. . .]" The organization of committees, public meetings, parades, or protests, outlawed strikes. [. . .] Insult, calumny or defamation towards public authorities in the exercise of their functions.'

These basic provisions were supplemented by decrees granting police powers to certain entities such as universities, and the authority to exclude a teacher or student for subversive activities inside or outside the university campus. For, although the category of internal enemy applied to the whole population, its most visible elements, aside from the urban guerrilla movement, were students, teachers, journalists and the clergy.

To impose this national security order, the intelligence services, modelled after the CIA, had the right of access to all private and public information, along with the right to interrogate and arrest anyone, the right to imprison in secret detention and the right to make people disappear.

A geopolitical project

The Brazilian officers had been plagued by the theoretical question of the army's role in nation-building ever since the Second World War.

They had actively participated in the war as members of an expeditionary corps sent to the Italian Front to fight alongside the Fifth United States Army; they were the only Latin American army to send a contingent. This direct contact proved essential.[7] On the one hand, it endured in the form of personal relationships, for example, with the future second in command at the CIA, Vernon A. Walters, the liaison officer who worked with the expeditionary corps and whose later role as military attaché to Brasilia was decisive in the *coup d'état*. It also continued in the form of institutional relationships. Brazilian officers were among the first foreign students to enrol in seminars at the American National War College in 1946. Three years later, they drew inspiration from that academy in founding the *Escola Superior de Guerra* (ESG), pompously nicknamed the 'Brazilian Sorbonne'. The American military mission attended its inauguration. From the start, however, the Brazilians intended to differentiate themselves, as an official history of the school recounts:

> We thought it was obviously not advisable to copy the American National War College. It would serve as an inspiration for the *Escola* but not the sole model. Indeed, the American school, operating in a developed setting, could choose to devote itself to the business of war without worrying about solving national problems, which were left to elites trained by an educational system whose effectiveness was proven. In Brazil, on the other hand, instead of preparing for war, the priority task would be to train elites to solve the country's problems in peacetime. From those considerations came the principles, formulated with unusual intuition, that marked the genesis and evolution of the ESG.[8]

The axiom governing this project to 'structure Brazilian political thought on realistic and scientific foundations' was that the country possessed the necessary conditions to achieve the status of a major power but its development had been delayed by successive governments' inability to plan and execute. Hence the need to develop a 'method for formulating national policy'.[9] Thus, the conceptual foundations of the doctrine of national security were redefined and clarified in their Brazilian version as policy and strategy in this school which, like its US prototype, was open not only to the military but also to civilians (civil servants in the central administration, magistrates, parliamentary representatives and businessmen).

Geopolítica do Brasil, a book written by one of the school's leading ideologists, General Golbery do Couto e Silva, and published in Rio de Janeiro in 1967, explains how and why the notion of national security became pivotal in the thinking of Brazilian strategists. A veteran of the Italian campaign, Golbery had taken courses at the US National War College. Under the dictatorship, he became the chief of the intelligence apparatus.

Golbery spoke from the standpoint of a regional power bearing a 'manifest destiny' conferred by its historical and geographical situation. He proclaimed Brazil's geopolitical position very clearly, going so far as to use the term 'empire' to designate the country's future status. Of course, he conceded, interdependence tied it to the United States and this alliance implied a loss of national sovereignty, but in no case would it be 'given away for a plate of lentils'. The bargain had to be 'fair' – a *barganha leal*. It had to be in keeping with Brazil's real stature in that part of the Atlantic world. The general's analyses were faithful to the definition of geopolitics provided by the so-called Munich School as 'the state's geographical consciousness'. Golbery drew the maps of worldwide and regional hegemony, positioned Brazil in relation to the dynamic centres of power in Latin America, assessed their potential, quantified communication flows, drew up a plan for new highway routes and outlined the possibilities for expansion and the areas of influence. He situated Brazil in relation to the 'West', concluding that 'a threatened West needs Brazil and, in turn, a threatened Brazil depends on the West'. The Brazilian geopolitics he outlined in 1960 was a 'geopolitics of participation in the defence of Western civilization, which is also ours', a 'geopolitics of continental collaboration', and a 'geopolitics of collaboration with the underdeveloped world here and overseas'. Before all else, however, it was a 'geopolitics of spatial integration and enhancement', a 'geopolitics of expansionism towards the interior and, towards the exterior, of peaceful projection'.[10]

The geographical consciousness of the state invoked by the Brazilian military went hand in hand with a belief in the fundamental role of communication networks in structuring the state. On that point, their belief was in line with a national tradition influenced by the positivism of Saint-Simon and Comte, which inspired the overthrow of the emperor and the establishment of the Republic in 1889. In 1962, two years before taking power, the military leaders applied pressure to have a telecommunications code promulgated, marking the beginning of a process of integration of the fragmented country. In 1965, they backed the creation of the public telephone company Embratel, ending the monopoly of a Canadian group. Its motto: 'Communication is integration'. This was the first step towards an overall strategy aimed at providing the country with an industry for processing and disseminating information and, at the same time, a civilian and military aerospace industry.[11]

However, communication only made sense in synergy with security and development, the latter notions being linked together by a 'relationship of reciprocal causality'. Directly in line with the original objectives of the ESG, it was in the name of 'development' that the military justified its coup against the constitutionally elected government.

If the concept of national security strategy was synonymous with a total strategy, it was because war had ceased to be strictly military and become 'total, global and indivisible' – and, Golbery added, 'apocalyptic and permanent'. It was a total strategy because it concerned individuals in all parts of the country, of every race, age, profession and belief. It erased the longstanding distinction between civilian and military, between interior (homeland) and exterior. It was total because the fronts on which the struggle took place and the weapons it used belonged to every level of individual and collective life and penetrated all its interstices. The weapons were of all types. They included diplomatic negotiations, alliances and counter-alliances, agreements and treaties with public or secret clauses, trade sanctions, loans, investments, embargoes, boycotts and dumping, as well as propaganda and counter-propaganda, slogans, blackmail, threats and terror. National security strategy was permanent because the distinction between wartime and peacetime had blurred. The view of war and the state of war that emerged from this perspective was one of abstract war, managed in an abstract world, or 'pure war' as Paul Virilio would say.[12] It was global because all the values that underlay Western civilization and made it the cradle of freedom were put into play in the fight against the 'communist East'.

Total war demanded a total response. To meet this requirement, it was necessary to mobilize the lifeblood of the nation, incorporating into the struggle the potential that Golbery called 'national power': all the physical and human resources available to each country, all of its spiritual and material capability and the whole of its economic, political, psycho-social and military resources. It was up to the state, the 'all-powerful warlord', as well as to each citizen, to 'maximize national power'. Golbery situated his approach in the history of strategic thought, invoking precursors' theories of the state of exception, including those of General Luddendorf and the political scientist Carl Schmitt, regarding 'total mobilization' within the framework of 'state pedagogy'. Loyalty to the mobilizing state had to take precedence over every other allegiance. All these political, economic, cultural and military efforts demanded that the entire population, who were all subject to the same dangers, agree to the same sacrifices and the same renunciation of its freedoms, many of them centuries-old, in favour of the state. 'Security and well-being, and, on a higher plane, security and freedom,' insisted Golbery, 'are the decisive dilemmas that have always faced humanity, but never as much as today, under such dramatic and pressing circumstances. [. . .] We are sure that defending Freedom also means, thank God, building national security on solid foundations.'[13] He recalled the slogan of Hermann Göring, Marshall of the Third Reich: in a state of emergency, 'Guns will make us powerful; butter will only make us fat.'

Mass indoctrination put to the test of mass culture

The Brazilian dictatorship was obsessed by the subject of psychological warfare, propaganda, the use of the media and other instruments of dissemination for purposes of indoctrination. Psychological weapons were at the heart of its 'psychosocial strategy'. The number of Articles referring to this topic in the founding Institutional Act is quite telling. As a Brazilian political scientist explained in 1976:

> The effort of national mobilization has taken on a fundamentally 'pedagogical' aspect of civic re-education of civil society and, to this end, the regime has made full use of the means of mass communication to touch the spirit of the nation with its messages. The messages combine an exaltation of civic spirit with national symbols, figures and dates to cultivate in the people a feeling of kinship and loyalty towards a single national community. In addition, there is the emphasis on scientific and technological education as a lever for lifting the nation. [. . .] In short, civic re-education is inseparable from the framework of 'psychological warfare'.[14]

The regime did not skimp on resources to carry out this task, but it encountered two stumbling blocks. First, the campaigns to exalt patriotic symbols did not succeed in offsetting the absence of popular organizations as indispensable 'transmission belts'. Given its inability to reproduce the pomp and ceremony of European fascist regimes, and in the absence of any strong backing from broad sectors of the population, the regime's propaganda slogans failed to win the support of the masses and merely filled the empty public arena with noise. In spite of the hype promoting the 'Brazilian miracle', the people felt excluded from a development model that favoured only one fifth of the nation, even though it was precisely around 'development' that the regime sought to mobilize them. The second stumbling block lay in the tension between the stated purposes of psychological warfare and the logic of the media in everyday life. The former addressed the citizen as a potential subversive, the latter as a consumer. Despite strict censorship, the country, which the government claimed to be under siege, could not afford to extend the state of exception to the point of drying up the flow of mass culture. Brazil had arrived at a new stage in the capitalistic development of its culture industries and was on its way to exporting cultural commodities. What had seemed possible a few decades earlier – 'seal up the theatre of psychological operations', as Goebbels said, was no longer feasible. Press releases, films, television series, magazines, commercials and the like continued to circulate, as demonstrated in my study with Michèle Mattelart, *The Carnival of Images*:[15]

> The novelty of the Brazilian authoritarianism was this: to assure a minimum of consensus for a political project that was forced to resort to coercion and police control, state power had to call in the commercial machinery of mass culture, the product of a society in which public opinion is a recognized actor in the public sphere. A mass culture linked to the idea of representative democracy and free access to the market economy of information, culture, and entertainment.[16]

The dark years of the dictatorship (1964–79) were thus a period of national integration through the unification not only of telecommunications networks but also of radio and television networks. Just as the military had been responsible for the telecommunications code prior to the *coup d'état*, they were the mentors of radio and television system regulation afterwards. As a result, the years of the dictatorship coincided with the emergence of the private monopoly of Globo, which climbed to fourth place in the worldwide hierarchy of television networks, and the explosion of the *telenovela*, which became the vector for introducing Brazilian fiction into international TV markets.

> The development of Globo contributed to Brazil's 'economic miracle', built on an ephemeral annual growth rate of 10 per cent but at the social cost of a dramatic concentration of wealth [. . .] Globo was at hand to communicate the idea of *Brasil grande*, which hid the political cost of the suppression of civil liberties and the cultural cost of censorship on creativity and intellectual activities.[17]

The irresistible ascension of television on a national scale was accompanied by the manifest growth of the advertising industry, thereby helping to discredit the economic commonplace that a rise in advertising expenditures is always associated with an increased standard of living and, hence, a 'growth of democracy'. What the centurions did not see was that Brazilian society, fascinated by the fast pace of technical events on which media logic is based, had already moved into the postmodern age.

Chile: the other September 11

Fascism is a historical phase into which capitalism has entered; in other words, it is both something new and something old. In the fascist countries, capitalism no longer exists except as fascism and fascism can be combated only as the most shameless, the most brazen, the most oppressive and the most deceitful form of capitalism. How, then, can one speak the truth about fascism, which one claims to oppose, without saying anything against capitalism which gave rise to it?[18]

These words, addressed to German writers in 1935 by Bertolt Brecht, still resound when one thinks of the legacy of the dark years of the Chilean dictatorship (1973–90), the other singular case of national security state acclimation. By adopting the extreme logic of capitalism in its ultra-liberal mode, the fascist regime produced by the *coup d'état* of 11 September 1973, which overthrew the socialist president Salvador Allende, demonstrated that the forced march towards integrating the local economy into a global area of free trade came necessarily at the cost of criminalizing basic freedoms. Chile under the boot of the military represented the avant-garde of this mode of 'development', subject to the diktat of monetarism. By their own admission, the criminal generals were not prepared to take power.[19] General Pinochet's book, *Geopolítica*, written in 1968 but republished after the *coup d'état*, paled beside the writings of General Golbery.[20] Brazil had had its ESG since 1949; Argentina, its Centro de Altos Estudios del Ejército Argentino since 1943; and Peru, its Centro de Altos Estudios Militares since 1950. In contrast, the Chilean army had no centre for the development of its own doctrine. It was only in 1974 that it set up an Advanced Academy of National Security and published an initial document on the question, borrowing considerably from existing doctrines, particularly in their Brazilian version.[21]

This lack of a track record did not keep the Junta from introducing some of the most strict and comprehensive legislation which, after silencing dissident voices, allowed the regime to 'extend the state of exception indefinitely, thereby transforming it into a "normality of exception"'.[22] A body of decrees, constitutional and otherwise, provided a framework for a model of economic growth based on over-exploitation of workers, who had become foreigners in their own country.

Brazil had opted for technological independence, as demonstrated by its policies in the strategic sectors of aerospace, information technology and armaments. Hoping to create its own version of Silicon Valley, it negotiated the terms of technology transfer every inch of the way with multinational corporations. While accepting huge foreign investments in numerous sectors – the very ones that gave rise to an illusory economic 'miracle' – for a long time, the government maintained firm control over telecommunication infrastructures and agreed to make concessions only when the regime was nearly at its end. Chile, on the other hand, had only a limited internal market and, aside from the copper mines already in operation, its natural resources were not sufficient to attract significant amounts of foreign capital. It therefore wagered on unrestricted opening to foreign capital, eliminating customs barriers and preferential tariffs, providing favourable conditions for the repatriation of profits, signing bilateral agreements, and so on. It sold off shares in the state sector and dismantled, piece by piece, existing welfare state provisions. It followed the wave of structural readjustments by privatizing social security, education and health care, and was one of the first countries on the South American continent to deregulate its telecommunications market. The model, drawn from the teachings of Nobel Prize-winning economist and University of Chicago professor Milton Friedman, was made possible by suspending liberties and setting the standards for labour output and profits incomparably higher than under normal conditions in a liberal economy. In 1980, Richard Nixon had this to say about the dictatorship his administration had actively helped put in place:

> In Chile, the ruling junta has embarked on what has been labelled 'a daring gamble to turn the country into a laboratory for free-market economics.' Investment has shot up, taxes have been cut, and tax reform enacted. Critics focus exclusively on political repression in Chile, while ignoring the freedoms that are the product of a free economy . . . Rather than insisting on instant perfection from Chile, we should encourage the progress it is making.[23]

For seventeen years, the regime plunged the country into a spiral of attacks on human rights, invoking the necessity of 'eradicating the Marxist cancer'. Military control was symbolized by erasing the old map of provinces inherited from the nineteenth century and replacing it with a topography broken down into military regions, each designated by a Roman numeral instead of a place name, based on the commander-in-chief's treatise on geopolitics. In the end, this economic model compelled lasting recognition as an enviable paragon of success – at the cost of excluding more than three-quarters of the population and causing a profound anthropological change in collective mentalities.

Chilean sociologist Tomás Moulian, one of the sharpest critics of neo-liberalism and its dramatic social consequences, gave a scathing assessment in a book symbolically entitled *El consumo me consume* (1999) (*Consumption is Consuming Me*):

> The obsession with wealth and fanatical consumption tend to relax the norms governing the relationship with money, which is converted into a contemporary idol, not only among society's rejects (marginalized people), but especially among the rich and powerful. What legitimacy can a society claim in punishing poor delinquents when its own extravagant passion for money has made immorality in business and influence-peddling commonplace, when cheating on taxes and on labour standards is acceptable? In these situations, neo-liberal ideology walks on its own tail. All these phenomena are extreme expressions of competitive individualism, which knows no other moral precept than attention to self-interest.[24]

The draconian 'anti-terrorist' law imposed by General Pinochet's dictatorship was not abolished by the centre-left governmental coalition known as the Conciliation, which succeeded him in 1990. The law was even invoked to sentence Mapuche Indian activists to prison in 2007 following a conflict with the major *latifundia* owners and multinationals, particularly logging companies, that occupy and exploit a territory which the indigenous communities of Araucania claim as the property of their ancestors.

The failure of the military dictatorships did not cause the doctrine of national security to disappear from the syllabus of American war colleges. The merciless war against terrorism since 11 September 2001 even gave it a second wind. The same holds for the US model of the 'National Security Council', which democratic regimes of a presidentialist character are tempted to see as the institutional formula most likely to help the executive branch protect its foreign policy preserve and its discretionary powers in the 'war on terror'. This was the schema for the concentration of the powers of defence and security in the hands of the head of state, at the expense of the government and the parliament, that President Nicolas Sarkozy chose to institutionalize in France in 2008. This 'national security strategy' aims to respond to 'all dangers and threats likely to damage the life of the nation'. It includes not only defence policy but also domestic and civilian security policy as well as foreign policy and economic policy. It is organized around five functions: knowledge, anticipation, dissuasion, protection and intervention. The first two functions, now assigned priority because of a 'world characterized by uncertainty and instability', command the restructuring of the civilian and military intelligence agencies.[25]

6

COUNTERINSURGENCY, THE CROSSROADS OF EXPEDITIONARY FORCES

The concept of 'insurrectional situation' matured with the repression of revolts against the colonial condition. The Second World War was barely over when the first clashes broke out between expeditionary forces and national liberation movements; revolutionary processes and popular uprisings erupted at the periphery of the world-system. Asia was in the forefront of this new type of conflict, against the backdrop of hope raised by the victory of the Chinese Revolution in 1949. The pockets of insurrection that developed in Indochina, the Malay Peninsula and the Philippines were formed by movements hardened during the war against Japanese occupation.

In 1950, the Philippine People's Army, made up of what were called in Tagalog the 'Huks', under the leadership of Luis Taruc and communist activists, launched a general offensive against the Philippine government.[1] The United States helped the Philippine army to hold the guerrilla group in check. The stakes were strategic for the US, which had signed a defence agreement with the government three years earlier to maintain permanent military bases for ninety-nine years. The Philippines, which they had taken from the Spanish Empire in 1898, had long been a US protectorate in Asia.

The adoption of the notion of 'counterinsurgency' resulting from the US involvement was not accompanied by even a summary formalization of a doctrine by US military commanders. This was symptomatic of a recurring inability to accumulate knowledge characteristic of counterinsurgency thinking in its US version. This amnesia forced US strategists, with each new crisis and each new wave of insurrections, to reinvent the wheel and get back up to speed, even if it meant borrowing from the experience of other Western armies. There was at least one explanation for this failing: the Pentagon had other fish to fry. At the time, strategic consciousness was totally absorbed in deterrence and the debate between partisans of 'massive retaliation' and those who favoured 'flexible response'. This tropism, which gave precedence to firepower and other technological factors in armed conflict, reflected the monopoly held by the Strategic Air Command (SAC) on military thinking. There was a prevailing belief in technological determinism, conducive to viewing the future from the perspective of nuclear apocalypse at the expense of 'human' factors.

In the Malay Peninsula, the Malayan Races Liberation Army defied the British Empire in 1948, setting off a struggle that was to last until 1960. The strength of this communist-inspired army lay in the strictly controlled network of villages it had developed in the course of resisting Japanese troops; it had deep roots among the population, which the Huks had lacked. To break this grassroots organization, the British undertook to transfer 400,000 of its most committed partisans into 400 'New Villages'. These fortified villages were surrounded by a wide security perimeter and each was equipped inside with a police station, which was the centre of a sophisticated intelligence system to control the population. Of the 4,000 insurgents who surrendered or were captured during the twelve-year struggle, 2,700 were turned into informants.[2]

The tactic of grouping together real or potential enemies was not new. It had been used by the British army in South Africa during the last quarter of the nineteenth century to cut off the Boers from their base of support among the civilian population. The country was sown with forty-four internment camps for Boers and sixty for Africans. They were called 'concentration camps' by South African historians, who viewed them as examples of barbarism. Boers and Africans lost their lives in equal numbers under deplorable detention conditions.[3] During the same period, the Spanish army used an identical tactic in Cuba to isolate the guerrillas fighting for independence.

For the British army, the Malaysian experience represented the beginning of a long accumulation of counterinsurgency practices that developed with each intervention in a new theatre of operation: on the island of Cyprus, against Colonel Grivas's National Organization of Cypriot Fighters (EOKA) beginning in 1955; in Kenya, against the Mau-Mau insurrection (1952–60); and finally, in their own territory, in Northern Ireland, against the Irish Republican Army (IRA), starting in 1970. This itinerary was perfectly reflected in the career of the general Sir Frank Kitson. After fighting in Malaysia, Kenya and Cyprus, Kitson was put in charge of a brigade in Ulster in the early 1970s.[4] It was in the course of these colonial wars that the Special Air Services Regiment (SAS) was forged. Set up during the Second World

War and dismantled when it ended, it was brought back in the 1950s specifically to fight the Malay guerrillas. The SAS would later serve as a model for numerous other special forces, particularly in Israel. From the 1970s onwards, the SAS acted both as a special military force and an anti-terrorist intervention group – a rare situation, since the two functions were usually performed by different units.

'Pacification': the French experience

In 1954, the defeat of the French expeditionary corps at Dien Bien Phu, which ended the war in Indochina, sparked the first strategic reflections of a prospective nature. This first, decisive war of decolonization (1945–54) was characterized by the colonial power as the 'first revolutionary war', the 'first face-to-face conflict with communism in action in a vast battlefield of an unprecedented style and size, heretofore unknown'. One question haunted the officers who took part and later drew up their assessments: 'How, with impeccable battalions, powerful armoured formations, artillery units, engineering and transmissions [. . .], how, with all this force intact, could we have ended up where we are now?' Colonel J. Némo formulated this question in 1956 in two articles published in the *Revue de la défense nationale*, the first entitled 'Warfare in a Social Environment', the second, 'Warfare in Crowds'. His answer:

> In Indochina, the French were unquestionably stronger and better educated from a technical point of view than their enemies. Yet the primary school certificates and the squad of student corporals of the latter defeated the university teaching degrees and the War College of the former. Perhaps it was because they were closer to the human reality, the one that cannot be betrayed with impunity.[5]

Adaptation to the 'social milieu' and 'immersion in the crowd' were what the French army could not master or did not know how to incorporate into its war potential, such that it was reduced to 'advancing its pawns on a chessboard of territorial forces that it could not see'.

Such considerations motivated the army to send officers to university to obtain diplomas in psychology and sociology, and immerse themselves in the classics of crowd psychology, including the works of Gustave Le Bon and Serge Chakotin's *The Rape of the Masses*[6] as well as Marxist texts on propaganda. These officers internalized the psychological dimension all the more as most of them had been subjected to re-education and public self-criticism while in captivity in Vietminh camps. One of those officers was Colonel Charles Lacheroy, a key figure in psychological action. Following his return from Indochina, he constantly drove home the message that the 'masses are for the taking', voluntarily or by force, and argued for 'new methods' of retaliation against the new enemy. He made his case as early as 4 August 1954 in an opinion piece published in *Le Monde* in which he explained that propaganda designed in accordance with the standards of a moderate democracy had only a 10 per cent chance of reaching its target, whereas propaganda that was part of a strict, powerful organization of parallel hierarchies offered the guarantee of maximum effectiveness. It was necessary to replace the adversary's clandestine structures with another, parallel, structure in the service of counterinsurgency strategy

By 1955, the integration of psychological action into military programmes had led to substantial changes in military structures, with the setting up of specialized administrative sections, made up of civilian and military personnel, both European and Muslim. It thus became an integral part of the French army strategy for fighting the Algerian insurrection (1954–62). Seeking to be 'pacification with a human face', it combined propaganda or psychological warfare, in particular through companies/military units equipped with loudspeakers, films and leaflets, and immersion in the population through 'civic action' in the form of literacy programmes, building dispensaries, food distribution and technical assistance. The Centre for Instruction in Pacification and Counterinsurgency-Guerrilla Warfare (CIPCG) was set up specifically in Algeria, with an agenda that included psychological action, psychological warfare, destruction of armed groups, destruction of the rebel infrastructure, political intelligence, investigation, police action and anti-terrorist action. As Marie-Monique Robin rightly notes in retracing this history:

> In this programme, it is important to note the role of 'political intelligence' and 'police action' – assignments normally given to the police or the gendarmerie, not to the army. When the 'pacification' policy proved incapable of stemming the spread of the insurrection, the military surreptitiously took over areas of police competence which they ended up claiming insistently as their own, calling in particular for tailor-made exceptional legislation.[7]

It was a complex situation, for unlike other processes of repression against insurgent movements, the Algerian War took place, except for brief periods, in a state of emergency when 'special powers' were granted, rather than in a state of war or martial law. Its legal framework was defined by the law of 3 April 1955, which supplemented the existing provisions by creating a 'state of emergency' in the event of 'imminent danger resulting from serious offences against public order or public calamities' – conditions vague enough to allow for various interpretations – and considerably broadened the scope of police functions. Articles 16 and 36 of the Constitution of 1958, which authorized the suspension of parliamentary safeguards, would be applied in 1961 at the time of the Algiers putsch fomented by four generals who were hostile to the idea of independence.

From the Battle of Algiers to 'village-posts'

The 'inhabitant', a factor scorned by the classical doctrines taught in war colleges, was the central subject of the analyses of Roger Trinquier, a colonel in the Second Colonial Parachute Regiment, in a book entitled *La Guerre moderne* (*Modern War*), published in 1961. In this text, destined to become a classic, he draws lessons from his combat experience in 'subversive war' or 'revolutionary war'. Trinquier began his career as a schoolteacher, then joined the army, enrolling in the officers' training school of Saint-Maixent. Assigned to Beijing during the Second World War, he went on to fight in the Indochina War and later in the Algerian War. What was new about these wars, he noted, was first of all the fact that the assailant strove to take advantage of the internal tensions of the attacked country, that is, the political, ideological, social, religious and economic oppositions likely to have a profound influence on the populations to be conquered. In this respect, it was a new form of total war. A further novelty was the diffuse, amoebic aspect of the enemy.

> In modern warfare, there is no material borderline separating the two camps. The boundary between friends and enemies cuts through the very core of the nation; within a single village, sometimes within a single family. It is often an ideological, immaterial boundary, which nevertheless must be clearly delineated if we want to be sure to reach our adversary and defeat him.[8]

In short, the organizations of clandestine war had 'infiltrated the population itself, like a cancer' and were 'manipulated by a small intellectual elite in the pay of foreign powers'.[9] A zone was to be 'treated' in the greatest depth possible, like a metastasis.

Surround the territory. Seal off. Comb. Clean out. Purge. Disinfect. Extirpate the cancer. This litany of sharp-edged terms summarized the

83

strategies for the so-called control and organization of populations. Beginning in cities, army units extended their action by 'throwing a huge dragnet across the city', which implied using existing police forces who 'continued to work within their normal framework'. And so it continued. Divide the territory into quarters. Divide the quarters into blocks. Note every building, every floor, every apartment or group of houses. At each level, designate leaders and deputies. The first natural leader, at the base of the pyramid, was the head of household, responsible for all the inhabitants of a home. Take a census of the population and give each inhabitant a census certificate, with one or two copies kept for the police. The certificate would include a photograph, the block number and letter (e.g., 3-B), the district number (e.g., 2). The whole (2B3) formed a 'veritable registration number', enabling frequent checks on individuals and detection of any attempts to infiltrate a territory, while establishing the responsibility of the heads of household upon whom everyone presumably depended. Such an organization made it possible to 'give a precise definition of an outlaw: any individual who, within a period to be determined, did not enter [the place where he or she was supposed to reside]'.[10]

The organization at the top of this hierarchical structure was at once 'an overt territorial intelligence service' and an 'action-intelligence service'. The former implied training a large number of inhabitants within a few days to act as agents in factories, building sites, administrations, public services and so on, while the latter put the information to use. It made agents talk the way it made actual suspects talk, by 'interrogating them persistently'. 'During the interrogation, [the suspect] will certainly not be assisted by a lawyer. If he provides the required information without any problem, the interrogation will end quickly; if not, specialists will have to pull the secrets out of him by any means.'[11]

In 1956, the newspaper *Le Monde* published an opinion piece on the Algerian 'events' which displayed a rare courage. Henri Marrou, a professor at the Sorbonne, wrote:

> I will pronounce only three words, quite charged with meaning: (concentration) camps, torture and (collective) repression. As regards torture, I cannot avoid talking about the 'Gestapo'; throughout Algeria – no one denies it – torture laboratories have been set up with electric bathtubs and everything else needed, and that is shameful for the country of the French Revolution and the Dreyfus Affair.[12]

Yet this was only the beginning of the escalation that led to the Algerian War. It was the eve of the Battle of Algiers, in which Colonel

Trinquier took part, and which ended in 1957 with the dismantling (effective until 1960) of the National Liberation Front (FLN) in the Kasbah. Resorting to torture was all the more common as, unlike in the Indochina War, the bombings carried out by Algerian fighters were a systematic feature of the conflict.

Trinquier reviewed the procedures to be used (roundups, checkpoints, ID verification) and warned against the problems encountered by broad police operations in large cities that took place in the very midst of the population, almost in public.

> Some unavoidable roughness will inevitably look like unacceptable brutality in the eyes of a sensitive public. And it is also a fact that, to extirpate the terrorist organization from within the population itself, the latter will have to be harshly shoved around, assembled, interrogated and searched. Day and night, armed soldiers will unexpectedly burst into the homes of peaceful inhabitants to make necessary arrests; fighting may even break out, which the inhabitants will be forced to endure.[13]

Moreover, the media visibility given to such operations in concentrated urban areas posed new problems for the armies. Trinquier lashed out at the critical attitude of the metropolitan press regarding the army's actions and exactions.

What is clear is that the repressive rationality of the 'pilot action' of the Battle of Algiers permeated all the army's methods of pacification. Preparing and conducting operations against the guerrilla fighters was the mission of the 'village-posts', which was a way of returning to the 'old system of fortified villages in the Middle Ages to protect the inhabitants against armed bands'. An observation post was set up in a village, sealed off with barbed wire or bushes and protected by a few blockhouses equipped with automatic weapons. The inhabitants could leave the villages only through guarded gates, and only for a few hours. Once the village was locked up, a police operation took place inside.

A population census was carried out and the inhabitants were attributed a certificate with a registration number which, aside from controlling their comings and goings, allowed each individual to receive a ration card to control the circulation of foodstuffs. Animals were counted (calves, cows and oxen were branded with the owner's number), a measure intended above all to cut off the adversary's access to supply sources. Each inhabitant was questioned individually and in secret, usually regarding two points: who collected funds in the village and who ensured surveillance. This was followed by another, more in-depth interrogation to determine who belonged to the local military-political organization and where weapons caches and food depots were located. The inhabitants of the closest or the most isolated villages were gradually brought inside these security perimeters. Other centres were created in order to group together and control all the inhabitants of rural areas.

A million and a half to two million people were thus displaced and enclosed in 'village-posts', 'compartmentalized and cleaned out', as General Jacques Massu put it. This sort of territorial control undoubtedly brings to mind the 'New Villages' formula applied by the British in Malaysia, but it was also the result of reflection undertaken by the French colonial troops following the pacification campaign in Morocco in the 1920s and 1930s.

As for psychological action, Trinquier believed its role during the operational phase should be 'limited to making the population understand that the severity of the measures sometimes taken is solely for the purpose of quickly succeeding in destroying the adversary' and, in the pacified areas, organizing and mobilizing the population. He was less forthcoming about the actions themselves, however. As a reader familiar with the classics of revolutionary propaganda, he thought that only propaganda through deeds – blows dealt to the enemy – was likely to be convincing. 'Until we have succeeded [in rendering the enemy harmless], any propaganda, however clever, or any proposed solution, even a very generous one, will have no effect on a population infiltrated by clandestine organizations that terrorize it, like a cancer.'[14]

The Pentagon's delayed awareness

[W]hen most of the world was focused on traditional ideas of general war and its doctrine of massive retaliation, the French were in Indochina struggling with Ho Chi Minh's legacy from Mao Tse-tung – the war of 'national liberation', the 'Communist revolution' . . . On the other hand, it should be remembered that most of the world, the United States in particular, has only recently become aware of the nature of wars of liberation. Only since Chairman Nikita Khrushchev's speech in January 1961, and President John F. Kennedy's reaction to his Vienna meeting with Chairman Khrushchev, had serious attention been given this problem at top levels of Government in the United States.[15]

It is highly significant that this article by Lieutenant-Colonel Donn A. Starry of the US army, published in 1967 in English in *Military Review*, was given a French title: '*La guerre révolutionnaire*'.

Starry's observation was so on the mark that in 1960, in the face of this gap, George A. Kelly exhorted 'the most qualified American military experts to make full use of the lessons of the French experience',[16] and repeated his warning two years later in the same theoretical journal of the US army.[17] After serving in the army's First Armoured Division from 1955 to 1957, Kelly had spent sixteen months in Europe, combing the writings of exponents of psychological action and the controversies they generated, in particular in daily newspapers such as *Le Monde*. It is interesting to note that he conducted this research as an assistant to Henry Kissinger at the Harvard Center for International Affairs, which had begun a research programme on counterinsurgency. From these observations on 'revolutionary war' in Algeria, he wrote an essay defining the notion of subversion. Its aim, he wrote, 'is to sap the credit and resources of the legitimate power by a variety of means'.[18] He went on to list these:

> Infiltration of agents into the public services. Agitation and manifestation against the existing authority, often for obscure causes. Creation of friction and factionalism within all possible elements of the society, so as to weaken them *per se*. Character assassinations of adverse political figures. Demoralization and sabotage of legal institutions and their capability of enforcing justice. Dramatic instances of civil disobedience. Provocations, leading to government repression, followed usually by the attempt to enlist the sympathies of political persons in front organizations. Propaganda of all types. Interception of communications to gain intelligence and to elicit apprehension. Encouragement of corrupt practices in political and legal systems, followed by blackmail. Creation of efficient information networks capable of gradually usurping power from the legitimate authority.

In 1961, the Kennedy administration updated its approach to this type of warfare by restructuring the Pentagon. The classics of 'revolutionary war' – Mao, Guevara and Giap – were included in the syllabi of the war colleges. In the background lay the problems encountered during the first phase of US intervention in Vietnam – still limited to sending military advisors – and the evident 'inevitability of wars of national liberation or popular rebellions', as the Soviet head of state put it in a speech quoted earlier, citing as examples the cases of Indochina, Algeria and Cuba (where the guerrilla forces had overthrown the dictatorship of General Fulgencio Batista in January 1959). The architect of this reshaping of the Pentagon was Robert McNamara, a former executive of the Ford Motor Company. Drawing on advisors from the business world, and think tanks such as the Rand Corporation, he introduced a managerial style in the military mega-machine. The result was the increased centralization of intelligence services relating to defence, logistics, communications and research. New specialized agencies were created to run programmes on 'counterinsurgency', which the dictionary of the armed forces defined as: 'those military, paramilitary, political, economic, psychological, and civic actions taken by a government to defeat subversive insurgency', while 'insurgency' was defined as 'a condition resulting from a revolt or insurrection against a constituted government which falls short of civil war. In the current context, subversive insurgency is primarily inspired, supported, or exploited by communists'.[19]

In research and development, priority was given to instruments for flushing out guerrilla forces and protecting the troops against surprise attacks. Irregular war thus became an extraordinary laboratory for technologies of localization, including portable electronic equipment to link troops in the field to their commanders by satellite; systems of reconnaissance; detection and surveillance from the air or the ground; aerial photography technologies; night-vision goggles; infrared olfactory detectors that reacted to body heat; acoustic and seismic sensors or captors. All the geophones that were later to be found on the 'walls of shame' were first used to install the 'McNamara Wall', that is, the virtual barrier intended to prevent the infiltration of Vietcong fighters.

A return to pacification

Recent experiences of irregular war were closely examined. The 'new villages' tactic in the Malay Peninsula inspired the creation of 'strategic hamlets' in Vietnam. Unlike the British original, however, in the US version there were no posts or police or soldiers inside the barricades. Protected only by day, the inhabitants were exposed at night to the vengeance of Vietcong cadres who lived and slept in the villages. As a result, the people felt threatened and were little disposed to provide decisive information. In addition, the rivalry among no less than eleven US and Vietnamese intelligence organizations was such that the Vietcong played them against each other.[20]

Pacification campaigns aroused similar interest. In a symposium on counterinsurgency organized by the Rand Corporation in 1962,[21] the head of the think tank's social sciences section commissioned Lieutenant Colonel David Galula, a former captain of the First Colonial Infantry Battalion during the Algerian War, to evaluate his experience of pacification. The research contract was signed while he was spending a sabbatical year as a research associate at the Harvard

Center for International Affairs. Two publications resulted: in 1963, a report of over 300 pages in Rand's own collection and, in 1964, a more commercial version.[22] The same year, the publisher of Galula's book brought out a US edition of Trinquier's *Modern Warfare*.[23] The backgrounds of these two officers and their form of involvement in Algerian operations were quite different, and so were their respective contributions. Trinquier was one of the major artisans of the Battle of Algiers, while Galula had helped design the pacification campaign in Kabylie. The former professed a commitment to defend Western values, while the latter avoided such slippery ground. Galula was a graduate of Saint-Cyr – the 'French equivalent of West Point' as the Rand Corporation was quick to point out. Before asking to be stationed in Algeria in 1956, he had been a military attaché from 1945 to 1948 in Beijing, where he was able to observe the progress of the Maoist guerrillas, and then in Hong Kong, where he frequented the British military forces who were fighting the guerrillas in the Malay Peninsula. Finally, he had been a UN expert on the Balkans, where he had observed the evolution of guerrillas in Greece.

Whereas the author of *Modern Warfare* constructed his report like a manual for counterinsurgency operations, Galula sought to produce a theoretical work and examine his own practices from a critical distance. His book combines a reflexive dimension with a record of the operations carried out under his command and discussions he had with his soldiers and members of the military hierarchy. Placing his diagnostic insights and analyses in context, he is attentive to the particular tensions, engendered by the state of emergency, between the territory controlled for military purposes and the administrative territory run by civil servants and subject to reforms. He points out the uncertainties of counterinsurgency thinking in action. His judgement of the army's handling of propaganda and psychological action is harsh:

In my zone, as everywhere in Algeria, the order was to 'pacify'. But how, exactly? The sad truth was that, in spite of all our past experience, we didn't have one single official doctrine for counterinsurgency warfare. Instead, there were various schools of thought, all unofficial. Some of them made a lot of noise. While the majority of officers lived in an intellectual vacuum, waiting for orders from above and meanwhile performing the routine combat tasks for which they have been trained all their lives, these different schools of thought were championed by minorities. At one extreme stood the 'warriors', who had learned nothing, challenged the very idea that the population was the real objective and maintained that military action pursued with sufficient means and vigour for a sufficiently long time would defeat the rebels . . . At the other extreme were the 'psychologists', most of them recruited among officers who had undergone Vietminh brainwashing in prisoner camps. To them, psychological action was the answer to everything. It was not merely propaganda and psychological warfare in addition to other types of operations, conventional or otherwise . . . They were convinced that the population could be manipulated through certain techniques adapted from communist methods.[24]

Galula's verdict is implacable: 'If there was one area in which we were definitely and infinitely more stupid than our opponents, it was propaganda.'

The 'warriors' in the Vietnam War paid scant attention to this attempt to provide a theoretical framework for thinking about methods of pacification. What they preferred from the French experience in Algeria was above all the patented model of the Battle of Algiers, which they transposed to Vietnam in order to destroy the networks of Vietminh partisans (or those suspected of being such) in Saigon and other cities. The pacification operation went by the code name Operation Phoenix and its agenda was called anti-VCI (Viet Cong Infrastructure). The campaign, which began in July 1968 under the direction of the CIA, mobilized all the military intelligence services and all members of the national paramilitary police, as well as mercenary units controlled by the CIA known as Provincial Reconnaissance Units. According to the hearings of the US Senate Foreign Relations Committee, the programme succeeded in its first year in 'neutralizing' 19,534 people, of whom 6,187 were assassinated, 8,515 were imprisoned and 4,832 went over to the side of the Saigon regime. Three years later, the number of people killed rose to 20,587.[25]

As in Algeria, the pacification campaign in Vietnam using torture and forced disappearances was balanced by a programme with a human face. The new mission assigned to the United States Information Agency (USIA), a civilian structure for producing and disseminating 'overt information' (as opposed to the covert information of the intelligence services), was to 'lend appropriate support in the psychological area to the high command in the theatre of active operations and provide it with daily advice and basic information material'. The USIA took on this mission in the field by creating, together with the high command of Operation Phoenix, the Joint United States Public Affairs Office (JUSPAO). Its aim: 'winning the hearts and minds of the Vietnamese people to support the efforts of the American war, by influencing journalists favourably, learning the tactics of psychological warfare used by the enemy and weakening its moral strength'.[26] Although the watchword of the 'Struggle for Hearts and Minds' had appeared in US army manuals around the time of the Korean War, its debut in public rhetoric came during the pacification campaigns in South East Asia.

Counterinsurgency software

The initial idea of the Kennedy doctrine for reforming the Pentagon was that advanced technology could not substitute for politics. This position justified large-scale bidding in 1962 on social science research contracts held by the Pentagon. Anthropologists, psychologists, sociologists, political scientists and economists were invited to fill the vacuum of knowledge in 'counterinsurgency software', to use the jargon of the period. The conceptual framework for these research projects known by the acronym 'Agile-Coin' (COunter-INsurgency), with the Rand Corporation as its primary intellectual hub and subcontractor, was to focus, for preventive and pre-emptive purposes, on the environments that produce 'insurgents' and cause them to prosper. Here, again, the diversity of the fields and objects proposed for observation in order to explore human behaviour in 'insurgency situations' testifies to the protean nature of this notion. It linked together studies on topics as varied as the religious forces opposing the Iranian dictatorship of the Shah, Washington's leading ally in the Gulf region, the popular front in Chile that was seeking power through elections, and countries battling urban guerrilla movements, such as Uruguay, or rural ones, such as Venezuela – not to mention, of course, the South East Asian countries confronted by similar movements.

To carry out these studies, a partnership was set up between local research teams and universities in the United States. The Camelot Project, launched in late 1964 by the University of Pittsburgh anthropology department, aimed to 'determine the critical social parameters capable of providing indications about the state of social agitation, identify the phenomena that precede the eruption of insurrectional violence, and evaluate the various actions that a regime in power could take to control this type of conflict', mainly in several Latin American countries but also in Iran and in Thailand, which was threatened by guerrillas at its borders. The project seemed so imperialistic to Chilean sociologists, who were among the first to learn about it, that they publicly denounced it. The issue was raised in the

Chilean Congress. In the face of protests from numerous representatives of the academic community both in the subcontinent and in the United States, President Lyndon Johnson in person suspended it *sine die*, but without touching the overall philosophy of the Defense Department-sponsored research programme, which continued in a different form.[27]

The purpose of this type of study was to provide the basic data – that is, scenarios for political alternatives – for so-called counter-subversive or counter-conspiracy simulation models. One of these models, which went by the code name of 'Politica', was developed in November 1965 by the 'Research and Engineering' section of the Defense Department, in collaboration with the Fletcher School of Law and Diplomacy and coordinated by Abt Associates, a think tank. This simulation game took place in an imaginary Latin American country named 'Patria', with copper mines belonging to Patria Minerales SA, an equally imaginary subsidiary of the very real Anaconda Copper Company, where three-quarters of the country's exports were produced. Although it claimed to combine the archetypes of diverse Latin American societies, the resemblance to Chile, one of the world's leading copper producers, was flagrant. The rules for building the scenario begin as follows:

> *Politica* is a game which simulates the process of internal national conflict leading to democratic change, revolutionary change, or reaction. It has been designed to reproduce the role of the military and other factions in the politics and economic dynamics of a nation by structuring the roles of major national actors and groups, placing them in conflict or cooperation in a game environment and identifying from the resulting interaction the societal and human variables relevant to a study of incipient insurgency. By sequential search of various patterns of variables under initial conditions, the game is designed to highlight those variables decisive for the description, indication, prediction, and control of internal revolutionary conflict.[28]

One of the essential features of the model was to reveal the possible attitudes of armed forces in relation to other actors (comprising no less than thirty-five categories, including the government, political parties, the middle classes, the working classes, multinational corporations, landowners, industrialists, the student movement, women's organizations, etc.): they could either disobey orders, voluntarily rebel against the government and repress strikes and 'terrorist activities'; or they could forge alliances.

Ironically, this *kriegspiel* of the age of so-called modern warfare presented national strikes, blocked communication routes, propaganda, sabotage, occupation of public buildings, occupation of the streets, assassination and terror as the preserve of leftist forces, christened 'Fuerzas de liberación nacional'. In reality, throughout the three years of the Popular Unity government (1970–3), it was the seditious front of right-wing forces, flanked by the mainstream media, professional and employers' organizations, multinational corporations and US intelligence agencies, that made intensive use of this range of subversive actions to create the conditions for the overthrow of Chile's constitutionally elected president, Salvador Allende, by the military on 11 September 1973.[29]

The body within the military apparatus that managed all federal research contracts intended to tighten the links between the social sciences and defence interests was called the Defense Advanced Research Projects Agency (DARPA). It was this group, for example, that commissioned David Galula's report on the pacification of Algeria. The agency was set up in 1958, when priority was being given to research on ballistic missiles and the detection of nuclear testing. Composed of civilian scientists under the direction of an academic, the DARPA was behind the creation of the Arpanet network, ancestor of the Internet, which was introduced in 1968 to facilitate exchange between research teams under contract with the Pentagon.

Iraq: permanent amnesia or a return to square one

The traumatism resulting from the disaster of Vietnam helped rehabilitate the Pentagon warriors' belief in the ability of modern technology to achieve rapid destruction of insurgent forces. It was a mechanistic doctrine that presupposed the need to set up a rapid, massive intervention force of troops, but it ignored the socio-historical environment in which such a force would be called upon to intervene. As Robert E. Osgood observed in 1979 in *Limited War Revisited*: 'The result of the gradualism in Vietnam was merely to prolong the war, while increasing its cost and the hostility of public opinion, without prospect for clear victory.' He concluded that 'the United States could have and should have won the war through a faster and more intensive escalation'.[30]

Our reading of Osgood's re-examination of the Vietnam War has obviously changed, a quarter-century later, with US expeditionary forces bogged down in Iraq. In 2003, in search of a strategic formula to overcome the urban guerrilla, White House advisors asked to see *La Bataille d'Alger*, the 1966 film by Gillo Pontecorvo and Yacef Saâdi. In 2004, the Praeger publishing house put out a new edition of David Galula's book. Two years later, the Rand Corporation followed suit with its report, accompanied by a new preface by Bruce Hoffman, vice-president of Rand, newly appointed to the corporate chair on counterterrorism and counterinsurgency. Hoffman wrote:

> The inability to absorb and apply much less even study, the lessons learned in previous counterinsurgency campaigns is a problem that has long afflicted the world's governments and militaries when they are confronted with insurgencies. Guerrilla groups and terrorist organizations, on the other hand, learn lessons very well . . . The recollections (of the then-Captain Galula) . . . have a remarkable, almost timeless resonance nearly half a century later. The parallels with America's own recent experiences in Iraq are striking.[31]

Hoffman, an expert who served as an advisor to the Coalition Provisional Authority in Iraq, who teaches at the Combating Terrorism Centre at West Point and is an adjunct professor in the National Security programme at Georgetown University in Washington, took up point by point the main lines of the analysis of the former colonial infantry captain who had died prematurely in 1967. According to Hoffman, Galula's thinking made it possible to establish the similarities between these two experiences of counterinsurgency. Among these:

> The absence of counterinsurgency doctrine, the perils of failure to recognize the signs of a budding insurgency, the insurgents' urban terrorist strategy, the imperative of separating the population from the insurgents, the concomitant imperative of not inadvertently alienating the indigenous population, the fallacy of a decapitation strategy to defeat an insurgency, the critical importance of an effective information operations campaign.

A further point in common was 'the importance of according humane treatment to captured insurgents'.[32] In both cases, this intangible principle was far from being respected.

What appears certain is that the failure to comply with this rule of conduct enabled torture and the forced disappearance of 'illegal' combatants to become part of the normal behaviour of both the ultras in French Algeria and the hawks in the Pentagon. In this regard, it is worth remembering Trinquier's stratagem for justifying aggressive interrogation methods:

The terrorist has in fact become a soldier, like the aviator, the infantry-man or the artilleryman. But the aviator who flies over a city knows that the anti-aircraft weapons that protect it could kill or mutilate him. He is ready to undergo the most atrocious suffering that the enemy's fire-power can inflict upon him. Wounded on the battlefield, the infantry-man agrees to suffer in his flesh. [. . .] Yet it has never entered the mind of either one to complain or, for example, to ask the enemy to give up using a gun, a shell or a bomb. [. . .] The soldier therefore admits physi-cal suffering as inherent in his condition. The risks he runs on the bat-tlefield and the sufferings he endures there are the ransom of the glory he receives. [. . .] The terrorist, however, lays claim to the same honours but refuses the same servitudes. [. . .] But he should know that when he is caught, he will not be treated like an ordinary criminal or a prisoner taken on the battlefield. Indeed, the forces of order that arrested him are not trying to punish him for a crime for which he is not person-ally responsible, by the way, but rather, as in any war, to destroy the enemy army or subjugate it. [. . .] Like the soldier, he will have to face the suffering and perhaps death that he was able to avoid thus far. The terrorist must know this, however, and accept it as a fact inherent to his condition and to the methods of war that his leaders and he himself have knowingly chosen.[33]

So much for the civilizational advances of the Geneva Conventions.

The makers of *La Bataille d'Alger* obviously thought of their film firstly as a manifesto against the atrocities committed by colonial power, and for that very reason the film could not be shown in France for a long time. The sequence of the film on the range of techniques used by the French military (electroshock, waterboarding, the rack, burning with a blowtorch) is absolutely unbearable. What gives cause for worry from an anthropological standpoint in the representation of torture since 11 September 2001 is that it has become fodder for the society of the spectacle. As Jane Mayer of *The New Yorker* has written:

Depictions of torture have become much more common on American TV. Before the attacks, fewer than four acts of torture appeared on primetime TV each year, according to Human Rights First, a non-profit organization. Now there are more than a hundred, and the tortures have changed. It used to be almost exclusively the villains who tortured. Today torture is often perpetrated by heroes.[34]

This is the case in the Fox Channel series entitled *24*, classified as a 'counterterrorism drama', which has had favourable audience ratings since 2001 and even received an Emmy Award in 2006. During its first season, the programme depicted no less than sixty-seven acts of torture, and not just any forms of degrading treatment: victims were beaten, suffocated, electrocuted, drugged, stabbed, abraded with a sanding tool, raped or hung by a meat hook. They were blackmailed through their wives or children. In one episode, the president goes so far as to ask a member of the Secret Service to torture his own national security advisor, who is suspected of treason, in front of him. The co-creator of 24, Joel Surnow, who makes no secret of his affinities with the most conservative circles such as the Heritage Foundation or those who feel nostalgic for the McCarthy era, presents the series as 'patriotic'. The Fox Channel makes a similar claim, having been the first to broadcast propaganda for the Bush administration's claim regarding the existence of weapons of mass destruction in Iraq. Confronting critics from human rights groups, Surnow justifies the programme as follows: 'Young interrogators don't need our show. What the human mind can imagine is so much greater than what we show on TV.'[35]

In contrast, the US-born writer Jonathan Littell, who made inter-rogation under torture and the role of the executioner during the Nazi period the central focus of his novel, originally written in French, *Les Bienveillantes*,[36] thinks that we cannot understand 'the rage to torture' if we confine ourselves to what goes on in the mind of indi-viduals. 'The day that a government, like the American government, lifts legal prohibitions by redefining what constitutes torture, there are plenty of people ready to torture and stage sexual fantasies as we saw in the photos from Abu Graib. It happens very quickly, imme-diately, and yet it occurs in a society considered to be democratic.'[37]

For the philosopher Pierre Pachet, who has worked extensively on this question, the act of torture is a

> new and terrifying figure of politics which has become, in certain parts of the world and at certain times, an experimentation ground for an exit from humanity, the laboratory for capitalizing the experience of the inhuman, placed in the service of prosaic ideals of management and the proper functioning of national affairs (. . .). Individuals who are put to the test of torture are being challenged to 'hold on', to maintain their convictions, attachments and quite simply their being; but what is being asked of individuals who undergo torture, in situations of colonial war, or civil war, or ideological conflict, is something even greater, if one dare say so. Indeed, it seems that every time, it is humanity as a whole that the act of torture aims to make disappear, to compromise.[38]

Venturing another interpretation, we might also see the banaliza-tion of torture as the result of a long-term strategic effort by certain media to break viewing records with productions that bolster the security order through the psycho-social motifs they mobilize. The transgression of the taboo on torture could be seen as the last step in the moral desensitizing of television viewers. Indeed, programmes such as *Big Brother* and its variants have prepared the way by blurring the borderline between the documentary and reality TV. By imposing no limits on voyeurism, exhibitionism and cynicism, and by giving free rein to the urges of targeted audiences, these programmes will not be the last to contribute to the decay of the idea of human dignity and to the corollary expansion of the desire for humiliation of the self and others.

Certain feature films recently released in the United States have vehemently denounced this legitimation of civilizational regression through the acceptance of torture, and more generally the exactions of intelligence agencies, as natural occurrences. It is no accident that Joel Surnow, co-producer of the series *24*, holds up as a counter-model the 2006 film *Syriana* by Stephen Cagan, starring George Clooney and Matt Damon, which sheds light on CIA strategies in the Middle East. He might also point to an even more explicit film, *Rendition*, by South African director Gavin Hood, starring Meryl Streep, which depicts the outsourcing of torture to centres abroad and the illegal detention of innocents. However, most recent films about Iraq and Afghanistan, such as *In the Valley of Elah*, *Lions for Lambs* and *The Kingdom*, have failed to recoup their investments.

— 7 —

THE INTERNATIONALIZATION OF TORTURE

The effect of counterinsurgency strategies was to connect local armed forces and police to a system of regional and global alliances and complicities, foremost among which were instruction and training systems. Once again, Latin America played the role of a pioneering laboratory.

In the United States, the fear of seeing emulators of the Cuban Revolution proliferate in Latin America reactivated the dormant project for an inter-American system of hemispheric security. In 1962, the Inter-American Defense College was founded at Fort McNair in the Washington, DC, area. The nine-month study programme, reserved for colonels and senior officers in Latin American armies or their equivalents in the civil service, was similar to those at the US National War College, the NATO Defense College in Rome and the Imperial Defence College of London.[1] While the United States provided the buildings to house the college, the cost of operations was borne by the member nations of the Organization of American States, whereas the chairman was appointed by the President of the United States. In 1960, the first annual conference of American armies took place with, as its subject, 'the security of South America'. The alliance's target was clearly designated: the 'common enemy' of communism and its variants within national borders. The meeting was held at Fort Amador in the military complex of the Panama Canal Zone. The next three inter-American conferences were organized in 1961, 1962 and 1963 at the same protected site, and the fifth in 1964 at the US Military Academy at West Point. At the sixth conference, which took place for the first time in a Latin American country, in Lima, Peru, the alliance decided that the location of subsequent meetings would be determined by alphabetical order of countries.

Argentina thus hosted the following conference in 1966. Bolivia should have been next in line, but, as a lieutenant-colonel of the US army wrote in *Military Review*, 1967 was the year of the 'Bolivian army's campaign against the insurrectional efforts of Ernesto [Che] Guevara',[2] which caused the conference to be cancelled.

The School of the Americas

The redeployment of the programmes for foreign military trainees (FMT) concerned above all the Panama Canal Zone, made up of fourteen forts that housed numerous schools, in addition to the head-quarters of the US Southern Command, in charge of coordinating military and intelligence activities, supervising assistance programmes and the logistics of US armed forces throughout Latin America. An Army Caribbean School, dedicated exclusively to Latin America, had already been set up at Fort Gulick in the Canal Zone in 1956. Classes there were taught in Spanish. In 1963, this school was transformed into the US Army School of the Americas (USARSA). For its sup-porters, it was the *Colegio de las Américas*; those who denounced it called it the '*Escuela de los golpes*' or school of *coups d'état*. Its four divisions – Command, Combat Operations, Technical Operations and Support Operations – emphasize armed counterinsurgency as well as civic action, with practical exercises conducted in the villages of the Panamanian countryside.

The programmes were run in parallel with those for US trainees at Fort Leavenworth, Texas, or the Special Warfare School section of the J. F. Kennedy School at Fort Bragg, North Carolina, headquarters of the Green Berets, the elite unit of the Eighth US Army Special Forces. The Jungle Operations Training Center, located at Fort Sherman on the other side of the Panama Canal, worked closely with them. The primary mission of this unit was to prepare Mobile Training Teams (MTT) for emergency interventions to advise and assist the military and paramilitary forces of the subcontinent. One such team with sixteen members was sent in total secrecy to Bolivia to ready local Rangers to interdict the guerrilla. The localization of the successive encampments of the *guerrilleros* and their movements from the air, using infrared cameras, was subcontracted to a private firm.[3] There was also the Inter-American Air Force Academy (IAAFA), located on the Albrook base in the Canal Zone, which inaugurated a joint course with the army on Special Air Operations in 1965.

The curriculum at the School of the Americas – some fifty courses ranging from two to forty weeks – was mainly taught by US citizens of Mexican, Puerto Rican or Cuban origin and the best trainees were invited to return as instructors. The school translated English-language manuals one after another into Spanish: between 25,000 and 30,000 pages per year, according to the school's administration.[4] Furthermore, every Latin American student could read *Military Review* in a Spanish edition (since 1945) or a Portuguese edition (since 1952). Upon arrival, each student was assigned a social sponsor who introduced him to the circle of military personnel residing in the zone, with whom he was expected to stay in contact once he returned home. In addition, each trainee agreed to give a lecture in the course of his stay on areas of conflict in his country of origin, and on the solutions proposed to prevent or combat urban insurgency or civil disorder.

In 1973, the School of the Americas could boast of an array of strategically placed graduates: 170 of its former students held positions in their respective countries, including head of state, minister, commander-in-chief of the army or head of secret services. The four members of the Chilean junta as well as the head of the *Dirección de Inteligencia Nacional*, the sinister DINA, created in 1974, had received advanced training at the school or in a military academy in the United States. General Pinochet had been trained at Fort Benning in Columbus, Georgia, and accepted invitations from the US Southern Command in 1965, 1968 and 1972, just prior to the coup that brought him to power.

By 1973, the school had received some 30,000 students since its foundation. At the top of the list were two staunch allies of the United States: Nicaragua (4,119 students), where the Somoza dynasty had imposed a reign of terror since 1936, and Bolivia (2,679), where the takeover by General René Barrientos in 1964 inaugurated eighteen years of *coups d'état* featuring the most repressive military dictatorships in its history.[5] And by 1973, the total number of Chileans who had been through the Panama Canal Zone School since its establishment reached 1,300 – considerably more than the number of Brazilian graduates (340) since Brazil had its own *Centro de instrução da guerra na selva* (Center for Instruction in Jungle Warfare), founded in 1964, the year of the *coup d'état*, in Manaus, in the heart of the Amazon region.

Military intelligence: control over life and death

What did trainees learn at the School of the Americas? The so-called theoretical lessons centred primarily on the 'nature of the Communist threat'. This was an omnipresent topic, presented in vulgarized form just as Senator J. William Fulbright had denounced it at roughly the same time in *The Pentagon Propaganda Machine* (1971). As a Chilean ex-black beret (*boina negra*) named Gonzalez testified in 1976 to two journalists from that same country: 'They talked to us about Marxism as a philosophical current of hate, of men possessed by the devil, people whose brains secreted the most diabolical ideas. [. . .] Ideas such as massacring and destroying the world, and sowing hatred. And our task was to fight against these ideas with guns. God would guide us in eliminating Communism.'[6]

Among the courses on practical methods, the most edifying were those concerning so-called 'military intelligence': for example, Course E-16 (combined with E-15), entitled 'Methods of Interrogation'. Graduates of the course, which lasted six weeks and was reserved for non-commissioned officers with at least the rank of corporal and six years of study and experience in this field, received the title of 'military intelligence interrogator'. Here is some more testimony from the same Chilean witness:

- *What does 'military intelligence' mean?*
- They taught us only up to a certain level. They did not teach us everything, obviously. [. . .] Military intelligence means two things: not to give out information and to receive information through interrogation. Either capture someone without the others knowing about it, interrogate him, kill him, get rid of his body, bury him. Or interrogate him while he can still talk, and once the guy dies, get rid of him so that the Reds [*los Rojos*] don't know we got the information out of him. That's what military intelligence is.
- *How were the torture classes?*
- Practical classes. They used us as examples, they put matches under our fingernails . . .
- *So Lieutenant Labbé tortured you?*
- Yes. Not only him, but the other officers and the conscripts; there were several instructors. They took us and hung us by our fingers with a very thin rope. They told us: when you have a rebellious guy who doesn't want to talk, you shouldn't waste time by systematically hitting him. You should let him suffer for a while, and think about it carefully, while suffering . . . His fingers fall asleep, his blood stops flowing, he suffers great pain. But at the same time, you don't kill him . . .
- *What else were you taught?*
- To strip them and make them run on stones, among thorns, barefoot. Threaten them with lighted cigarettes, on the cheeks, near the eyes, the mouth, the lips . . . to come as close as possible so that he feels the heat, that his skin burns, but without applying the cigarette.

101

- But doesn't that leave marks?
-Yes. They taught us to bring the burning tip as close as possible, so that the flesh burns, but the cigarette doesn't go out. Bring it close to nipples, testicles, pinch the nipples . . .
- Of women, too?
- There were different systems for women. They told us that when women were in the guerrilla, they were extremely dangerous. They insisted a great deal on that point. They were all passionate and prostitutes and were looking for men . . . and that's why they were there. The best way was to find the person the woman loved most, her man or her children, and hit them or torture them in front of her.[7]

All existing reports on torture indicate that 'the female body has always been a "special" object for torturers', writes anthropologist Elizabeth Jelin:

The treatment of women included a dose of sexual violence. The women's bodies – their vaginas, their uteruses, their breasts – linked to the women's identity as sexual object, as spouses and mothers, were clearly objects of sexual torture. [. . .] For men, torture and prison implied an act of 'feminization', in the sense that it transformed them into passive, powerless, dependent beings. Sexual violence was part and parcel of torture, as were constant references to the genitalia – the mark of circumcision among Jewish victims as a factor aggravating torture, references to the size of the penis for everyone, electroshocks applied to testicles, etc. It was a way of turning men into inferior beings, and in so doing, establishing 'military virility'. The men had to 'live like women'.[8]

First-hand accounts like these explain why, for people who had experienced other 11 Septembers, the revelation of such violent acts in the new global 'war on terror' was nothing new.

The corporal admitted that in training to become an 'interrogator', the first link in the chain of military intelligence, he was not taught the overall plan that gave meaning to the practices. Thus, immediately after the *coup d'état* in Santiago, the Brazilian intelligence services arrived at the offices of the DINA to interrogate day and night fellow Brazilians who had taken refuge in Chile following the *coup d'état* against President Goulart.[9] Two years later, with the full knowledge of the US intelligence services and Henry Kissinger, President Nixon's national security advisor, the heads of the intelligence services under the dictatorships in Argentina, Brazil, Chile, Paraguay and Uruguay inaugurated Operation Condor, a veritable international association for torture, clandestine kidnapping and forced disappearance.[10] Its aim was to collect, exchange, classify and compare information on

102

opposition leaders in each of these countries and organize joint operations to eliminate them. The discovery of the 'archives of terror' of the secret police of Paraguay in 1991 only confirmed this plan. Already in 1977, the trade journal *Computer Decisions* had published an article with the provocative title 'Would You Sell a Computer to Hitler?' by two US computer technologists who addressed serious questions to the manufacturers and suppliers of these data-processing systems.[11]

Building a repressive police force

The decision to give priority to modernizing the equipment of military forces, training them and sending advisors to the field, also concerned the police and security services. The Office of Public Safety (OPS), established in 1962 as a division of the US Agency for International Development (USAID), had as its mission 'to anticipate immediate threats to domestic order and set up civil police institutions capable of guaranteeing the internal stability essential for economic, social and political progress'. Economizing resources was also a consideration, because the mission statement also called for preparing police forces 'to prevent threats to domestic order from developing before they turn into explosive problems requiring military action'.[12]

The Public Safety Project thus enabled the Brazilian government to retrain roughly 100,000 agents and train more than half a million officers between 1969 and 1972. Foremost among the beneficiary institutions were the National Police Academy, the Institute of Criminology and Identification, and the National Telecommunications Center. One of the main objectives of the aid programme was to unify the police forces under a national command and facilitate the circulation and exchange of information; hence the importance of a communication equipment plan for the acquisition of computers, radios, automobiles and helicopters. The point was to develop 'mobile communication capability in times of civil disturbance' while 'increasing the efficiency of control by police patrols'.

Another textbook case that indicates the large scale of the OPS programmes is the infamous Operation Phoenix. Within this framework, the Vietnamese national police force saw its ranks multiplied by five between 1963 and 1971, and restructured in order to assume paramilitary responsibilities. Its mission was to keep tight control over the flow of people and resources from village to village by extending a network of checkpoints to even the most remote roads and waterways and, above all, to establish a national identification system to register everyone over the age of fifteen, including fingerprint records and files on individuals' political affiliation. Public security programmes thus helped to format more than a million police agents throughout the world, not only in Latin America, but also in Saudi Arabia, Iran, the Congo under General Mobutu, Pakistan and the Philippines.

The Inter-American Police Academy, too, opened its doors in 1962. The original 'Inter-American' appellation changed a few years later to 'International', thereby extending the scope of its audience. The course titles at the academy are as telling as those taught at the schools of war, as witnessed by this sample list of courses and lectures related to internal security, taken from the January 1967 issue of the *International Police Academy Review*: 'Introduction to Internal Security', 'Nature of Insurgency', 'Basic Framework for Counter-Insurgency Policy', 'Operational Views on Insurgency', 'Introduction to Civil Disturbances', 'Records and Internal Security', 'Planning for Riot Control', 'Riot Control Formations', 'Photography in Civil Disturbances', 'Special Equipment for Control of Civil Disturbances', 'Police Baton', 'Chemical Munitions', 'Environmental Factors of Insurgency', 'Economic View of Insurgency', 'Legal Considerations in Crowd and Riot Control', 'Targets of Insurgency', 'Tactical Communications in Control of Civil Disturbance', 'Crowd and Mob Psychology' (*sic*), 'Counterinsurgency Intelligence', 'Anti-terrorist Measures', 'Causes and Characteristics of Riots', and so on.

Most of the information on OPS operations filtered out of hearings conducted in 1971 by the Congressional committee working in closed session and chaired by Senator Frank Church, and had to do with the agency's connections with regimes showing little concern for human rights.[13] Public opinion had been alerted by the revelations following the 1970 execution in Montevideo of Dan Mitrione, an OPS agent who specialized in aggressive interrogations, by the Tupamaros urban guerrilla movement. This expert, on detachment to the Uruguayan police, had previously served the same function for nearly eight years in a Brazilian police centre in Belo Horizonte. A parallel investigation, launched by a Uruguayan Senate commission, had concluded that torture was a normal, frequent and customary occurrence, and listed twelve types of techniques used by the local police. A manual distributed to members of the police force was actually entitled: *How to Keep People under Torture Alive*. In 1972, the film-maker Costa-Gavras dramatized the Mitrione episode of the anti-subversive struggle in his film *State of Siege*. It was filmed in Santiago – a sinister omen – when Salvador Allende was still president of Chile.

The consequence of the US Senate investigations was to prohibit training and assistance programmes for foreign police. They resulted in 1976 in the amendment of Section 660 to the Foreign Assistance Act (FAA) of 1961, prohibiting 'the use of security-assistance funds to train, advise or offer financial support to foreign police forces, prisons, internal intelligence programs or other law enforcement forces'. The legislators did, however, provide for a set of exceptions, to be approved by Congress on a case-by-case basis and contingent upon respect for human rights, but no such procedure was followed to counter the actions of armed forces and intelligence services during the 'dark years' of the Latin-American dictatorships.

The French network

We know from our own painful experience that what is sometimes described as subversion is often merely political disagreement, which is normal in a democracy. We know that such struggles can lead to using methods that hardly conform to military methods and traditions. At such times, citizens are kidnapped and disappear; others are imprisoned for long periods without being sentenced or charged with any crime; some are tortured; prisoners' families do not know where they are being held. [. . .] We earnestly ask you to see to it that the Republic of General José de San Martin never presents, under your presidency, the oppressive image that too many military governments are giving elsewhere in the world.

The above is a short passage from a letter sent to the Argentine president by three French reserve field officers, General Beccam (former commander of the National School of Aerial Warfare), General Binoche (former governor of Berlin), and Vice-Admiral Sanguinetti (former inspector general of the navy). It was included in an article published in *Le Monde* in August 1977 that revealed the connection between the 'counter-guerrilla methods in the manuals by French authors' and the dirty war launched in 1976 by the Argentine dictatorship against its opponents, which was to last seven years. Indeed, the journalist who broke the news of the French officers' message, went beyond the letter itself, which sought to avoid offending the local military, reporting that 'some Argentine officers invoked the Indochinese and Algerian "examples"', boasting that they had 'succeeded in achieving better results'.[14]

The Spanish edition of Roger Trinquier's work *La Guerre moderne* had indeed been published in 1963 by an Argentine publishing house specializing in military writings, and a compilation of his writings on subversion and revolution came out the year before the *coup d'état*.[15] *Les Centurions* by Jean Lartéguy, which drew on the French colonel's descriptions in the writing of its most graphic chapters, became a bestseller. This type of anti-subversive literature was passed on to Argentine officers by French advisors recruited directly by the country's military leaders or by other Argentine officers trained at the Ecole Supérieure de Guerre in Paris. The French Embassy in Buenos Aires, and its successive military attachés in particular, were also unsparing in their assistance.[16] After the Second World War, Argentina was the land of exile for collaborators of the Vichy regime who had been sentenced to death in France. After the Algerian conflict, it became a haven for activists in the OAS (*Organisation Armée Secrète*) who continued their bombings and targeted assassinations following their failed putsch in Algiers on 21 April 1961 to prevent the signing of the Evian Accords concerning the ceasefire and self-determination for Algeria.

The first French advisors arrived in Argentina in 1957. They published articles in the *Revista militar* and organized lectures and simulated combat exercises at the war college in Buenos Aires, the gendarmerie and ESMA (the national school of naval engineering), which was to become one of the main centres of torture under the dictatorship. These crusaders of anti-subversive warfare, who had earned their stripes in Indochina and Algeria, became propagandists for the concepts of 'internal enemy' and 'psychological action'. In the military journal, one of them even recommended setting up a 'centre for counter-guerrilla instruction'. Unlike its neighbour Chile, which was more subservient to the training system in the Canal Zone, Argentina sent few officers and cadets there (no more than 565 during the first ten years of the school's existence).

In 1961, the national war college in Buenos Aires organized the first 'inter-American course on counterrevolutionary warfare', concocted by the French advisors together with an Argentine officer who had received military training in France. By the next year, the school of war had its first manual, entitled *Instructions for the Struggle against Subversion*, based on a document written by two members of the French mission. The transplant took. Some were worried about the direction it was taking. Among them was Lieutenant-Colonel Mario Orsolini, who presciently detected in the enthusiasm of his superiors the sign of a 'crisis of the army':

A definite tendency was already developing within the military hierarchy to embrace the most extreme political ideas, imitate the adversary's

terrorist methods and consider those who raise their voices against this
state of collective insanity as enemies. Hatred is becoming the main
driving force for action and fear is its secret foundation [. . .] causing
the advent of the *dictator*.[17]

'Hatred' was the recurring word that readers of Trinquier's book who
lived under dictatorial regimes during the 1970s used to characterize
his anti-subversive doctrine.[18] The experts' dissection of the Battle of
Algiers was to constitute an unprecedented ideological effort, culminating in making the practice of torture natural, like the use of any
other weapon of warfare. The French advisors did not hesitate to
show Gillo Pontecorvo's film *La Bataille d'Alger* over and over in the
barracks.

The transplant of a decontextualized concept of anti-subversion
was particularly successful because it took place in ground ferti-
lized by the long history of the relationship between the French and
Argentine Catholic extreme right-wing circles. They were united
around the project of a holy alliance between the cross and the sword,
the guarantee of a 'Christian' order to bar the anti-Christian revolution of communism. They read the same texts as the ideologues of the
'Catholic order' (*la Cité catholique*). During the dictatorship, and in
contrast to Chile where the Curacy of Solidarity took up the defence
of the victims and denounced human rights violations, part of the
hierarchy of the Argentine Church approved of torture and 'death
flights', that is, the elimination of detainees by dropping them into the
sea from a plane.[19]

The technique of 'forced disappearance of people' was one of the
characteristic features of the clandestine repression introduced by
the junta's project for militarizing national institutions, the '*Proceso
de reorganización nacional*'. The practices included selective kidnapping, detention and torture at clandestine centres (nearly 340
throughout the country), execution and hiding the remains. In choosing their victims, the apparatus of repression applied 'extremely
broad criteria extending to individuals with family or affective ties to
the targeted person. Such ties were sometimes assimilated to participation and these relationships also offered a way to gain access to the
"target".[20] The ultimate horror of this system of deliberate annihila-
tion of individuals and eradication of any other political project was
the theft of children kidnapped along with their parents or born in
clandestine centres during their mothers' detention.

The system was not only repressive but also coercive – a mode
of exercising power, since it had effects of control and deterrence

on the entire population.[21] It combined visibility with clandestinity. Kidnappings were carried out in broad daylight in public places and in front of witnesses. Unidentified corpses turned up bearing traces of brutal torture. The newspapers talked about them. But what happened to those considered to be 'seditious individuals or elements', 'delinquents', 'criminals' or 'subversives', who were said to have 'died in confrontations', remained hidden along with the reasons for their kidnapping. This mode of disseminating terror became a mechanism of social control through fear.

To counter the damning reports of Amnesty International, the dictatorship's Ministry of Information called upon a large multinational public relations agency in 1977 to organize a campaign from its headquarters in New York 'to project throughout the world a new progressive, stable image' of the Argentine regime and to retrain in this spirit the officials in charge of media relations posted in embassies and consulates.[22] This operation in institutional communication also prepared football supporters for the World Cup championship that Argentina was to host in its stadiums the following year. That global event, according to one sports commentator on French television who recounted the 'fabulous story of the World Cup', was a great success:

> Before the beginning of the championship, General Videla wanted to win the battle for Argentina's brand image, and César Luis Menotti [coach for the host country] wanted to win the World Cup. Both of them succeeded beyond their wildest dreams, for seldom has a world competition been as well organized at every level. It's a pity the quality of the playing was poor, but that was not Argentina's fault.[23]

A manifesto against torture

In the 1970s, citizen organizations set an example for what should be the obligation of states to account for their strategies of terror. The Russell Tribunal II, named after the philosopher Bertrand Russell, who had gone to war against war in 1914, commissioned investigations and brought indictments against Latin American dictatorships between 1974 and 1976. The first Russell Tribunal, also known as the International War Crimes Tribunal, had acted in similar fashion in 1966–7 to denounce the crimes of US forces in Vietnam (Operation Phoenix, the spraying of forests with exfoliating agents, the use of napalm). These two experiences resulted in the Universal Declaration of the Rights of Peoples, adopted on 4 July 1976 in Algiers by a group of jurists, economists, political figures and leaders of national liberation movements. At the same moment, the International League of Rights and Liberation of Peoples, a non-governmental organization, was born. The Permanent Peoples' Tribunal (PPT) was established three years later in the wake of these events; it has since convened nearly forty times to judge violations of human rights in countries as diverse as Colombia, Algeria and the Philippines. The 'judgment' pronounced at each of the sessions of the citizens' tribunal is less a verdict than a process of explanation of the mechanisms underlying illegal actions and their impunity. It aims not only to 'state the law publicly' but also to raise awareness. Thirty years later, these grassroots initiatives are still hard at work. This was demonstrated by the 2006 proclamation by the International League for the Rights and Liberation of Peoples of the 'People's Manifesto against Torture', drafted by the Uruguayan writer Eduardo Galeano in an international context marked by a resurgence of such practices.[24]

As a counterpoint to repressive policies, networks of solidarity and denunciation of human rights violations sprang up during the 'dark years' at the global and regional levels, and have subsequently continued their work.[25] Testimony to this effort can be found in the long, tortuous process begun in 1981 at the first congress of the Latin American Federation of Associations for Relatives of the Detained-Disappeared in alliance with other regional federations, particularly the Asian Federation against Involuntary Disappearances (AFAD), which culminated in the International Convention for the Protection of All Persons from Enforced Disappearance in December 2006. This international legal instrument, officially supported by Argentine and French diplomacy and approved by the 61st UN General Assembly, stipulates that forced disappearances constitute crimes against humanity. It recognizes the right not to be subjected to forced disappearance, with all the consequences and obligations that implies for governments: the right to the truth, i.e., the right to know the truth about the fate of a disappeared person and the circumstances of the crime; the right of relatives to recover the remains of the disappeared; the establishment of guarantees regarding the prohibition of clandestine detention of any person in any place; the right to justice for the relatives and friends of the disappeared, guaranteed by making forced disappearance punishable under domestic criminal law. Furthermore, the Convention extends the status of victim to the relatives and friends of the disappeared, confirms the multiple dimensions of the right to reparation and ratifies the right of child victims of forced disappearances to recover their identity. The symbolic impact of this Convention is especially powerful as it was adopted in a troubled context, marked by the scandal of the 'secret prisons' maintained by the US intelligence services as part of the fight against terrorism.

Finally, the return to democratic institutions in the Latin American republics opened up a vast field of unanswered questions regarding the 'memories of repression' and the 'work of memory', as Elizabeth Jelin explains. First, it involves 'trying to understand memories as subjective processes, rooted in symbolic and material frameworks'. It further entails:

> recognizing memories as a subject of disputes, conflicts and struggles, which leads to paying attention to the active role, involving production of meaning, of the participants in those struggles, who are situated in power relations. Finally it requires 'historicizing' those memories, in other words recognizing that there are historical changes that affect the meaning of the past, as well as the place assigned to memories in different societies, cultural environments and spheres of political and ideological struggle.[26]

In attempting to answer these questions, one discovers not only the various 'extreme situations' experienced by the countries of the Southern Cone of Latin America, but also those of the Shoah or the Spanish Civil War. For, as Claudia Feld notes:

> in this regard, what happened in Argentina is akin to earlier experiences undergone by other countries, in which horror put language and the mechanisms of representation to the test. In that sense, the question formulated by Elie Wiesel regarding the extermination of the Jews under Nazism is also valid for the Argentine experience under dictatorship: 'How can we tell the story when the event, by its dimensions and the weight of horrors, defies language?'[27]

'Security cooperation': post-Cold War reorganization

What became of the School of the Americas? Renamed Western Hemisphere Institute for Security Cooperation (WHINSEC), it was brought home to the United States in 1986 and re-established at Fort Benning, Georgia, in preparation for the devolution of the Canal Zone to the Republic of Panama planned in 2000, pursuant to the treaty signed by US president Jimmy Carter and Panamanian president Omar Torrijos in 1977. Classes of officers and cadets from Latin American countries continued nonetheless to graduate from the school. Chile, even after returning to democratic rule, did not cut its ties. The doctrine of national security still has a place of honour, along with courses on 'civic action' which have added the adjective 'humanitarian' to the title. Every year, demonstrators organize sit-ins in front of the school gates, demanding that it be closed.

The Pentagon has invested in new military bases on the islands of Aruba and Curaçao, in Comalapa, Salvador and in Manta, Ecuador. It has extended its radar system mainly to Peru and Colombia.[28] Joint operations involving the armies of the northern and southern hemispheres have not been discontinued. The aim of the simulation carried out in the Aguila III exercises in 2003 under US command was nothing less than to 'annihilate an insurgent commando'. The Organization of American States (OAS), which includes the countries of the subcontinent and the United States, has approved the principle of intervention by foreign troops.

While the governments of the Southern Cone (Argentina, Uruguay and Chile) have been reluctant to allow the participation of the armed forces in the area of domestic security, some Latin American countries have called upon the military to perform tasks of policing and civil protection by combating organized crime or repressing social conflicts that the authorities are unable to control. This militarization suggests how difficult it has become to draw a clear dividing line between organized crime and social conflict, since organized crime, in the regions where the phenomenon is most developed, goes hand in hand with endemic poverty. This is the case in Brazil where the government of President Lula da Silva has sent the Special Police Operations Regiment (BOPE), a kind of SWAT team, to fight drug traffickers in the *favelas* of Rio de Janeiro. It also occurs in Central America where a supranational force was created by Washington in 2005 to fight against youth gangs (*pandillas de maras*), drug trafficking and traffic in illicit migration. As for Colombia, submerged in an endless civil war between guerrillas, paramilitary forces, drug traffickers and the military, it crystallizes all the possible uses of the armed forces.[29]

Before the global war on terror was declared, Latin America was the first to receive news of another war, also described as global, declared in 1989 by President George H. Bush against drug traffic. It was called the 'Colombia Plan', at once an anti-narcotics and counterinsurgency scheme. The military base in Manta was created to provide logistical support to the plan. Manta has the added advantage of being located in a country rich in hydrocarbons and minerals. More than ever, the geopolitics of energy and natural resources, at the worldwide as well as regional level, plays a key role in the redistribution of platforms for intervention.

The US argument concerning the existence of terrorist 'sleeper cells' in the regions where the borders of Argentina, Brazil and Paraguay join hastened the signing of an agreement between the three countries and the United States in 2003 to authorize joint operations patrolling the Iguazú and Paraná rivers. The real issue remains, however, control over another natural resource – water, since that is where the Guaraní Aquifer System, a veritable ocean of underground potable water, is located. Everything related to surveillance or satellite detection of regional resources, whatever their nature, is in the sights of the US government. This was demonstrated by its manoeuvres in 1994 to secure the SIVAM (System of Vigilance for the Amazon) contract with the Brazilian government to operate a vast system of infrared surveillance, enabling observation of the slightest movement beneath the foliage. Informed by Echelon, the planetary eavesdropping system, that a transaction was under way between Brasilia and the French firm Thompson (now Thales), the Americans barely succeeded in preventing the signing of the contract. They accused the French firm of trying to bribe Brazilian officials and President Clinton personally contacted his Brazilian counterpart. As a result, the SIVAM project with its 25 radar installations, 87 satellites and 200 receiving platforms was awarded to the US firm Raytheon, one of the Pentagon's leading suppliers, better known for its Patriot missiles. The stakes were both geo-economic and geopolitical. The electronic surveillance of the Amazon serves several purposes: monitoring the environment, protecting the indigenous populations, controlling land occupation and use, and updating maps. At the same time, it is intended to keep watch over an area with vast water reserves and potential for wealth thanks to its biodiversity, and to control river navigation and air traffic as well as borders through which all sorts of contraband and traffic pass, particularly as Brazil shares a border with the Colombian region in which heroin traffickers – but also guerrilla movements – operate.

As a counterweight to the militarization of security cooperation plans such as Plan Colombia under the authority of the Pentagon, the US State Department worked closely with the Justice and Treasury Departments, the FBI and the Drug Enforcement Agency (DEA) to set up the International Law Enforcement Academy (ILEA South) in El Salvador in 2005. This Central America ILEA is the fifth link in the network of US academies: ILEA-Budapest, inaugurated in 1995, covers post-communist Central and Eastern Europe; ILEA-Bangkok, created in 2000, covers Asia; ILEA-Botswana, set up in 2001, is located near sanctuaries of terrorist networks in East Africa; ILEA-Roswell, in the state of New Mexico, hosts graduates from the other academies. The mission of these academies is to train police officers, judges and prosecutors. The courses and practical training emphasize topics related to the struggle against suspicious financial transactions, arms and drug traffic, and terrorism. For this reason, the Department of Homeland Security, created shortly after the attacks on the World Trade Center, was immediately associated with the development of these programmes. ILEA-South has also incorporated data on clandestine migration. It thus includes immigration officers among its teachers and students.

The creation of the Salvadoran branch did not occur without difficulties. When the idea was launched in 1997 under the Clinton administration, the headquarters of this regional academy were supposed to be in Panama, but that country quickly declined the offer. The president of Costa Rica then agreed to house the new institution, but the country's Congress, supported by the National Human Rights Commission and civil society organizations, refused to ratify the agreement between the two presidents, in view of the sinister memory of plans for police cooperation introduced in Latin America during the 1960s and 1970s. What Washington wanted to avoid at all cost was precisely setting up the ILEA in Salvador, a politically marked country which had received millions of dollars in US aid to liquidate guerrilla movements in the 1970s and 1980s. It was indeed during the Salvadoran civil war, which resulted in 80,000 victims, that US advisors had developed the methods they sought to apply in the fight against Iraqi insurgents under the code name 'Salvador Option'. As an unswerving ally, El Salvador distinguished itself from the rest of Latin America by sending a token contingent to Iraq alongside the American-British coalition. According to the State Department, the creation of this type of international academy on the other continents had thus far never met with any political objections!

In recent years, the rise of leftist or progressive regimes in the American subcontinent – most particularly in Venezuela, Bolivia and Ecuador – has provoked worry in Washington. The new president of Ecuador had barely been sworn in when he held an international conference in Manta in March 2007 on the worldwide system of US military bases. The Ecuadorian authorities set an example by deciding not to extend the authorization given when the base was established.

Part III

Securitizing/Insecuritizing

— 8 —

THE NEW DOMESTIC ORDER

Crisis, exception, security – a trilogy inseparable from the socio-political configuration of the so-called advanced industrial societies in the 1970s. The period of exceptional growth from 1945 to 1973 led to the belief that crises had become obsolete and could be easily explained and neutralized. The oil shock, when the price of crude oil quadrupled in 1973 and tripled in 1979, refuted this assumption. Then came the shake-up of the international monetary system with the deregulation of capital transactions and the loss of momentum of the Keynesian state. There was also a crisis of the mode of production of the general will, heralded by French students in May 1968 who, as Roland Barthes noted, seized the opportunity to speak out as if they were 'taking the Bastille'. In an essay written after the events outlining a 'sociology of the crisis', Edgar Morin described May 1968 as a genuine 'explosion' that 'paralysed the state and authority, starting with the students' revolt against gerontocracy and paternalism, and as it spread weakening the essence of authority within families and the workplace'.[1] He concluded by saying: 'We should think about the international character of the student revolts, and interpret May 1968 not so much in a strictly French context but rather within the scope of virtually planetary movements.'

Upsetting 'traditional means of social control'

Is democracy in crisis? This question is now being raised with increasing urgency by some of the leading statesmen in the West, by columnists and scholars, and – if public opinion polls are to be trusted – even by the general public. In some respects, the mood of today is reminiscent of the early twenties, when the views of Oswald Spengler regarding 'The Decline of the West' were highly popular.[2]

So began the report on the 'governability of democracies' by the Trilateral Commission, an informal brain trust made up of business-men, politicians and liberal intellectuals from the three centres of the world economy (Western Europe, North America and Japan). The statement reflects distress in the West and shows that the crisis it is undergoing affects the very foundations of the system. It was signed by Zbigniew Brzezinski, the future national security advisor under President Jimmy Carter. The body of the report, written by three experts – Michel Crozier for Western Europe, Samuel P. Huntington for the United States and Joji Watanuki for Japan – largely echoed this pessimism.

> The more democratic a system is, indeed, the more likely it is to be endangered by intrinsic threats . . . Yet, in recent years, the operations of the democratic process do indeed appear to have generated a break-down of traditional means of social control, a delegitimation of political and other forms of authority, and an overload of demands on government exceeding its capacity to respond.[3]

'The effective operation of a democratic political system', the report continued, 'requires some measure of apathy and non-involvement on the part of some individuals and groups.'

The new challenge arose from the development of an 'adversary culture' among intellectuals, including students, literary circles, and the media, who were assumed, by definition, to be cut off from practical affairs and therefore irresponsible. 'In some measure', the report read, 'the advanced industrial societies have spawned a stratum of value-oriented intellectuals who often devote themselves to the derogation of leadership, the challenging of authority, and the unmasking and delegitimation of established institutions, their behaviour contrasting with that of the also increasing number of technocratic and policy-oriented intellectuals.' The expansion of secondary and university education, pervasive media and the dis-placement of manual labour by intellectuals and professionals have had the combined effect of confronting democratic governments with a challenge that was 'potentially at least, as serious as those posed in the past by the aristocratic cliques, fascist movements, and com-munist parties'.[4] The media were no less dangerous: 'There is, for instance, considerable evidence to suggest that the development of television journalism contributed to the undermining of government

118

authority . . . Television news, in short, functions as a "dispatriating" agency – one which portrays the conditions in society as undesirable and as getting worse.'[5] Only shock therapy could prevent the 'suicide of democracy': 'We have come to recognize that there are potentially desirable limits to economic growth. There are also potentially desirable limits to the indefinite extension of political democracy.' To put it plainly, in order to counter the 'abuse of power by the press', it was necessary to 'restore the balance between government and the media':

> In due course, beginning with the Interstate Commerce Act and the Sherman Antitrust Act, measures had to be taken to regulate the new industrial centres of power and to define their relations to the rest of society. Something comparable appears to be now needed with respect to the media. Specifically, there is a need to insure to the press its right to print what it wants without prior restraint except in most unusual circumstances. But there is also the need to assure to the government the right and the ability to withhold information at the source.[6]

It should be kept in mind that the Interstate Commerce Act (1887) was the first law to restrict freedom of enterprise in the United States. It was passed in the midst of the first great international recession and it aimed to regulate railroad oligopolies. President Richard Nixon expressed similar wariness of the major media in *The Real War*, his memoirs about his experience of international negotiations. In the chapter devoted to 'secrets', he noted:

> 'Freedom of information' has become a sacred cow. Secrecy is considered sinister and wrong. Yet common sense ought to tell us that publicity that leads to bad results is not necessary good, and that secrecy that leads to good results is not necessarily bad. We need more effective legal sanctions to discourage harmful disclosures. Even more important, we must quit making national heroes out of those who illegally disclose top-secret information.[7]

During his terms of office, the second of which ended abruptly in August 1974 as a result of the Watergate scandal, Nixon had to counter numerous leaks. The most famous of these occurred in July 1971, when the *New York Times* published the *Pentagon Papers*, secret documents passed on by a former CIA agent that revealed manoeuvres in the military and civilian spheres designed to lead the country into an irreversible military commitment in Vietnam.

Computerizing society as a way out of the crisis

'A crisis of civilization' was the diagnosis formulated in 1978 in a report on the computerization of society by two high-ranking French civil servants, Simon Nora and Alain Minc, at the request of President Valéry Giscard d'Estaing. This official document was destined to become an international reference. It noted the 'first signal' given by the 'student explosion of 1968': the 'displacement of conflicts to other subjects of confrontation such as the city, health care, education, etc.', which 'has begun to be perceptible in most modern countries'.[8] The scenario they proposed as a way out of the crisis was to promote a network society or 'information society' as the sole solution capable of bringing to an end centralization, which was 'publicly criticized and yet obscurely demanded'. The dynamics of technology would upset the 'nervous system of organizations and society as a whole' and undermine the 'elitist distribution of powers'. But the authors warned:

> If there is irresponsible upsurge of convivial and cultural aspirations that is incompatible with the constraints, it would reduce the collective project to a minimum, or provoke a sudden reaction on the part of the high priests of the kingly order. [. . .] Socializing information therefore means introducing the mechanisms by which constraints and freedoms can be managed and harmonized.[9]

The 'management and harmonization of constraints and freedoms' is what the authors emphasize when they discuss the dangers of collecting and filing information on people.

> The general public experiences keeping computerized records as a form of 'surveillance of individuals' and thus a violation of privacy and freedom. This is one of the most emotive and most thoroughly explored aspects of the consequences of computerization. It is the most emotive because computers and files have taken on a symbolic value that crystallizes allergic reactions to modernity. It is the most thoroughly explored due to the remarkable work carried out by the National Commission on Information Technology and Freedom, the parliamentary debates this work has made possible, and the laws that came out it. [. . .] In this area, the quality of the social fabric, the pluralism of forces and the play of counter-powers override the 'freedom-threatening traps' of technology.[10]

This was indeed a period in which significant social mobilization succeeded in forcing the French state to introduce legal control mechanisms to establish a balance between the progress of information technology and the preservation of the right to privacy and freedom. The Ministry of the Interior had concocted in complete secrecy a technocratic project, which was leaked by the press and members of the French parliament. As a result, between 1972 and 1974, the citizenry became aware of the 'freedom-threatening traps' of information technology: the computerized system of administrative files and directory of individuals known as *Safari*, based on linking together some 400 different files using a 'single identifier', the Social Security registration number. This personal, permanent number assigned to each person is made up of thirteen digits which can be broken down into six parts: the first indicates the person's sex (1= male, 2 = female); the second is made up of the last two digits of the year of birth; the third is the number of the month of birth (preceded by a zero until October); then two numbers identifying the department of residence, followed by three digits corresponding to the township of birth; the last three are the entry number in the civil status registry.

In 1974, the 'Safari affair' forced the government to suspend the project and appoint a National Commission on Information Technology and Freedom (CNIL) associated with the Ministry of Justice. Its mission was 'to propose measures to the government within six months to guarantee that the development of information technology in the public, semi-public and private sectors would respect the right to privacy as well as individual and public freedom'.[11] The issue of the 'single identifier' as a surveillance tool was all the more sensitive as it had first been used during the Occupation and thus carried a highly negative connotation. It was indeed under the Vichy regime that the national statistics service inaugurated this device to constitute a register of the entire population, since 'it was necessary to implement laws governing trade, university quotas and the entry of Jews into public service'.[12] The population register was abandoned at the time of the Liberation, but the project of instituting a single identity number was taken up again and materialized in 1945 when INSEE (the French National Institute for Statistics and Economic Studies), charged with putting electoral registers in order, constituted a new register to identify all persons born in France. The Social Security health-care insurance programme, which had just been created, adopted this system of individual identification and used it massively. Subsequently, several ministries adopted it,[13] foremost among them the ministries of National Education, the Armed Forces and Finance. It is interesting to note that 'these operations, in themselves timely and carried out with great care, were based on quite uncertain legal grounds in the governmental decrees of 14 June 1946 and 13 May 1947'.[14]

121

The Information Technology, Files and Freedom Act

The French debate over the single identity number as a tool for linking files took place early by comparison with most other advanced industrial societies, and with good reason. At the time, many countries still refused the very principle of the identity card, despite recurring pressure from police authorities such as the FBI in the United States at the time of 'Red' hunting after the First World War. France had made the identity card mandatory after the Second World War, following an initial failed attempt in 1939. Moreover, it was one of the first democratic societies to formulate a project for a computerized, unfalsifiable identity card on the pretext of combating terrorism. In the late 1970s, the Bill to institute this card was sent for an opinion to the recently created CNIL. After some hesitation, it gave the project the green light. In the process, it imprudently gave its approval to legalizing identity checks.

This first public debate on the protection of privacy and personal data culminated in a set of concrete measures in the Information Technology, Files and Freedom Act, passed on 6 January 1978. The CNIL was given the status of an independent authority, to be composed of members from the parliament, the *Conseil d'État*, the judiciary, the order of barristers and higher education. Its mission was to seek a compromise between the various interests of administrative bodies, corporations and citizens. The processing of personal data and its storage in files had to be declared to the CNIL and even required the Commission's authorization in the case of public files. Interconnections among files were strictly limited and regulated. 'Right of access' was confirmed in three modes: the right for individuals to know about the existence of files and any personal information concerning them, the right to know the content of this information or the right to access it in the strict sense, and the right to challenge it. The sole caveat was that the right of access was to be the rule and impossibility of access the exception: 'Exceptions to the right of access are. . . required for processing computerized personal information of interest to national defence, state security and public safety.'[15] In all the official reports, in particular the Nora-Minc Report, the diagnostics and recommendations stop where the exclusive preserve of national security and repressive apparatuses begins. As an analyst for *Le Monde* noted when the CNIL report was published:

> One of the weaknesses of the Information Technology and Freedom Act is that it allows the administration to use personal files without any real

controls when those files are of interest to defence and 'public safety', in the broad sense of the term. The temptation is great to hide behind this exception to prohibit citizens included in such files from exercising the 'right of access' recognized by law.[16]

During the same period, several countries – Austria, Denmark, the Federal Republic of Germany, Luxembourg, Norway and Sweden – adopted measures tending towards 'habeas data' as in France. In contrast, countries such as Portugal and Spain raised citizen protection against the encroachment of information technology to the level of constitutional guarantees.

The public debate also called attention to the danger of seeing certain multinational corporations escape the constraints of the protective national system by setting up 'data havens', along the lines of 'tax havens', in countries with no legislative protections. At the international level, several measures were adopted to deal with this legal challenge. In Europe, Convention 108 of the Council of Europe (1981) enacted mandatory rules and specified, on a decisive point, that any person could claim the enumerated guarantees and rights, 'regardless of nationality or residence'. A decade later, the framework proposed by the European Union directives on telecommunications data (1995 and 1997) was added. The international legal arsenal was supplemented by OECD guidelines in 1980, the regulations of the World Trade Organization (WTO) in 1995 and the International Labour Office (ILO) in 1996. These rules require member states to refrain from adopting regulations which, on the pretext of protecting privacy, would impede the free circulation of personal data. The United States interpreted and continually invoked this argument in its own favour before international bodies, in order to legitimate strategies of traceability and consumer targeting by global geomarketing enterprises.

The notions of 'vulnerability' and 'vulnerable society' became a constant in diagnostics and in the preambles to measures taken to regulate the relationship between security and liberty. Beyond considerations of individual liberties, they conveyed apprehension about the danger of collapse inherent in a network society. Several pioneering reports identified this vulnerability in detail. Whether from Paris or Stockholm, which proposed a 'decree on vulnerability', everyone warned of interference that was likely to hinder the functioning of the new reticular economic structure: acts of war, riots, terrorism, economic embargo and international crises.[17] Vulnerability also referred to crises that made the catastrophic scenario of a 'major technological risk' less virtual, such as the Three Mile Island nuclear accident in Pennsylvania in March 1979; the derailing of a train carrying chemicals in Mississauga, Ontario, also in 1979; the large-scale oil spill that followed the 1978 sinking of the *Amoco-Cadiz* off the coast of Brittany in France; and the chemical accident in Seveso, Italy, in 1976. Defiance towards major techno-scientific systems began to appear. At the core of fears linked to environmental considerations lay civil nuclear energy.

The post-Fordist corporation under siege

The events of May 1968 foreshadowed challenges not only to state authority but also to the entire mode of rigid, hierarchical management, materialized for decades in the so-called Fordist order. Throughout the world, the crisis of confidence in the institutional realm coincided with the beginning of the dismemberment of the industrial firm and the emergence of a managerial and financial neo-capitalism whose main rules were adaptability, responsiveness and flexibility in a competitive global market. Corresponding changes occurred in the socio-psychological sphere of power within the firm: a decision-making system of controlled autonomy, allowing vast, complex ensembles to be governed from a distance; internalized rules and principles, in keeping with the logic of organizations, without orders and prohibitions; the organization as the locus of a corporate religion; the psychological hold of the organization as both a pleasure-producing and anxiety-producing machine.[18] It was a mode of subjection of individuals in tune with the world of new information and communication technologies.

The vanguard of this corporate paradigm – at once flexible and global – was embodied at the time by IBM, the leading trade name of the 'information age'. The Nora-Minc Report described this firm as the symbol of the main enemy against which the nation-state had to protect itself. Its control over the global computer technology market and its projects for alliances with the telecommunications industry justified adopting a national industrial strategy to counter the danger to the country's 'collective memory' posed by dependence on the US network and data banks. Throughout the decade, the 'IBM empire' gave shape to the threat against individual liberties and national sovereignty. In 1968, Stanley Kubrick's film *2001, A Space Odyssey* had already pictured the totalizing grip of the computer HAL, a clone of the IBM system. The mega-corporation's discourse on its philosophy of action and its products fostered such perceptions: on the one hand, the prophetic proclamations concerning its commercial activities: 'World Peace Through World Trade'; on the other, the realism expressed, for example, in an advertising brochure on its latest computer model in 1980, the IBM 3750:

> Its multiple functions make it the nerve centre of a versatile telephone network. [. . .] For companies in a single region, all the information indicating who entered and exited which company building, by which door and at what time, is available for subsequent computer processing. [. . .] Finally, and here is a way of further increasing the effectiveness of the security functions, the access rules can be modified instantly at the control panel of the 3750. Similarly, a person can be authorized to access certain areas for a predetermined amount of time.[19]

Convinced that security was the name of the game in a highly competitive market, IBM applied the security shock treatment to itself. It incorporated security into its managerial approach by soliciting the aid of the International Association of Chiefs of Police (IACP) to protect the company against exposure to kidnappings and ransom demands by 'extremists'. This resulted in a course given to all employees at its subsidiaries: *Security. A Management Style. A Course of Instruction in Corporate Protective Services. IBM as a Target for Terrorists.* Here is an excerpt:

> Simply because it operates overseas, IBM will have some vulnerability to terror or violence there. Add to this simple fact of location the fact that IBM is identified with Western technological supremacy and, to some degree with so-called 'American Imperialism', and the overall assessment of IBM's future overseas vulnerability must be placed relatively high on a scale of judgements . . . IBM at CHQ and Site levels thus will face some hard decisions about how to define and institutionalize this very necessary intelligence capability. An important element of a counter-terror intelligence system will be its ability to generate analyses of incident data and use them to formulate response scenarios. IBM is unusually well qualified to develop such scenarios. In doing so it can draw upon accumulated expertise intelligence and analysis within the Defense research and development community.[20]

The computer manufacturer advised its employees to read the urban guerrilla manual by the Brazilian revolutionary Carlos Marighela, who was assassinated by the São Paolo police in 1969.[21]

IBM's mobilization against the 'terrorist threat' was not an isolated phenomenon. It was widespread in the outposts of the multinational economy. Seminars, think-tank reports and articles in management

125

revues enshrined its entry into the science of 'global corporate intelligence'.[22]

State insecurity: the dramatization of criminality

'Not the exception/ but the state of exception/ confirms the rule/ What rule?/ In order not to/ answer the question/ one proclaims the state of exception', wrote the German poet Erich Fried in 1978 in *100 Poems without A Country*.[23] His words echoed what was happening in liberal European democracies at the time. Regimes of exception or permanent emergency took hold, police powers were expanded, judicial powers were reduced and political opposition was criminalized. A whole range of rights and liberties and a series of domains of freedom lost ground, giving new meaning to the idea of 'limited democracy'. Numerous works appearing in the second half of the 1970s sounded the alarm on the extension of a new arsenal of repression in just a few years.[24]

In France, the drift towards the abuse of liberties was one of the characteristic features of the project of 'advanced liberalism' promoted by President Giscard d'Estaing between 1974 and 1981. After the election of his successor, socialist François Mitterrand, in May 1981, the French League of Human Rights reviewed the evolution of rights and liberties in France in a 'black book' (*Livre noir*) describing Giscard's seven-year term. Obviously, the departing president could not be held directly responsible for all of the elements in this document, but the Giscard administration's use of laws and institutions after 1974, which the opposition had fought from the start, clearly revealed their harmfulness. Over that seven-year period, the 'procedures for domestic protection to be enforced in the event of a crisis' were revised to protect the existing order against the dangers of 'a destabilized society and world that might react in a disorderly or anarchistic manner', according to the terms of the government project to reorganize territorial security. By introducing concepts such as 'state of exception' and 'reinforced state of exception' into legislation in order to fill the gap between state of emergency and state of siege, the authorities indicated their determination to zero in with ever greater precision on any 'hot spots' and 'sensitive points' of domestic security that might endanger the 'integrity of national structures'. It was at this time too that a special force called the Intervention Group of the National *Gendarmerie* (GIGN) was set up.

To counter the threat of the 'enemy within', the armed forces were redeployed throughout the country. According to Vice-Admiral Antoine Sanguinetti:

In May 1968, there was no army in France in any usable form, only a few skeletal barracks. General de Gaulle wanted it that way, after the warning of an attempted takeover by the OAS (Secret Army Organisation) during the events in Algeria, in order to shield the country from a putsch by officers of the extreme right ... All French troops were stationed in Germany or at the borders, without any permanent organic link to the civil administration network inside the country.[25]

Under the new army redistribution plan, the whole of French national territory was covered by twelve of the fifteen active divisions. The aim of this redeployment was 'to ensure security against enemy infiltration within the territory'. Finally, the agents at the intelligence agency known as the SDCE (Foreign Documentation and Counter-espionage Service), who were traditionally assigned to work outside national borders, also began being assigned to domestic intelligence work. Thus, a new sector specializing in 'anti-subversive research' was created within the 'counter-espionage' division.

In 1976, a series of Bills on illegal possession of weapons, criminal association, vehicle searches and criminal code provisions was endorsed by the Council of Ministers. Among those subsequently approved by the parliament, only the measure regarding vehicle searches was rejected by the Constitutional Council.[26] This prohibition was to be circumvented by a law authorizing alcohol tests – the first law allowing people to be stopped without having committed any violation. The high point of this process arrived with the gestation of the law entitled 'Security and Liberty'. On 23 March 1976, a 'committee assigned to study violent forms of delinquency in contemporary French society and draw relevant lessons' was created by governmental order under the authority of the prime minister. In July 1977, a report entitled *Reponses to Violence* was submitted to the government; it was immediately published in paperback, sold at news-stands and widely discussed on television. From this diagnosis of the 'manifestations of violence' and its 'root causes' the new law arose. The feeling of insecurity stemming from economic causes was channelled towards the ideal traditional scapegoat: 'criminality'. This was also the time when the economic crisis closed the parenthesis of three decades of labour immigration to France. The borders were sealed and the immigrant population was held responsible for all the country's ills.

'France is afraid' was the laconic but sensational opening line of the evening news on the French television channel TF1 on 18 February 1976. Media overkill and opinion polls took over the topic of insecurity and dramatized it. Whether the acts of deviance were small or great was immaterial; the 'body social' had to be protected from the 'pathology' supposedly threatening it. Security was defined solely in physical terms rather than in terms of uncertainties regarding wages, medical care or education. 'Social control developed according to a "eugenic" perspective and the growing concern with social prophylactics required the regular production of internal enemies, thus simultaneously rationalizing and strengthening the process.'[27] By promulgating the 'Security and Liberty' law shortly before the 1981 presidential elections, the government counted on reaping the dividends of fear, believing it had found the best argument to rally the majority of ordinary citizens to the incumbent president, who was running for a second term against the Socialist candidate. This so-called 'special legislation' was in line with existing measures that already provided for responses to any situation of threat to the state. These included the law on the state of emergency passed during the Algerian War; two supplementary laws adopted in the wake of May 1968, which reinforced the repressive arsenal of measures of exception: the 1970 'anti-rioter' law that allowed the state to attribute responsibility for any collective action to certain individuals (originally, acts committed by 'leftists'; later on, trade union actions and protests); the law against drug trafficking (1971) aimed at individuals suspected of 'using drugs in social situations'. The armed forces maintained military tribunals (with no possibility of filing claims for civil damages or appealing a decision) in peacetime, despite eighty years of demands by the League of Human Rights to put an end to them. The Socialist Party-led government thus had to take on a long list of reforms, including the repeal of liberty-threatening laws and the suppression of courts of exception. The left government sent a strong signal when it stopped plans to adopt a computerized identity card.

Without attempting to establish a strict causal link, clearly, Michel Foucault's analyses of imprisonment and the concepts that legitimate and organize it, in *Discipline and Punish*, should also be read against the political backdrop of the 1970s. Prison guards, judges and, of course, prisoners joined together to form the Prison Information Group (GIP), which included Foucault and other intellectuals such as Gilles Deleuze and François Châtelet. The group engaged in an explosive combination of thinking, protesting and formulating proposals on incarceration.

New emergency systems

The 1970s were marked by the actions of groups that recommended and used violence as a method to achieve political ends, including the Baader-Meinhof gang or Red Army Faction (*Rote Armee Fraktion*, RAF) in the Federal Republic of Germany, the Red Brigades in Italy and the IRA in the United Kingdom. There was also the operation on 5 September 1972 in which members of the Israeli delegation at the Munich Olympic Games were taken hostage by a Palestinian group called Black September, whose name referred to the massacre of armed Palestinian groups on Jordanian territory by King Hussein in September 1970. With the actions of these groups in mind, the member states of the European Community constructed the notion of 'terrorism'. Paradoxically, the term was never defined in criminal law. As a result, it served as the heading for a list of new crimes without becoming a legal category itself. Nor is there any legal definition of terrorism under international law. The G7 referred to it for the first time in 1978 in pragmatic terms in calling for the suspension of all flights to and from countries that supported terrorism. In spite of its vagueness, the expression 'international terrorism' came into vogue at the time, amalgamating movements that developed in very different countries and thus different political contexts: the Euzkadi Ta Akatasuna (ETA) in Franco's Spain, the Tupamaros and Montoneros, under the military dictatorships in Uruguay and Argentina respectively; the Palestine Liberation Organisation (PLO); Ahmed Jibril's Popular Front for the Liberation of Palestine-General Command (PFLP-GC); the Red Army in Japan, which introduced kamikaze practices in the Middle East by sending a three-man commando to massacre twenty-six people and then commit suicide at Lod Airport in Israel. This amalgam was used and abused by the media to establish the idea of a new 'age of terrorism'.[28]

The role played by media in complicity with the state apparatus to construct an official notion of terrorism was revealed by three British sociologists in their research on the emblematic case of Northern Ireland. Examining a sample of reports, documentaries and fiction films on the subject, they concluded:

We reject the counter-insurgents' claim that television gives extensive publicity to 'terrorist' views and mobilises sympathy and support for their causes. We also reject the commonplace radical characterisation of broadcasting as a largely uncritical conduit for official views. In opposition to these one-dimensional accounts we have drawn attention to the diverse ways in which television handles 'terrorism' and the problems this question poses for liberal democracies. We have shown that some programmes are relatively 'closed' and work wholly or mainly within the terms set by the official perspective. Others, though, are more 'open' and provide space for alternative and oppositional views. However, the extent of this diversity should not be overstated. Although television is the site of continual struggle between contending perspectives on 'terrorism', the contest is not an equal one. 'Open' programmes appear far less frequently than 'closed' ones and they reach smaller audiences.[29]

In essence, terrorism was represented by the media as the extreme case of the 'violent society' syndrome. Since the other 'forms of violence' were merely steps on the same ladder, it was justifiable to extend the enforcement of special legislation beyond 'terrorist attacks'.

In the conclusion of his critical evaluation of anti-terrorist measures adopted during the 1970s, Gérard Soulier, a philosopher of law, confirmed that

> terrorism is first of all a mass-media concept. A terrorist is someone who is designated as such by the media. It has become a standard reference, a notion of anti-crime policy in the context of the fight against terrorism. [. . .] This formal retreat on the conceptual terrain, which began with regard to terrorism, is of considerable importance for the theory of law (it is both a sign and an agent of the decline of law), as well as from a practical standpoint: such informal practices have quickly spread within the domain of concepts, and have been extended, quite naturally one might say, to the area of procedure.[30]

The withdrawal of procedural guarantees (regarding the right to defence, preventive detention, or prison conditions) was also a common feature of the Reale Law in Italy, the anti-terrorist decrees in the Federal Republic of Germany and the Prevention of Terrorism Act in the United Kingdom. In 1971, London reintroduced 'administrative internment' (imprisonment without indictment or trial). The United Kingdom placed the fight against the armed movements of Ulster within the militarized framework of Low-Intensity Operations, refusing to grant prisoners the status of political prisoners and instituting courts of justice without juries, authorized to find defendants guilty without evidence, solely on the basis of their confessions. Defendants were subjected to interrogation methods in flagrant violation of both Article 3 of the European Human Rights Convention concerning 'torture' and 'inhuman and degrading treatment' and Article 14 on 'discrimination' (in this case, against the Catholic minority). Following a complaint against the United Kingdom filed by the Irish government in 1976, the European Human Rights Commission in Strasbourg concluded:

> The systematic enforcement of methods aimed at inciting a person to provide information is very similar to methods of systematic torture that have been known for centuries. Although the five methods – also known as 'disorientation' or 'sensory deprivation' – do not necessarily leave serious after-effects, the Commission sees them as a modern system of torture that falls into the same category as systems applied in previous eras to obtain information or confessions.[31]

Many countries experimented with new forms of detention such as special prisons or special high security facilities. In Germany, roughly thirty changes in the laws concerning the right to legal defence resulted in the presumption of innocence being replaced by the presumption of guilt, while also prohibiting parole, excluding defendants from their own trials and not allowing them to choose their own counsel. Informing on others was promoted to the status of civic action. The notion of complicity in criminal law was interpreted in a broad sense, as illustrated by the notion of 'sympathizer' in Germany, and that of 'connection', ratified by the anti-terrorist law adopted by post-Franco Spain in 1978, the same year that country adopted a Constitution establishing the rule of law.

In the feverish atmosphere of Germany's judicial hunt, reality TV seized on insecurity, stoking fears and transforming every television viewer into a police informer. The programme *Case XY. . .* projected a short film retracing an enigma confronting the police in an unsolved criminal case, listing a series of questions based on a clue or an identikit likeness and inviting the public to join in the game. Viewers with any information were asked to call the studio, where a police officer would answer the phone. All the complaints filed against the show by citizen organizations were dismissed from the courts. In November 1973, the programme was discussed in an article in the official publication of Interpol, the *Revue internationale de police criminelle*, and two years later the film-makers Margarethe von Trotta and Volker Schlöndorff used it as a vehicle for their scathing attack on the strategies of rumour fomented by the state of exception in *The Lost Honour of Katharina Blum,* based on a novel by Heinrich Böll.

The use of tracking technologies followed the same slippery slope. In 1979, acting on the assumption that the members of the Red Army Faction did not use credit cards or cheques in order to avoid detection, the Frankfurt police asked the electric power company to provide a list of customers who paid their bills in cash. There were

18,000 people in this category. By cross-checking this information against data from other organizations such as rental agencies, they succeeded in identifying two individuals and two apartments, one inhabited by a drug dealer and the other by an RAF militant actively sought by the police.[32]

New measures of exception were added on to others, creating a snowball effect. The West German government reinstituted professional prohibition practices (*Berufsverbot*) for failure to respect norms of discretion or loyalty.[33] Introduced via the Adenauer decree in 1950, this mechanism was used to purge government service of any 'civil servants, employees or agents of the state belonging to organizations or participating in undertakings directed against the free, democratic state'. Anti-terrorist laws went further by authorizing suspension for political reasons; the private sector was encouraged to do the same. As early as 1955, the Federal Republic of Germany had already begun

> its first preparatory work for the emergency laws promulgated in 1968. In the 1950s, there was even talk of extending the jurisdiction and increasing the technical resources of organisations such as the *Bundeskriminalamt* (BKA) – the infamous criminal investigation department designed to prevent a domestic state of emergency. It was the student movement, however, and the social movements that followed the first economic recession of 1964–1965 that finally spurred the government to adopt these measures in 1969.[34]

In 1972, the attacks at the Olympic Games in Munich precipitated the creation of a special anti-terrorist unit, which was attached to the border police (GSG9).

What did these 'dark years' ultimately yield? Here is the assessment of a legal expert:

> Terrorism was one of the stages in the general trend. It was part of a chain of causalities. It was not the primary cause of the hardening attitude assumed by governments determined to combat it. It was merely one component of a more general process that reflected the crisis of liberal democratic states in the twofold sense of a crisis of democracy (considered as a political system recognizing the legitimacy of conflict and proposing methods to resolve it without resorting to violence) and a crisis of legal-political liberalism according to which any proceedings against violations of the law must comply with certain fundamental principles.[35]

What about the projects for intra-European law enforcement cooperation? The Council of Europe was the first body to take a step in this direction. In 1977, it proposed a European Convention for the

Prevention and Repression of Terrorism to its members. To facilitate extradition measures, it voided the notion of political offence of its traditional meaning: 'None of the offences referred to in Articles 5 to 7 and 9 of this Convention, shall be regarded, for the purposes of extradition or mutual legal assistance, as a political offence, an offence connected with a political offence, or as an offence inspired by political motives.' The project for a European judicial area proposed by President Giscard d'Estaing, which was proposed even before France ratified the Convention, greatly exceeded the content of this document. The French project pushed the disqualification of the notion of political offence to its logical conclusion by proposing simply to eliminate any political criteria. It thereby made possible 'automatic extradition' for any acts qualified as 'terrorist', which were directly assimilated to violations of common law.[36] The member states did not go very far in this direction, concerned as they were that the creation of a common judicial area should not short-circuit their national sovereignty in particularly complex domains. In fact, the construction of a European policing area would overtake the project for a judicial area. It was to take more than two decades for the European Union to be endowed with a genuine programme of coordination and harmonization in the realm of justice and domestic affairs.

The theological discourse of global war and the global market

A pivotal year if ever there was one, 1979 set the stage for a geopolitical and geo-economic shift on a planetary scale. In February, the overthrow of the Shah of Iran and the proclamation of the Islamic Republic by Imam Khomeini marked the beginning of the Islamist Revolution throughout the Muslim world. In December, the Soviet Union began its invasion of Afghanistan, which ultimately brought about its demise. Finally, in the United Kingdom, Margaret Thatcher came to power as the paragon of monetarist policies, which steered the world economy towards neo-liberal economic principles. This turn to deregulation, which was consummated the following year with the election of Ronald Reagan as president of the United States, dissolved the concept of politics into market logic, with the doctrine of free trade inaugurating a new mode of governability. In 1986, together with Michèle Mattelart, we outlined an initial assessment of the first years in which markets, previously regulated, switched to what *Business Week* called the 'animal instinct of capitalism':

133

The biological reference has lodged itself in the heart of deregulation. It is deployed against the background of the new Darwinian theatre. The new freedoms granted by the market consecrate the 'freedom to triumph': may the best man win. The tension between freedom and equality that had marked American democracy since its origins has been resolved to the advantage of the former; the discourse of freedom has taken off like a rocket and become hyperbolic while equality has failed to leave the ground.[37]

The destitute were advised to 'help themselves'. In economic and political discourse, 'performance' became part of the doxa of new social norms. In the physical domain of the 'technology of the self', the liberalization under Reagan of the sale of products to 'improve' performance – muscle mass, stamina, memory, breathing, sexuality, rejuvenation, etc. – boosted whole industries and markets. The range of legally permitted substances (for example, creatine, which is not authorized in the European Union) was gradually extended. In the process, the idea of 'maximizing performance' in sports became naturalized and the cascade of revelations about doping had no effect on attendance at athletic events.

In 1985, in the midst of the Reagan era, the German-born economist and theologian Franz Hinkelammert, who settled in Costa Rica after working in Chile for many years, noted the convergence of two discourses on freedom that tended towards the theological. The first promoted the legitimacy of total market politics; the second called for a new intensification of the Cold War against the 'evil empire' or the worldwide communist enemy. (It should be remembered that in 1983 the president of the United States launched the Strategic Defense Initiative (SDI), also known as 'star wars', a satellite-based anti-missile system designed to operate as a sort of global electronic shield). 'The new motto', Hinkelammert points out, 'describes what happened:

'The welfare state enslaves, the police state liberates'. This development was based on an ideology of the total market, which is also an ideology of combat. By interpreting and treating society as a whole from the angle of progress towards a total market, the mystique of the total market became a mystique of struggle among markets, to which every sphere of society had to be subjected. In this totalizing perspective, there now appeared a mystique of war against those who resist subjecting every sphere of society to market struggle. Thus emerged the image of an enemy, which was the very product of this mystique of market struggle. This enemy is not a competitive adversary in the struggle among markets, nor even a participant in the market, except

134

as an adversary of the establishment of the total market and its results. The enemy is anyone who resists the transformation of market struggle into the unique principle and organizational basis of society as a whole. This explains the totalizing conception of subversion. Everything turns into subversion when the values being affirmed and defended conflict with the unrestricted validity of the total market and the unlimited accumulation of capital. [. . .] A Manichean dualism appears between the total market as Good and as the law of nature, and revolt as Evil and contrary to nature. [. . .] The more wicked the evil empire appears to be, the more legitimate the goal of a total market becomes along with all means to impose it.[38]

In 1981, the theologically inclined discourse on the total market inspired the American Enterprise Institute (AEI), the think tank of the neo-conservatives and other partisans of extreme deregulation, to publish a seminal text entitled *The Corporation: A Theological Inquiry*. In this work, the modern enterprise is treated as an 'incarnation – an object of extreme scorn – of the presence of God in the world'.[39] It is a crucified God, precisely because its incarnation on earth is scorned. Note the irony of market newspeak in AEI's complete name: the American Enterprise Institute for Public Policy Research!

For more than two decades, the gospel of the total market has been undermining the principle of public policies oriented towards collective interest. The explosion of the speculative bubble on 'Black Monday' in September 2008 provoked a moment of truth in politics. The failure of one bank led to a cascade of other bank and institutional failures, destabilizing enterprises of all sizes and impacting the lives of ordinary people with full force. The disastrous effects of these 'negative externalities' (to use the customary economic term) of manipulative bank practices gave credibility to the idea that the world's complex, interdependent financial system should be treated as a 'global public good': financial security must become a global right, guaranteed by multiple government bodies. From a long-term perspective, according to historian and sociologist Immanuel Wallerstein, what is unprecedented in the new situation and distinguishes it from earlier economic crises, is that:

capitalism no longer succeeds in forming a system in the sense in which the physicist and chemist Ilya Prigogine (1917–2003) used this term: when a biological, chemical or social system deviates too far and too often from its stable situation, it can no longer recover its equilibrium and we observe a bifurcation. The situation becomes chaotic and uncontrollable for the forces that dominated it up to then.[40]

If we add to this systemic depression of the capitalist world-economy, the energy, food and climate crises, we can speak – this time justifiably – of a 'crisis of civilization', a crisis of meaning through the exhaustion of a mode of living and working together.

After serving to boost market forces, the messianic narrative examined above, tinged with a religious spirit, was to underlie President George W. Bush's crusade against another crusade known as *jihad*.

— 9 —

WAR WITHOUT END: THE TECHNO-SECURITY PARADIGM

For the United States, the implosion of the communist regimes in Eastern Europe raised the issue of preserving its status as the sole superpower. That power rests on four pillars: technological, economic, military and cultural supremacy. Control over information and communication networks in wartime as well as peacetime – known as 'global information dominance' in the strategic jargon of the 'revolution in military affairs' and 'revolution in diplomatic affairs' – became the principle of a new doctrine of hegemony. It was accompanied by discourse on cyberwar as a 'clean war' or a 'zero-death war', transfigured and sublimated by the cybernetic artefact, with 'surgical strikes' and 'collateral damage'. This discourse first appeared during the first Gulf War (1991) and again during the NATO aerial bombing campaign in Kosovo eight years later. The ubiquity and fluidity of information flows, thanks to new information systems organized under the acronym C4ISR – Command, Control, Communications, Computing, Intelligence, Surveillance, Reconnaissance – transformed the theatre of operations into a panopticon of worldwide dimensions. Its priority target: the so-called 'rogue states'.

As soon as the Internet emerged as a public access network, geo-strategists sought to define the stakes and the protagonists involved in *noopolitik*, i.e., the politics of knowledge in the broad sense. This notion, introduced in 1999, encompasses the civil ('netwar') and military ('cyberwar') aspects of strategies for control of information, knowledge and know-how, with a view to achieving given global political and economic objectives.[1] They drew up a list of new enemies who made intensive use of reticular tools, including transnational, non-state actors such as activists, non-governmental organizations, drug cartels and terrorist groups.[2] Without neglecting its military espionage mission, the Echelon system of planetary eavesdropping was reoriented towards civilian espionage objectives.[3] These included gathering political, economic, technological and commercial information to give an advantage to US firms involved in weapons and civil aviation contracts, and anticipating the actions of environmental groups. Paradoxically, despite the sophisticated planetary remote surveillance system, cyberwar and netwar thinkers could not foresee the new battlefield of asymmetric confrontations that opened with the attacks on the World Trade Center towers on 11 September 2001. The exclusively technological approach to intelligence-gathering, at the expense of human intelligence, thus revealed its limitations. What became obvious was the lack of coordination between agencies in charge of security (failure to share information, lack of common terminology and even incompatible equipment, not to mention the absence of translators and the deficiency of decryption methods for examining millions of pieces of information). As for the myth of clean war, there was to be no further mention of it.

What is meant by 'terrorism'?

This question suddenly returned to the fore in September 2001 and once again the answer remained incomplete. 'As strange as it may seem, there is no definition on which all of the actors from the member states agree,' noted the OECD working group created in 2002. There was no valid, univocal notion that could be used internationally as jurisprudence. For anyone familiar with the history of policies of exception, there is obviously nothing odd about this gap. The United Nations itself did not reopen the debate until after the bombings in Madrid in March 2004 and in London in July 2005. This debate had lain fallow for a decade due to the objection of several member states who argued that national liberation struggles, even if they result in civilian victims, cannot be described as terrorism. The UN definition of the phenomenon was to be minimal: 'The targeting and deliberate killing of civilians and non-combatants cannot be justified or legitimized by any cause or grievance.'[4] Were this definition to be taken literally, many of the states seeking to curb terrorism would be indicted by international courts.

The OECD experts added that the only definitions of terrorism are national in scope – a point of view that appears to be contradicted by a detailed, convincing argument presented by legal expert Mark Burgess, currently the director of the Brussels office of the

World Security Institute. On the website of the Center for Defense Information (CDI), a Washington-based organization made up of academics and a few retired high-ranking military officers, which engages in critical analysis of US defence policy, Burgess asserts: 'Often, a uniform definition of terrorism will not even exist across the various concerned agencies of a given country. Such is the case with the United States, where the range of definitions listed below is currently applied.'[5] For the Pentagon, terrorism is defined as 'the calculated use of unlawful violence to inculcate fear, intended to coerce or to intimidate governments or societies in the pursuit of goals that are generally political, religious, or ideological'. For the FBI, it is 'the unlawful use of force and violence against persons or property to intimidate or coerce a government, the civilian population, or any segment thereof, in furtherance of political or social objectives'. The State Department considers it to be 'premeditated, politically motivated violence perpetrated against non-combatant targets by subnational groups or clandestine agents, usually intended to influence an audience'. Burgess concludes:

> Defining terrorism has become so polemical and subjective an undertaking as to resemble an art rather than a science. . . Such definitions are made more equivocal by the rhetoric surrounding the so-called 'Global War on Terrorism,' as the current American administration describes the series of military campaigns and other initiatives that were provoked by the Al-Qaeda attacks of Sept. 11, 2001. As with the journalistic tendencies . . ., such a broad reading of 'terrorism' as this usage engenders risks rendering the term meaningless. It also lays the government open to charges that it is undermining its own counterterrorism efforts through the use of such wide terminology in compiling the statistics attached to them.

The problem lies in the fact that this ill-defined concept serves as a referent for another: 'illegal enemy combatant', a category that includes not only 'anyone who commits an act of terrorism' but also 'any individuals who voluntarily or materially support terrorists engaged in a hostile action against the United States'. This is a 'dangerously broad' definition, as a *New York Times* editorial rightly asserted on 28 September 2006 in the wake of the approval of the formula by Congress, since it could 'subject legal residents of the United States, as well as foreign citizens living in their own countries, to summary arrest and indefinite detention with no hope of appeal. The president could give the power to apply this label to anyone he wanted.'[6] A very extensive notion of terrorism, without necessarily mimicking the bellicose language of the US administration, has become globalized, encouraging numerous governments to adapt their laws to the new geopolitical situation by broadening the circle of suspects. These countries may not be targets of al-Qaeda actions; their leaders tend to think first of all of internal enemies, real or potential.

A new global enemy: the recycling of national security

The US government's choice to confront terrorism by military means explains why the balance between the protection of liberties and the reinforcement of security measures was so severely disrupted. Measures at first taken arbitrarily and illegally were later ratified in October 2006 by Congress, which gave the executive branch a blank cheque regarding military tribunals, denial of habeas corpus, coercive interrogations, internment camps, kidnappings and the outsourcing of clandestine prisons to foreign countries. Congress also broadened the president's power to call upon the armed forces and the National Guard (military reserve units controlled by each state but equipped by the federal government) to maintain order on US territory. Such authority had formerly been restricted by two laws: the Posse Comitatus Act of 1878 and the Insurrection Act of 1807. These extra-judicial logics, which civil liberties defence groups had never ceased denouncing, revived a dark past of the reason of state gone astray and called to memory the excesses made possible by the doctrine of national security that had marked the Cold War era.

No global, pre-emptive and preventive war, without fixed limits in time or space, could be waged against the new global enemy without mobilizing the entire information and technology complex. Such was the imperative dictated by the surveillance scenarios developed by geostrategists of the anti-terrorist struggle in the immediate post-9/11 period. The military apparatus had to disseminate its influence throughout society. Whether in the battlefield or in society viewed as a battlefield, it meant linking all the systems together in a communication and information network so that those at the head of the system of systems would have precise knowledge of each theatre of operations, its actors and their trajectories in order to anticipate the plans and actions of the new global enemy and organize the retaliation accordingly in real time. The chain of control involved every link between the citizen in daily life and the national security state and between the combatant in the field and the central command post. Such civil-military pairing has allowed the defence industry increasingly to produce systems and devices for both domains at once.

This is what Raytheon, a corporation that manufactures this type of hybrid system, describes as the integration of all the components of the 'Kill Chain'. This high-density, reticular structure of surveillance is the result of the extrapolation to the social whole of a 'paradigm' developed by the military in the late 1990s and actively promoted during the lightning invasion of Afghanistan under Taliban rule in 2002: 'network-centric warfare'. In the words of a cyberwar and netwar specialist, it was 'a form of military superiority similar to that used by some American companies to gain competitive advantage'.[7] Clearly, as the editorialist of *Aviation Week and Space Technology* reckoned at the time of the first measures of exception:

> To apply the Pentagon's network-centric warfare concepts to homeland defense implies that information will have to be shared by military, intelligence, law enforcement and corporate organizations, and with grassroots groups and private citizens. In network-centric warfare, the aim is to move targeting data rapidly from any sensor on the battlefield to any shooter in real time. In network-centric homeland defense, the power of networks will be brought to bear to correlate information so terrorists can be detected, attacks prevented and incident responses coordinated. Networking is about people and how they will interact in a new virtual culture that crosses organizational boundaries.[8]

Such close surveillance makes it possible to anticipate the moves of the enemy and take preventive action. This is an excessively ambitious project, of course, which shows that the struggle against terrorism has caused the Dr Strangeloves of 'dataveillance' to work hard spawning configurations that tend to militarize the civilian population.

The intersecting of systems for data gathering and analysis corresponds to the organized convergence of institutions focusing on domestic security. In late October 2001, the US Congress overwhelmingly approved a law known as the USA Patriot Act. The name is an acronym for the mission the law was intended to accomplish: 'Uniting and Strengthening America by Providing Appropriate Tools Required to Intercept and Obstruct Terrorism'. To implement it, another law, the Homeland Security Act was passed in early 2002, to found the Department of Homeland Security (DHS). As a gauge of its importance, this was the first government department to be created since 1947, when the Pentagon was brought into being by the National Security Act. The new department's mission was 'to detect, prepare for, prevent, protect against, respond to, and recover from terrorist attacks within the United States'. The twenty-two previously independent federal agencies and programmes dedicated to fighting terrorism, employing some 170,000 people, were regrouped and divided into five directorates: Border and Transportation Security, Emergency Preparedness and Response, Science and Technology, Information Analysis and Infrastructure Protection, and Management. DHS melded together agencies as varied as the Coast Guard, the Customs Service, the Immigration and Naturalization Service and the Transportation Security Administration. The law specifies that 'American homeland' or 'homeland' means the United States, in a geographic sense. Alongside the creation of this new department, the entire intelligence-gathering apparatus was restructured. The need to connect domestic security with external security, the civilian world with the military world and the police force with the military forces resulted in authorizing the foreign intelligence agencies such as the CIA and Defense Department programmes to gather intelligence within the United States. The FBI, traditionally confined within national borders, was allowed to set up a network of offices abroad.

The fall of the Berlin Wall was highly symbolic of the entry into an era of open societies and the end of sources of entropy through communication and information technologies. It signalled the advent of universal democracy through free trade, but also 'the end of history'. The new global war shook these beliefs, marking the return of real history with the erection of new barriers of fear and hatred. The redemptive discourse of ultra-liberals on the free, uninhibited movement of persons was demystified by the effects of reciprocal closures: on the one hand, privileged classes and groups surrounded themselves with walls and electronic devices to escape from the Other, seen as a permanent threat; on the other hand, the multitude of rejects of the project of global integration were crammed into the ghettoes of techno-apartheid.

In an avowal of its powerlessness, the US army erected a security barrier in Baghdad around the 'Green Zone' to prevent attacks. At home, the United States barricaded its border with Mexico. In September 2006, Congress passed the Secure Fence Act, authorizing the construction of a wall equipped with watchtowers, cameras and detectors covering over 1,200 km of the border zone. The government paid no attention to symbols. In 1994, when the North American Free Trade Agreement between Canada, the United States and Mexico came into force, it had already approved a programme called 'Gatekeeper', one of whose measures was to build a wall along the border between Mexico and California with surplus materials from the first Gulf War. Yet, as early as 1970, a virtual barrier had been tested along the same border; it included the same seismic captors used in the 'McNamara wall' in Vietnam. Since then, illegal

142

immigration, drug traffic and terrorism have been invoked, separately or together, to justify closing the borders. The most recent project is unusual in that it testifies to the rapid militarization of this type of surveillance, since it has been not just under the official control of the National Guard but also supported extra-officially by the 'Minutemen', the new vigilantes made up of members of far-right groups who take discourse on the new global war literally and consider illegal immigrants 'terrorists'. Moreover, a few months before the adoption of the Secure Fence Act, another Bill had been adopted by the House of Representatives – H.R. 4437 or the Sensenbrenner Bill – whose purpose was to criminalize illegal immigrants and anyone suspected of giving them aid.

The Bill did not become law. The return to real history also brought with it, in the spring of 2006, a wave of demonstrations of Latino immigrants and their supporters, who forced Congress to back down on this Bill to criminalize them. On 1 May, in Los Angeles, the historic cradle and centre of the Mexican-American population, the *Movimiento pro-derechos de los inmigrantes* launched the 'Great American Boycott of 2006' or 'A day without an immigrant', the first national strike to reveal the weight of the immigrant population in the US economy and to denounce the exploitation to which they are subjected.

The US Patriot Act

The scope of this law is very broad. It authorizes eavesdropping, the search and seizure of computers, tracking the profile of readers at local libraries, and other intrusive procedures left to the discretion of federal agents. It allows officials to bypass the requirement of a court warrant to issue 'security letters' to banks, Internet access providers, telephone companies, credit organizations, travel agencies and libraries, all of which are obligated to provide information about their clients.

The title of the programme of individual databank crosschecking is telling: TIA or Total Information Awareness. In presenting the programme in August 2002, the director, John Poindexter, declared:

> The main point is that we need a much more systematic approach. A variety of tools, processes and procedures will be required to deal with the problem, but they must be integrated by a systems approach

built around a common architecture to be effective. Total Information Awareness – a prototype system – is our answer. We must be able to detect, classify, identify, and track terrorists so that we may understand their plans and act to prevent them from being executed. To protect our rights, we must ensure that our systems track the terrorists, and those that mean us harm. [. . .]

Technically, TIA aimed to develop 'novel methods for populating the database from existing sources, create innovative new sources, and invent new algorithms for mining, combining, and refining information for subsequent inclusion in the database; and revolutionary new models, algorithms, methods, tools, and techniques for analyzing and correlating information in the database to derive actionable intelligence'.[9]

The Information Awareness Office in charge of the programme was housed by DARPA (Defense Advanced Research Projects Agency), the agency where the Internet was born, and whose mission, we may recall, was to develop synergy between university research and defence during the Cold War. John Poindexter is the vice-admiral who was convicted of multiple felonies in 1990 for having instigated the Iran-Contra affair, involving illegal weapons sales to the opponents of the revolutionary government of Nicaragua.

The programme was to keep the acronym TIA but its name changed in 2003 to 'Terrorism Information Awareness', after Congress's refusal to allocate the funds deemed necessary to expand to its full scope, but also because of the numerous protests staged by associations for the defence of civil liberties. Its aim remained in any case to build an integrated system of databank networks to centralize and crosscheck all personal information on citizens (social security, credit cards, FBI records, local police records, bank accounts, hospital and insurance records, etc.). The hunt for terrorists set off an orgy of data gathering and storage by official institutions and private agencies, although the tools that made such data relevant were not up to the task. Such was the case of the so-called 'risk assessment' model, which was particularly highly rated by information hunters. The criteria of evaluation proposed by data-mining programmes to sort an ocean of information and generate suspect profiles were either quite vague or they were kept secret.[10] The prodigious development of intelligence activities capable of assessing economic, political and military risks is just one sign among many of the 'privatization' of sovereign functions of the state (army, police). It has a parallel in outsourcing activities such as recruiting foreign volunteer soldiers for Iraq with promises of naturalization at the end of their tour of duty, the subcontracting of

144

activities of policing and repression, and other modern forms of mercenary activity. Former CIA agents, police and military officers move from the public to the private sector. One of the major laboratories of this privatization has unquestionably been the global war on drug traffic. In 2006, there were more than 180 private security companies in Iraq, employing about 50,000 agents who performed missions for the US and British armies, ranging from operating telecommunications networks to protecting diplomats and interrogating prisoners. The head of one such company, specialized in training armed security agents to operate in conflict zones, provided this account:

> Private military companies are going to replace the blue helmets [UN peacekeeping troops]; it's inevitable, because the current system doesn't work. On the one hand, the contingents sent by the democratic countries get bogged down in political and ethical considerations that tie their hands. On the other hand, when underdeveloped countries are asked to provide contingents, they don't send their best troops. Far from it.[11]

One of the priorities of the Department of Homeland Security has been investment in research and development programmes for the security arsenal (its budget reached 50 billion dollars for fiscal year 2006 and 40 billion for 2008). The programmes focus on techniques for tracking and decrypting electronic messages, video surveillance, securitizing data transmission, developing technology for the surveillance and detection or inspection of luggage and cargo, in accordance with the Safety Act (2002). 'Safety' is an acronym for 'Support Antiterrorism by Fostering Effective Technologies'. High-tech companies in Silicon Valley rushed to fill these niches of protean innovation, working particularly on biometric systems of access and chemical detection of contaminating agents such as anthrax. Not to be outdone, research centres convened specialists representing the full range of disciplines within the social and behavioural sciences, including cognitive and clinical psychology, criminology, anthropology, communication, linguistics, sociology, economics, geography and political science. This agenda is being pursued at the National Consortium for the Study of Terrorism and the Responses to Terrorism (START) at the University of Maryland, College Park. According to its website, the objective is 'to provide timely guidance on how to disrupt terrorist networks, reduce the incidence of terrorism, and enhance the resilience of US society in the face of the terrorist threat'. The consortium is a US Department of Homeland Security Center of Excellence, tasked by the Department's Science and Technology Directorate. To

SECURITIZING/INSECURITIZING

achieve its goal, START has assembled a network of researchers from various institutions across the United States and around the world. They study the formation and recruitment of terrorists, the persistence and dynamics of terrorist groups, and societal responses to terrorist threats and attacks. They map out the world of blogs and examine the semantic content of websites. They also explore the pathology of terrorists, the pyramidal structure of groups, the relation between leaders and sympathizers and supporters, the unconscious motives that cause people to opt for violent action, and the role of the media in amplifying the effects of a terrorist attack. They attempt to devise methods for countering *jihadist* ideology among detainees and evaluate the effects and effectiveness of deradicalization programmes, and undertake modelizations of future terrorist attacks and negotiation scenarios with hostage-takers. They further examine the perception of risk by the public and likely behavioural responses to future terrorist attacks. They seek strategies for mitigating negative psychological effects and enhancing resilience of the citizens in the face of the terror threat. The consortium has also constructed an open-source database named Global Terrorism Database (GTD), which includes systematic information on terrorist (international and domestic) events around the world since 1970 (date and location, weapons used, nature of the target, number of casualties, and – when identifiable – the identity of the perpetrator). These areas of study reflect a return to the questions that interested the counterinsurgency research network sponsored by the Department of Defense in the 1960s and 1970s, but which had been abandoned after the war in Vietnam. Thus, the experimental programme of the Pentagon's Human Terrain Team, set up in late 2003 as part of the counterinsurgency strategy, aims to 'embed' teams of anthropologists and social scientists in combat units in Afghanistan and Iraq, just as journalists had been embedded in the same units during the invasion of Iraq earlier in the same year.

The range of clients and suppliers in the security market was also protean, for it was built on fear and the irrational. *Thinking the Unthinkable* was the title of an official document that the newly created Department of Homeland Security hastened to send out to companies to encourage them to ensure their own security in the event of a natural catastrophe or a terrorist attack. The inclusion of the terrorist threat merely generalized a recommendation that global corporations such as IBM and the major oil companies had already implemented on their own initiative in the 1970s when they began to redouble the protection of their enclaves against urban guerrilla movements, calling on private surveillance companies and carrying

146

out the vertical and horizontal integration of this new risk into their management scheme.

The Department of Homeland Security's Science and Technology Directorate is situated at the intersection of processes for developing technical standards regarding security. It is an important part of the Homeland Security Standards Panel, created six months after the 9/11 attacks. Open to representatives of industry, government, professional societies, trade associations, standards developers and consortia groups, this cooperative project between the public and private sectors resulted in the creation of the Homeland Security Advisory System, a colour-coded terrorism threat advisory scale. The five colours are intended to reflect the probability of a terrorist attack and its potential gravity: red stands for a 'severe' risk; orange is 'high', yellow is 'elevated' or 'significant'; blue is 'guarded' or 'general' and green is 'low'. The various levels of threat or risk call for different actions to be taken and different forces to intervene (federal agencies, state or local governments) in order to secure airports and public facilities.

The panel's mission is first and foremost to protect US territory. However, since there is no way to dissociate the national from the international in the cybersecurity era, it seeks to transform the multiple technical standards invented and tested to secure the homeland into transnational references. The war on terror has thus been turned into a powerful means of pressure to standardize security systems, procedures and protocols. It has also been decisive in shaping and consolidating a market of worldwide dimensions. In 2007, spokespersons for global securities industries evaluated the international market in this sector at approximately 350 billion euros: roughly 150 billion for US companies, 110 billion for European companies, 60 billion for Asian companies and 30 billion for the rest of the world. The OECD forecast an 8 per cent rate of annual growth for this industry in the coming years. All agree that the US is in the vanguard of standardization, since it controls fully a third of the market and is thus in a position to 'determine its direction'.[12]

Economic concentration, the ally of warfare

Concentration contributes to the tightening of institutions, first of all at the level of the entire techno-informational complex. This structural principle helps to explain why the National Security Agency (NSA) had no trouble obtaining lists of telephone calls made by millions of US citizens from the leading telecommunications group AT&T. Indeed, it was hardly by chance that the country's regulatory authority, the Federal Communications Commission, voted unanimously in 2006 in favour of the merger between AT&T and Baby BellSouth, the largest such combination in the history of telecommunications in the United States. This operation was in stark contrast to the dismantling of the old AT&T by the anti-trust authorities in 1984, a pivotal year for deregulation. The giant firm was thus transformed into seven local telephone companies known as 'Baby Bells', and one company for long-distance calls. Three of those companies survived – AT&T, Verizon and Qwest – while four others came back under the control of AT&T. The last of these was precisely Baby BellSouth. The new AT&T (with 120 billion dollars in revenues in 2006 and 300,000 employees) has 67.5 million landlines, 58 million mobile phone customers and 11.5 million broadband Internet users. In 2008, a law expanded the possibilities of eavesdropping on private individuals and granted immunity from prosecution to the companies that assisted in wiretapping on instructions from the government.

In the name of anti-trust regulation, the US administration had vetoed in 1998 the merger between two mega-corporations – Northrop Grumman (defence-related activities) and Lockheed-Martin (civil and military aviation). Since 2001, however, the merger process has started up again with renewed vigour in the arms industry and security sector. As one economist noted: 'The determination to control the entire technological sector and therefore to impede the entry of possible competitors resulted in certain companies being placed in a position of near-monopoly. Their ability to influence public authorities was thereby strengthened, which contributed to the militarisation of foreign policy.'[13] When trading reopened on Wall Street after the 11 September attacks, high-tech shares jumped by 15–30 per cent on the first day. Since then, the steady rise of the Space Defense Index (DXS), comprising the fifty-seven corporations most representative of the defence and security markets, is evidence that the financial euphoria has continued unabated. A law adopted by the US Congress in July 2007, in the name of national security, reinforced the control of the government and intelligence services over the acquisition of US companies by foreign investors.

In the media, concentration has proved to be a strategic ally. A media ownership Bill considered by Congress in 2003 aimed to reinforce monopolies at the expense of the diversity of information sources. That year, the Federal Communications Commission authorized a single group to control up to 45 per cent of the national audience (compared with 35 per cent previously) while lifting the prohibition against owning newspapers, radio and television stations in a single location. However, protests from civil liberties advocacy organizations succeeded in having the new rule overturned. In late 2007, the FCC was back on the attack to relax the limits on concentration. Such policies went against the concerns expressed in 1975 by the Trilateral Commission, which was worried about the media's role in destabilizing 'traditional means of social control' (more specifically, in contributing to a negative image of US involvement in Vietnam) and called for rulings to limit media concentration. It must be said, however, that, unlike in the 1970s, in 2003 the media establishment eagerly endorsed the government's 'just war' argument. Reporters were still 'intimidated by accusations of being "anti-American" and "unpatriotic", inherited from the Vietnam War period' and 'in the case of Fox News and CNN, they were explicitly warned against this risk'.[14] Fox went even further: every morning in March and April 2003, it issued instructions to its journalists. Secrecy, lies and fake news generated a loss of media credibility and a growing state of information insecurity.[15] The media establishment distilled lies about the existence of weapons of mass destruction in Iraq without changing so much as a comma in the information disseminated by the government, allowing the Fox News of the Murdoch group and the *Wall Street Journal* to set the tone of unconditional support for the invasion. As the expeditionary forces encountered problems on the ground, governmental propaganda and manipulation only increased. Testimony to this fact can be found in a report published by the US media reform advocacy group Free Press in late 2005 concerning the Bush administration's relations with the press. The report called attention to governmental infiltration of public radio broadcasting, the dissemination by local and national television channels of fake news reports produced by federal agencies, the corrupting of journalists and the suppression of many forums of public discussion in media programming. It also denounced the expanding state monopoly over matters related to security (a notion whose elastic character is thus manifested once again), resulting in more information being labelled 'classified', 'sensitive' or 'for official use only', and the violation of journalists' right of access, making it more difficult for them to cover important sectors of government activity. For any deviation from this new standard of secrecy, recalcitrant journalists were threatened with legal action under the Espionage Act of 1917.

Return to the ideology of modernization

Propaganda was also a component of the US government's communication strategies to rally the populations in Middle Eastern countries around its plan to reorganize the region. To understand fully the role and scope of these strategies, it is important to remember that what changed with the entry into the new global war was the geopolitical status of information and, more broadly, of the products of mass culture as a vector of global hegemony. With the disappearance of the Soviet superpower, US strategists thought they could enlarge the so-called community of democracies, integrated into the world market, by relying on the symbolic investments, realized throughout the world since the Second World War, in shaping collective mentalities via US culture and information industries and the multiple networks taking part in the global circulation of symbols of the 'American way of life'. The power these cultural vectors were assumed to exercise over the network of networks – global information dominance – lent credence to the dogma.

However, the events following 11 September 2001 discredited the doctrine of the pre-eminence of soft power as a means of inducing the entire world to join the global democratic marketplace. The doctrine suggested that the dividing line between friends and enemies was fading. At the end of the Cold War, the theoretician of international relations Francis Fukuyama proclaimed that the world was entering the era of the end of history and planetary democracy would inevitably come about through the incorporation of more and more nations into the global market. After advocating the overthrow of Saddam Hussein, Fukuyama finally broke with the neo-conservatives and today he asserts: 'One of the main problems is how to redefine soft power. It was originally based on image, principles and values. On these questions the damage has been considerable. In the Third World, the American model, the market and democracy, are no longer taken seriously. When we speak of human rights, people answer "Abu Ghraib".'[16] The revived use of the media for propaganda purposes needs to be understood in this structural context.

The US superpower was forced to abandon its status as an unquestioned cultural force. Faced with a deteriorating image in the region, it had to invest in a proactive strategy of persuasion. Hence, the launching of an official television channel in Arabic, Al-Hurra ('the Free'). The channel proved to be a failure, for it was too propagandistic and reproduced the same errors of judgement, the same ignorance and the same disregard for the cultural dimension of Middle Eastern societies that had motivated the invasion and occupation of Iraq.

History stutters. It may be remembered that in the 1950s, the United States, seeking to prevent the so-called underdeveloped countries from yielding to the solicitations of the communist camp, had turned the Middle East into a laboratory for policies of 'Westernization' of so-called traditional societies. The media was the centrepiece of this strategy to secure these countries' loyalty by promoting attitudes and behaviour in keeping with a certain idea of modernity. At the time, the Voice of America had even commissioned in various countries of that region the first sociological study of international radio audiences. A half-century later, this conception of development made a new appearance in the Bush administration's plan to establish a democratic 'Greater Middle East'. The same old worn-out ideas of development and modernization were recycled; the population was invited to join a consumer society based on a Western model, artificially transposed to the complex and changing reality of the region.

The novelty of today's situation is that the emergence of the pan-Arab channels has made this complexity visible. The world of continuous news service, heretofore dominated by the British and US channels CNN and BBC World, must now take into account such new players as Al-Jazeera in Qatar, LBC in Lebanon, along with MBC and Al-Arabya in the United Arab Emirates, which, in their efforts to offer a different version of the news, are also contributing to the construction of a pan-Arab identity. Like it or not, the trend has been gaining ground, as evidenced by the conclusions of a two-part seminar organized in 2005 and 2006 on the topic of 'Open Media and Transitioning Societies in the Arab Middle East: Implications for US Security Policy'. The seminar, organized by two think tanks, the Stanley Foundation and the Institute for Near East and Gulf Military Analysis, both specializing in peace and security issues, was attended by experts from the region and the United States. The seminar gave rise to a publication whose introduction begins as follows:

> The increased presence and growth of Middle Eastern media, particularly satellite television, raises pertinent questions about the nature and influence of this information explosion. For US decision makers, the most pressing question is how the realities of expanding open media sources and transitioning societies affect issues such as the US presence in the region, regional stability and growth, democratisation, and transnational terrorism. The complexity of the Middle East media landscape needs to be better understood by US policymakers if more productive security policies and solutions are to be developed. This encompasses

151

the growing sophistication of the media outlets and audiences, how new Middle East media compares and contrasts with US media norms and trends; and what, if any, impact the media revolution has on the region's social, economic, and political realms.[17]

The participants obviously had in mind the failures of the official Al-Hurra channel.

Yet those who had rightly criticized the propagandistic approach proved to be strangely uninspired in proposing an alternative, as one of the core recommendations by conference participants – namely, to introduce advertising – clearly shows:

> Recognize that advertising revenue helps free the media from its reliance on government-only sponsorship and also acts as a force for 'objectivity' in reporting. Encourage advertising by multinational companies via emphasis on the size and modern tastes of the region's Pan-Arab population, especially the burgeoning youth population.[18]

The old schemas of modernization and development as conceptualized by diffusionist theories of mass communication had apparently weathered the decades without a wrinkle.

Policing global flows

At a conference held in 2002 on 'homeland security and defence', the US Secretary of Transportation declared: 'All of us ought to understand that we have entered a new era in transportation, an era in which a determined and remorseless enemy has challenged one of America's most cherished freedoms – namely, the freedom of mobility.'[19] Initiatives to thwart terrorism gave rise to a global logic of 'interoperability' and interconnection aimed at maintaining surveillance over all means of moving goods, persons and messages, with results that were soon felt at the international level. Problems were settled either by unilateral measures or by multilateral agreements. Here are a few landmarks in this process.

The US authorities invited the head officials of major ports and shipping companies to align themselves with the rules prescribed by the Coast Guard administration or risk being struck from the list of cooperating parties and no longer being allowed to take part in trade. In order to securitize the international logistics chain of international transport, the European Union was forced to adapt by imitating US 'reliability' standards for operators, enacted immediately after 11 September 2001 to prevent products considered dangerous to national security from entering US territory. From that point on, in order to be certified as an 'approved economic operator' and avoid endless and abusive customs paperwork, any firm seeking to import or export goods had to comply with strict rules. Among other measures, they had to carry out background checks on employees assigned to 'sensitive' positions and establish a programme to raise employee awareness about security.

After applying various forms of pressure and threatening sanctions against airlines, Washington imposed on them the obligation to communicate thirty-four types of confidential data, including postal and e-mail addresses, telephone and credit card numbers, itineraries and even food preferences, for every traveller flying from Europe to the United States. Filtering passengers through the Computer-Assisted Passenger Prescreening System – CAPPS II – went against the 1995 EU directive on the protection of personal data and also violated the Council of Europe's European Convention for the Protection of Human Rights and Fundamental Freedoms, which prohibited the use for security purposes of data gathered for commercial reasons. The European Court of Justice challenged the legal grounds for the agreement (without, however, taking a firm position on its content) and required the governments to revise it. As a result, a compromise was reached between the EU and the United States in June 2007, whereby the number of types of data to be communicated was reduced to nineteen, but the period of conservation of this data rose from three and a half years to fifteen years. Furthermore, any agency associated with the US Department of Homeland Security could have access to the data. To cap it all, in the United States, under pressure from civil liberties advocates and the Congress, the Bush administration had to withdraw CAPPS II in 2004 and postpone its replacement by the Secure Flight program until 2010, because too many passengers were being mistakenly listed as suspects.

To define the new airport security policy in 2006 with reinforced passenger checks, the European Union held an emergency consultation with a committee made up of European experts, flanked by their US counterparts. Measures were adopted to prohibit carry-on luggage containing more than 100 ml of liquids, gels, creams, sprays and toothpaste – spectacular but anxiety-producing measures that have little effect, according to many security specialists, who are more concerned about the inadequate surveillance of airport complexes including runways, terminals, warehouses and underground car parks. All these passenger control measures were soon adopted at international and domestic airports in the rest of the world.

On the subject of information flows, the United States has systematically refused any reform of 'Internet government'.[20] The Internet is managed by the Internet Corporation for Assigned Names and Numbers (Icann). Operating with an unusual status (a non-profit company under California law), this body controls access to any virtual domain, whether generic (.com, .org, .gov, .edu, etc.) or national. In the final instance, it actually comes under the authority of the US Department of Commerce. The leverage that allows the US administration to exert its worldwide control over the Internet and theoretically gives it the prerogative to exclude countries from the World Wide Web, is first of all technical: it resides in 'root servers', the bridgehead of the addressing system. In spite of the strong alliance that exists between the governments of the South and the European Union (although they are motivated by different interests), the World Summit on the Information Society, organized at the initiative of the International Telecommunication Union in Tunis in late 2005, failed to undermine the principle of control over the Internet by the United States, which continues to cling to its doctrine of global information dominance. A compromise solution was reached by creating an Internet Forum, an intergovernmental body to foster dialogue but without any decision-making authority, bringing together spokespersons for the private sector and organized civil society.

The European Union had already had another occasion to measure the intransigence of the United States regarding the use of cyberspace. Under US pressure, but also with a push from certain member states, the EU had agreed that its future positioning system, Galileo, which was likely to compete with the United States' Global Positioning System (GPS), would remain strictly civilian and not be used for military purposes. It further agreed, first, to place the keys to the system partially in Washington's hands, and, second, to choose frequencies that the US authorities could jam as much as they saw fit in a theatre of operations. The enlargement of the EU from fifteen to twenty-seven member states considerably strengthened the power of the United States and its numerous lobbies that gravitate around the European Commission in Brussels. Any foreign policy initiative that does not meet with their approval is liable to be opposed by the majority bloc of 'Atlanticist' or pro-US governments.

For the Pentagon, the Internet is a 'vulnerable weapons system', according to the report issued in October 2003 by the then Secretary of Defence Donald H. Rumsfeld and entitled the *Information Operations Roadmap*. While it was important to take advantage of the Internet's full potential, it was just as important to 'fight' any deviations. As the report stated: 'We Must Fight the Net. DoD [the Department of Defense] is building an information-centric force. Networks are increasingly the operational center of gravity [. . ..] DoD's "Defense in Depth" strategy should operate on the premise that the Department will "fight the net" as it would a weapons system.'[21] With its interventions in the Middle East, the army's need for electronic communication in the field has risen at a dizzying rate. During the first Gulf War (1990–1), some 500,000 combatants were able to benefit from 100 megabits per second (Mbps) in the satcom bandwidth. Ten years later, when 'Operation Enduring Freedom' was launched in 2001 in Afghanistan, 10 per cent of the forces had at least seven times more capacity, prompting Lieutenant General Harry D. Raduege, director of the Defense Information Systems Agency, to declare: 'That's dramatic evidence that we're making the leap into the information age and network-centric warfare, and that space is growing in critical importance.'[22]

As for the Echelon system, it showed itself once again to be highly useful, not only because it had enhanced its technical potential for information gathering and analysis and made significant headway in Asia using Japan as a springboard, but also because the partnership between the United States, Great Britain, Canada, Australia and New Zealand enabled each of these countries to avoid judicial control by having partner countries spy on their citizens. A hub was set up, again outside judicial control, to exchange information, excerpts from wiretapping and computer files. In a document accompanying its 2005 report, the International Campaign Against Mass Surveillance (ICAMS) noted: 'Recently such an agreement was cited by U.S. officials who seized computer servers in London hosting the websites of Indymedia (the Independent Media Centre) in twenty countries, purportedly at the request of the Swiss and Italian police.'[23] We have here no more than a glimpse of the many formal and informal agreements for police cooperation and their contours and interconnections. It is mostly via indirect paths that information filters out to the public. Such was the case, for example, of the revelations in 2005 regarding the existence of a Western counterterrorist intelligence centre called 'Alliance Base', involving six countries (the United States, France, the United Kingdom, Germany, Canada and Australia), based in Paris. The struggle against terrorism encourages the globalization of formal exchange of national security doctrines and practices. It is in this context that one can understand the network of International Law Enforcement Academies (ILEA), created by the State Department and other US agencies, which groups together regional training institutes for police officers, magistrates and prosecutors in Hungary, Thailand, Botswana, El Salvador and the state of New Mexico.[24]

Tracking the financing of terrorist networks has furthermore opened global flows of bank funds to monitoring by intelligence services. The US Treasury Department reluctantly acknowledged this, following the publication of an article in the *New York Times* on 23 June 2006 which revealed the existence of a secret system of financial transaction surveillance, monitored by the CIA. The Terrorist Finance Tracking Program, as it is called, tracks both US citizens and foreign nationals throughout the world. The programme could not exist without the close cooperation of Swift (Society for Worldwide Interbank Financial Telecommunication), a private cooperative under Belgian jurisdiction with headquarters near Brussels, through which 6 billion dollars pass each day, providing services to some 8,000 financial institutions in more than 200 countries. While it offers a unique window to detect signs of security threats to the United States, this observatory of global flows is – like the satellite espionage system Echelon – a means of access to strategic information for the actors of the US economy.

Last but not least, there are the omnipresent logistics of the worldwide system of US military bases. According to official figures, there were 737 such bases in 2005,[25] but the unofficial tally puts the number at 1,000. Indeed, US military statistics omit many important infrastructures built in the Near East and the surrounding region after 11 September 2001, especially in the former Soviet republics, as well as others administered by the host country army. Colombia is one example, but the United Kingdom, which has housed US military and espionage installations disguised as Royal Air Force bases since the beginning of the Cold War, is another. With the war on terrorism, the United States accorded itself the right to expand the area covered by its system of military bases in the name of the doctrine of pre-emptive intervention. Since 2003, the so-called Proliferation Security Initiative (PSI) authorizes US battleships anchored at naval bases abroad to intercept any ship on the high seas suspected of transporting 'weapons of mass destruction' as well as the components or ingredients used to manufacture them. It is highly symbolic that the United States chose to locate the internment camp for 'unlawful enemy combatants' on its base in Guantánamo Bay, Cuba. This base was established following the first US imperial expedition, launched in 1898 on the pretext of delivering from the yoke of the Spanish Empire a people that was already in the process of liberating itself. The symbol is all the more telling in view of the fact that, at the time, the press magnate William

Randolph Hearst, alias Citizen Kane, organized a campaign of war hysteria in the press to encourage the McKinley administration to intervene militarily on foreign territory. Hearst summarized his state of mind in a famous message to Frederic Remington, a reporter and well-known artist he had sent to Havana. When Remington cabled him saying 'Everything is quiet here. There is no trouble. There will be no war. Wish to return,' he replied, 'Please remain. You furnish the pictures, I'll furnish the war.'[26] Orson Welles immortalized this moment of history in a sequence of news briefs in the opening scene of *Citizen Kane* (1941).

Israel: the genesis of a garrison society

In Israel, Jewish settlements are surrounded by ramparts and networks of surveillance cameras. A so-called security fence – in fact, a concrete wall 8 or 9 metres high, with an electronic alarm and surrounded by moats and covered with barbed wire in certain places – is intended in its final form to run some 700 km along the 'green line', that is, the border established in 1967 following the Six Day War.[27]

Among the regimes that can be described as evolving under a dominant sign of national security, the state of Israel lays claim to one of the few experiences of long-term struggle against a movement classified as terrorist, thereby allowing for some historical perspective on a permanent regime of war and a permanently mobilized population. The paradox here is that the specifically Israeli mode of putting the concept of national security into practice developed outside any official ad hoc doctrine. At least that would be the interpretation of David Rodman, a specialist in Israeli diplomatic and military history, who has written:

> No state in the post-Second World War era has been more concerned with its national security than Israel – and it is not hard to fathom why. . . [But] the lack of a formal national security doctrine notwithstanding, the combined effects of the state's environment and experiences convinced Israeli defence planners to formulate a set of basic security concepts. On the one hand, these concepts have been Israel's response to the geographic, diplomatic, and resource environment in which it has had to survive. On the other hand, they have also been shaped by the state's experiences in both wartime and peacetime. Developed at various points in time, and not integrated into a set of closely linked propositions that could be called a systematic and

157

coherent 'theory' of national security, these concepts have nevertheless clearly driven Israeli thinking and conduct over the course of the state's existence.[28]

Rodman illustrates this specificity point by point. First and foremost among the factors that help to explain these concepts' operational capability is the postulate of superpower patronage. When Israel was created in 1948, Prime Minister David Ben-Gurion established this founding geopolitical principle by choosing to ally with the United States. Within this framework, Israel sought to develop another of its cardinal principles, the need for self-reliance to ensure its security. From the outset, Israeli defence and security planners chose the option of a 'militia-army' to compensate for its demographic handicap and avoid destabilizing the economy by provoking a labour shortage (in 1948, the Jewish population of Israel was between 600,000 and 650,000). The peacetime army consists of a limited number of professional soldiers, a large pool of young male and female conscripts under a system of mandatory military service, and a limited quota of reservists mobilized for one month of the year (or more, depending on their speciality). This nation-at-arms has two functions in peacetime: first, to ensure the day-to-day security of a country facing low-intensity conflicts, border skirmishes, terrorist organizations and mass uprisings; and second, to prepare for war, in other words, to maintain an ongoing system of rapid, flexible mobilization of conscripts and reservists. The weakness of the militia-army is that it cannot face an extended period of crisis without endangering the economy. In addition, the new weapons systems tend to foster increased professionalisation of the armed forces.

Historically, the tactical and strategic knowledge of the Israel Defence Forces (IDF) has been shaped by the type of confrontation they have had to face. Few officers were trained in foreign military academies and those who were sent abroad went primarily to learn how to handle new weapons systems. The combined experience of large-scale and low-level conflicts has led IDF strategists to think continually in terms of 'conventional warfare' without ruling out 'unconventional warfare'. The war of October 1973 (or Yom Kippur War) pitting Israel against its neighbours led to a complete revision of its initial tactical and strategic conception of conventional war, whereas the Intifada of the 1987–1993 period and the rise of Hezbollah in the 1990s made it aware of the challenges of unconventional war. The IDF was to be one of the first armies to update, on the basis of experience on the ground, the doctrine and practice of counterinsurgency in an urban environment. The evolution of the defence and security doctrine coincided with the creation of a research and development strategy oriented to respond to both types of conflicts. Large-scale warfare brought about a quantitative and qualitative leap in the Israeli armaments industry, which was now able to produce tanks and other land vehicles as well as reconnaissance satellites, missile launchers, warheads and medium- and long-range missiles (of the Jericho series), antiballistic missile defence systems and all sorts of electronic systems (radar, communications, etc.) – not to mention nuclear weapons. On the other hand, aircraft and ships were imported, mainly from the United States. Israel's arms dependency on the superpower went much further, as demonstrated by its use of the US base in Diego Garcia in the Indian Ocean as an air bridge during the July 2006 war in Lebanon, as well as the importing of Patriot missiles in the previous wars. The need to adapt to low-intensity conflicts drove research and production of devices for remote surveillance and targeting of adversaries, including drones or UAVs (Unmanned Air Vehicles) for espionage, which are being miniaturized along with the missiles they carry, explosive detection systems, etc. By the turn of the century, Israel had become the world leader in the UAV technology industry.[29] For security sector manufacturers offering their know-how in the international market, the experience of Israel's antiterrorist struggle became a sales argument. This can be seen in the following excerpt from the presentation of a product known as 'Cogito 1002', an automated test station produced by SDS (Suspect Detection Systems), a company founded by former senior Israeli security officials and experienced veterans of the high-tech industry:

> The SDS concept is supported and enhanced by knowledge acquired and assimilated from the analysis of thousands of case studies related to suicide bombers in Israel and worldwide, gathered by Israeli authorities and the academic community. [. . .] The 'Cogito 1002' Test Station is an automated kiosk-like station that enables the profiling and screening of passengers based on biofeedback indications. Relying on unique and proprietary technology the system is designed to identify malicious intent. SDS develops and markets the 'Cogito1002' to be used by law enforcement agencies for the detection of suspects harboring malicious intent at border control and/or other checkpoints. Our mission is to assist law enforcement agencies and employers all over the world in their war against organized crime and terrorism by providing innovative solutions that can be deployed today.[30]

This form of prolonged conflict also led to the formation of special operations units such as *Sayeret Shimson* and *Sayeret Duvdevan*, which make the tracking down of terrorist leaders one of their top priorities. It also encouraged a review of passive defence methods. Following the Gulf War, a 'Domestic Front Command' was set up to ensure the self-defence of the population against weapons of mass destruction; it operates in parallel with the 'Strategic Command', which groups together the different armed forces and intelligence services to confront foreign aggression. In this area as well, expertise acquired in the field is exported. The Israelis were inspired by the British SAS model to create their own special force, *Sayeret Matkal*. The major advances achieved in anti-terrorism by the United Kingdom since the beginning of the twenty-first century reflect a reversal in the direction of exchanges. Scotland Yard adopted the rules of engagement in force in Israel to confront suspected suicide bombers. Those rules resulted in a change whereby anti-terrorist intervention squads, accustomed to a 'shoot to stop' procedure (that is, identifying themselves by shouting and announcing the intention to open fire, aiming at the torso and re-examining the situation after each shot fired), switched to a 'shoot to kill' method by aiming at the head. The first innocent victim of the new procedure was a young Brazilian man who was shot down in the London Underground shortly after the July 2005 bombings.

As confrontations grew in intensity, Israeli courts had to go to great pains to rule on the legitimacy of certain rampant national security practices, such as 'targeted assassinations' of people 'directly involved in terrorist activities'. Such assassinations were made technically possible by combining new weapons systems with miniaturized targeting, including UAVs. The Israeli Supreme Court took five years to reach a verdict on the appeal filed in 2001 by two human rights organizations concerning the danger of killing innocent people inherent in this type of operation. In a 62-page decision, the court ruled that one could not 'determine in advance whether every targeted assassination violated international law, just as it was impossible to state *a priori* that each targeted killing was authorized by international law. The legality of each assassination must be examined on a case-by-case basis.'[31] The decision further directed that an independent investigation should be conducted after each targeted assassination to determine its relevance. If it proves to have been an error, the victims have a right to compensation.

The Israeli state, having become a laboratory of national security theory in action, has been led to dismantle the democratic safeguards that protect a society of citizens from the logic of reciprocal savagery inherent in the terrorism–anti-terrorism dialectic. In its punitive expeditions, it has unwittingly confirmed the premonitory intuition of the philosopher Walter Benjamin that the destructive methods used in future wars would annihilate 'the most important foundation of international law': the distinction between the civilian population and the combatant population. Israel has not signed any of the conventions on the law of war that prohibit the use of chemical weapons, cluster bombs or antipersonnel mines. Nor has it adhered to the nuclear non-proliferation treaty or ratified UNESCO's International Convention on the Protection and Promotion of the Diversity of Cultural Expressions, which was approved in October 2005 by 148 countries, with only two opposed: Israel and the United States.

What is the toll taken on people for this ongoing state of war? Here is the answer given by Israeli writer David Grossman in a lecture at the PEN American Center in May 2007:

> The shrinking of the 'surface area' of the soul that comes in contact with the bloody and menacing world out there. The limiting of one's ability and willingness to identify, even a little, with the pain of others; the suspension of moral judgment [. . .]. The despair most of us experience of possibly understanding our own true thoughts in a state of affairs that is so terrifying and deceptive and complex, both morally and practically. Most of all, I'm better off not feeling too much – at least until this shall pass. And if it doesn't, at least I relieved my suffering somewhat, I developed a useful numbness, I protected myself as best I could with the help of a bit of indifference, a bit of sublimation, a bit of intended blindness and large doses of self-anesthetization. In other words: Because of the perpetual – and all-too-real – fear of being hurt, or of death, or of unbearable loss, or even of 'mere' humiliation, each and every one of us, the conflict's citizens, its prisoners, trim down our own vivacity, our internal mental and cognitive diapason, ever enveloping ourselves with protective layers, which end up suffocating us. Kafka's mouse is right: when the predator is closing in on you, the world does indeed become increasingly narrow. So does the language that describes it.

From the conflict in the Middle East, Grossman extrapolated the idea of 'the conflict's citizens' to the billions of people across the world today who 'face a "predicament" of one type or other, in which personal existence and values, liberty and identity are under threat, to some extent. We all feel – or can intuit – how our special "predicament" can rapidly turn into a trap that would take away our freedom, the sense of home our country provides, our private language, our free will.'[32]

— 10 —

THE EUROPEAN POLICE AREA

The European Union, unlike the United States, does not view the fight against terrorism and organized crime from a military perspective, hence the importance of its common judicial and police areas. However, the EU's determination to prevent terrorism has not led to any innovation in the definition of the concept. The European summit on 'Democracy, Terrorism and Security', held in Madrid in 2005, a year after the bombings in that city by al-Qaeda supporters, proposed the following definition: 'Any act intended to cause death or grave bodily injury to a civilian or a non-combatant, when this act, by its nature or its context, is aimed at intimidating a population or constraining a government or international organization to accomplish or refrain from an act.'

It was not until 1999, at a conference in Tampere, Finland, that the EU introduced what it calls its third 'pillar' of regional integration, covering issues relating to judicial and police cooperation, asylum, and immigration. (The first pillar, known as 'the Community pillar', consists of the EU's three founding treaties; the second is the Common Foreign and Security Policy.) In 1985, France, Germany and the three Benelux countries signed a treaty to create an open-border area called the Schengen Area. Although it took ten years for the Schengen rules to be enforced, the area was subsequently extended to include, currently, twenty-five of the twenty-seven member states. The area embodies the principle of free movement within the Union, without distinction of nationality, while at the same time reinforcing the surveillance of its common external borders. This necessitates improved judicial and police cooperation among the member states as well as increased surveillance of external borders to prevent criminals from taking advantage of the newfound freedom of movement. As an indispensable prerequisite to eliminating border controls, a central database was created. The Schengen Information System (SIS), as it is known, lists individuals wanted for criminal activity in each member state. In 1999, the European Antifraud Office (OLAF) was also created, in order to combat fraud that could harm the financial interests of the Union, including contraband, money laundering and other suspect transactions – in short, a whole illegal economy that had become globalized as a result of the deregulation of financial markets.

Europol, an intelligence service

Interpol (International Criminal Police Organization), the intergovernmental organization founded to facilitate police cooperation, has been in existence since 1923. It operates autonomously with funding from its members and its own investments and includes 186 participating countries. The secretariat, located in Lyon, manages a network of six regional offices (Argentina, Ivory Coast, Salvador, Kenya, Thailand and Zimbabwe) and national offices in each member country. Interpol pioneered a system of information exchange on criminals, setting up an international radio communications network as early as 1935. Today the organization manages databanks on lost or stolen passports, stolen vehicles and works of art, and on criminals (their full names, fingerprints and DNA profiles). It oversees a large network of experts and working groups in the areas of police science, fraud control, drug trafficking, security and so on.

Europol (European Police Office) is a fruit of the Maastricht Treaty or 'Treaty on European Union' of 1992. Based in The Hague, Netherlands, it began limited operations in 1994 in the form of the Europol Drugs Unit (EDU), whose mission was to fight against drug traffic and associated money laundering. The Europol Convention was ratified by all EU member states and came into force on 1 October 1998. Europol commenced its full activities on 1 July 1999 and has gradually extended its scope of action. The founding of Europol represents a cornerstone in the efforts of the EU to strengthen law-enforcement cooperation in a 'Europe without borders'. The aim of the organization, as defined in Article 2 of its Convention, is to:

> improve . . . the effectiveness and cooperation of the competent authorities in the Member States in preventing and combating terrorism, unlawful drug trafficking and other serious forms of international crime where there are factual indications that an organized criminal structure

is involved and two or more Member States are affected by the forms of crime in question in such a way as to require a common approach by the Member States owing to the scale, significance and consequences of the offences concerned.[1]

The controversial point is how to define 'criminal organization'. The 1998 European Union 'Joint Action on Making it a Criminal Offence to Participate in a Criminal Organization' defines a criminal organization in Article 1 as 'a structured organization, established over a period of time, of more than two persons, acting in concert with the view to committing offences . . . whether such offences are an end in themselves or a means of obtaining material benefits and, where appropriate, of improperly influencing the operation of public authorities'. As Jean-Claude Paye notes, it was the German approach that prevailed here, and in particular that of the German criminal police, the BKA:

> It introduced a directly political notion to describe a penal action. [. . .]
> This definition is criminological and is designed to serve police investigation. The use of this type of definition for penal incrimination represents an extension of the scope of such investigations. Contrary to the penal approach in the strict sense, a criminological definition enables very broad incrimination. [. . .] Such penal language is opposed to the principle of equality, which requires that punishable facts be precisely defined.[2]

The comment is particularly relevant because this Belgian sociologist observed the drift towards security-oriented and repressive approaches associated with this type of definition when Belgium launched its 'federal security plan' and judicial and police reforms in 1998.

As the embryo of a European police force, Europol's mission resembles that of an intelligence service: exchange and coordination, data collection and analysis, creation of files not only on persons suspected of having committed or taken part in crimes, but also individuals presumed likely to commit them. In other words, it anticipates offences in a 'proactive' fashion. Its mission is also to produce reports on emerging trends in organized crime. Finally, it lends support to the training of national police forces in technical and scientific police work as well as investigation techniques. The intelligence function and its corollary, secrecy, have earned Europol a special status in the architecture of European institutions. The office is independent of the judicial authority of the various member states and European jurisdiction (in particular, the Court of Justice), and largely escapes political control. The European Parliament plays only a consulting role; it may question the recourse to police cooperation. As for the European Commission, it has the right to attend meetings of the Europol board of directors but cannot vote. In fact, the autonomous development of Europol is similar to the independence acquired by the European Central Bank in the area of economic and monetary policy.[3]

At the same time as Europol, in early 2001, the European Police College (CEPOL) came into being. This network of cooperation, made up of national training institutes for high police officials, aims to develop a common approach to the main problems of prevention and the fight against criminality through courses and seminars for qualified police agents. It is paradoxically located in Bramshill in the United Kingdom, which, like Ireland, has refused to join the Schengen Area and jealously preserves its sovereignty in security matters. In fact, the creation of the first European counterterrorist network, TREVI, by the ministries of the interior in 1971, in response to terrorist acts such as the hostage-taking during the 1972 Olympic Games in Munich, was also a British initiative.

A 'culture of security': the Schengen Area at fever pitch

'To adopt a culture of security': that is how the European Commissioner in charge of research defined in 2004 the objective of a new programme to 'mobilize the forces of the security industry and the excellence of European research'.[4] The Commissioner for Information Society and Media followed suit, declaring: 'Events have put security among the foremost practical concerns in Europe and the world. [. . .] Strong research is the indispensable substratum of competitive business. Communication is a decisive step towards a consistent European approach to research in the area of security'. The EU adopted the recommendations of a group composed of twenty-seven European industrial leaders and decision-makers. Although the initial budget dedicated to this programme of several years' duration was far below the funding of the Department of Homeland Security, it has constantly increased. Following invitations to tender, consortiums were set up, associating university laboratories with the defence and security industry. This has not kept defence manufacturers from taking a very active part in American programmes while collaborating on those in Europe. In fact, under pressure from these groups, the EU decided to end the protectionist policy that prevailed for decades in European weapons markets. A European Defence Agency was set up in 2004 to foster the creation of a competitive European market in this sector. In line with the trend in the United States, major groups underwent restructuring. As a result of the ensuing alliances, mergers and privatizations, three European groups emerged which now rank among the top ten worldwide: British Aerospace (United Kingdom), EADS (European Aeronautics Defense and Space, Netherlands) and Thales (France). These groups also forged ties with US groups.[5]

The 'security' issue led the European Union to widen its scope of action to encompass projects contiguous, and sometimes mingled, with defence. EU doctrine on military and security programmes, which led it to extend the frontiers of its 'security zone' and thus of its interventions outside its territory, necessarily tended to link the two domains together.[6] One example of this connection between defence and security was the programme known as GMES (Global Monitoring for Environment and Security), designed to gather data provided by observation satellites, airborne devices and onshore and offshore sensors – an essential tool for controlling borders, among other uses. Although the principle of military use of the European GSP, another major programme, was not officially approved, there is nothing to prevent it from serving such purposes.

Two other factors contributed to tighter security measures within the Union as a whole: first, the management of migration flows and the presumed dangers in this respect of EU enlargement towards Eastern Europe; and, second, the management of the police computerized record system. The latter had become so complex that a delay in introducing the second generation of databases, SIS II – indispensable for external border control – forced the entry of the ten new member states into the Schengen Area to be postponed for several months. By 21 December 2007, it was in place, however, when eight Eastern European countries and Malta were included in the area; Switzerland joined them in December 2008. The Schengen control centre, located in Strasbourg, is the brain of a system that manages data concerning stolen documents, vehicles and individuals wanted in a territory with a population of 400 million. Initially planned for the end of 2007, the implementation of the whole SIS II project of technical connections will not be in operation until late 2009. The programme involves incorporating into the central file biometric data such as photographs, fingerprints and DNA, increasing the amount of information available on asylum seekers, extending the period of data storage, and broadening the right of access to the files. These developments have resulted in critical reports by the Commissioner for Human Rights of the Council of Europe and by citizens' organizations such as Statewatch and the European Civil Liberties Network (ECLN), particularly regarding the protection of newly integrated data.

New components were added to the system of police and judicial cooperation, despite the slow and partial development of the powers of the European judicial area. Eurojust (officially known as the 'European Judicial Cooperation Unit'), an embryonic European prosecutor's office made up of national magistrates, was assigned in 2001 to solve drug-trafficking and money-laundering cases and investigate the networks of those involved. In the same year, the Financial Action Task Force on Money Laundering (FATF), created in 1989 by the G7 at its summit in Paris, joined with Europol to monitor and report suspect financial transactions in European countries. Then, in 2002 and 2003, two protocols to its Convention gave Europol new powers to assist the member states, including coordinating joint investigation teams, requesting investigations and allowing third countries (with which Europol has concluded operational agreements) to take part in groups that conduct analyses. In 2002, the European warrant for arrest was introduced, giving material form to the principle of mutual recognition on which operational cooperation between Eurojust and Europol was based. In 2004, the rules giving these two bodies access to files were relaxed. In 2005, a new organization called Frontex was set up, with headquarters in Warsaw, to ensure better cooperation among member states for the management and surveillance of the European Union's terrestrial and maritime borders and airspace. In 2007, two bodies, composed of border guard officers of member states, the European Patrol Network (EPN) and the Rapid Border Intervention Teams (RABIT), completed the security cordon. The mission of the latter body is to act in the event of 'the massive arrival of illegal immigrants'.

One thing is certain: in 2004, under the shock of the Madrid bombings, the European anti-terrorism system was reinforced to improve cooperation within the EU. A coordinator position was created and its occupant reported directly to the High Representative for the common European foreign and security policy. Yet, five years later, this body has failed to provide satisfactory answers to the questions of the European Parliament concerning clandestine flights – nearly 1,250 of them – organized by the CIA on chartered planes, to transport suspects to various locations for interrogation and detention. In late 2007, the programme prompted the following warning from the Council of Europe's Commissioner on Human Rights: the European States practise 'a double standard policy', a 'form of hypocrisy'.[7] As a result, they have lost their credibility when 'they point out the problems posed by the other regions of the world (. . .)'. In 2008, the Parliamentary Assembly of the Council of Europe challenged the black lists of the UN and the European Union, declaring that the criteria for including individuals and entities on terrorist 'lists' violate human rights and make a mockery of the rule of law. Indeed, names are placed in the files without any hearing, be it public or behind closed doors.

The London bombings of July 2005 led to a major expansion of measures involving the ongoing interference of technology in private life. The rapid identification by Scotland Yard, thanks to video camera images, of the four presumed authors of the attempted attacks in the underground and in a bus, impressed European Union police forces, who hastened to install their own video surveillance systems in public transport and other public places. It must be said that the United Kingdom had an ample head start on the continent in using this means of deterrence and identification, with 10 per cent of all security cameras installed in the world, which means that any London resident may be filmed more than 300 times a day. In its 2006 Report, the Surveillance Studies Network, an independent research body established to promote access to official data and to protect personal information, expressed concern at seeing the United Kingdom evolving into a 'surveillance society'. Such a society, the Network wrote, 'is premised both on state secrecy and the state not giving up its supposed right to keep information under control while, at the same time, wanting to know as much as it can about us'.[8]

The attacks also precipitated decisions that resulted in new anti-terrorist provisions to regulate security intercepts, which now target every potentially usable means of communication. In late 2005, a large majority of the twenty-seven member states agreed on a draft European directive, initiated by the British government, ordering mandatory preservation of certain data relating to telephone or electronic communications. (On 1 January 2008, a new European directive came into force, requiring telephone and Internet providers to record and store telephone numbers, Internet addresses and the dates and times of telephone and electronic communications for six months. This information can be made available to the police, the courts and intelligence services. In Germany, especially, the new legislation provoked a wave of protest in the streets of more than forty cities, in answer to a call from the Working Group on Data Saving, a citizens' group that includes members of various associations and organizations. The reinforcement of security apparatuses is a sensitive issue in this country because of its Nazi and later Communist past.)

What is paradoxical about the British initiative is that the United Kingdom has spearheaded security policies in the European Union without belonging to the Schengen Area. With the law on criminal justice (2003), the law on terrorism prevention (2005) and the law on investigation procedures (2005), it has pushed for measures that continue to upset the institutional balance, in a process which began with the struggle against armed groups in Northern Ireland in the 1970s and 1980s.

As for the surveillance of Internet users, France has by no means lagged behind in developing its own Big Brother fantasies. This was demonstrated by the public outcry over the June 2004 law on digital economy, known as 'the law for confidence in the digital economy'. Prepared in secret, the measures decided in the wake of this law required website editors, hosts, land and mobile telephone operators and Internet access providers to save all traces of Internet users and mobile phone subscribers for one year, and to hand them over to police detectives (*police judiciaire*) or the state upon request. This meant saving passwords, pseudonyms, confidential access codes and other identifying data, bank card numbers, payment details, telephone numbers, email addresses, the numbers of computers or telephones used, the means of network access, and the dates and times of calls, connections or a person's visit or contribution to a website. Once this personal data was gathered, it could be saved for up to three years in the files of the Ministries of the Interior and Defence. These announced measures provoked the combined opposition of defenders of civil liberties and the major French website editors. As the president of an online editors' group, Geste, declared in an opinion piece in *Le Monde*: 'On the pretext of fighting the genuine threat of terrorism, the French state is running the risk – like no other country – of killing a significant part of the country's future, without any qualms and in the deafening silence of a presidential campaign omnipresent on the Internet but mute regarding Internet development.'[9]

Projects for a Biometric ID

The European Union began paving the way for a global identification system by following the US model of a 'biometric passport with global interoperability', containing a digital photograph on a chip for automatic electronic facial recognition. The issue of securitization and harmonization of passports was of course already under discussion in the EU prior to the 2001 attacks in New York, but the decision to incorporate biometric components into Schengen Area passports (a measure with which non-EU countries such as Iceland, Norway and Switzerland were also associated) responded to the need for member states belonging to the Visa Waiver Program to align themselves with US legislation, so that their citizens would be authorized to continue travelling to the United States without a visa for stays of up to three months. This exemption programme, inaugurated in 1986, applies exclusively to the nationals of twenty-seven countries, primarily in Western Europe, but also Australia, Brunei, Singapore and New Zealand. After the enlargement of the European Union to include twelve new member states, mainly from Eastern Europe, Brussels asked Washington to extend the programme to the newcomers. However, the US federal authorities preferred to decide individually on a case-by-case basis, according to restrictive criteria: any country with a 2 per cent rate of visa rejections would be disqualified. To be in the good graces of the US administration, countries such as the Czech Republic, Hungary and Poland chose to go it alone, emphasizing the quality of their cooperation in the fight against terrorism – especially since, in exchange for maintaining or expanding the programme, the United States intended to tighten controls and impose new conditions regarding the information exchanged on passengers and procedures. This is the aim of the Electronic System for Travel Authorization (ESTA), modelled after the Australian system, which became mandatory in January 2009: travellers are required to fill out an Internet form when purchasing their tickets and, on the basis of the information contained in their passports and on their credit cards, a central computer verifies that they are not on a suspect list – roughly the equivalent of a visa.[10]

The irony of this adoption of the US model of the interoperable passport is that the US government opted for the least reliable technology. Indeed, the technique of facial recognition can produce a rate of error as high as 10 per cent. There are many other biometric recognition techniques, five of which offer a high level of security: DNA or genetic print analysis; scanning of the retina or the iris (the two unique eye 'signatures'); fingerprints and their cousin, palm prints; and, finally, hand geometry. The probability of finding two individuals presenting the same traits is virtually nil (about one in several billion for DNA or iris recognition, and one in sixty-four billion for fingerprints). Two other procedures, voice and handwriting recognition, like facial recognition, have a lower capability of differentiating people because they depend on the software used and on the quality of the initial photograph.

Europe has embraced identification techniques with great zeal. In the United States, citizens still have no national identity card; they can use their driving licence or another document for identification. In Europe, however – from Spain to France and Portugal all the way to Estonia – many countries have already replaced old paper identity cards with a biometric ID. Countries that had previously refused the very principle of the identity card, on the grounds that it is a police state practice, are now switching without transition or discussion to the biometric version. In Great Britain, the Home Secretary publicized its proposals for the introduction of a national identity card in November 2003, as part of its strategy for addressing 'the growing threats to the nation's security and prosperity from illegal immigration and working, organized crime and terrorism, identity theft and fraudulent access to public services'. In March 2006, the Identity Cards Bill received royal assent and became the Identity Cards Act. The project involved introducing by 2010 an electronic identity card, including fingerprints, digitized facial scan and iris scans, and instituting a national biometric identity register called the NIR, in spite of objections from the Conservative Party and human rights and civil liberties advocates. Prior to this controversial law, national identity documents had been required only twice in the United Kingdom, both times under exceptional circumstances: during the First World War, and again from 1939 to 1952, for military conscription and the management of food rations. In 2008, the government modified its plans for the introduction of identity cards: these would not be required for UK citizens. It was planned that everyone over the age of sixteen applying for a passport would have their information – including fingerprints and facial scans – added to a National Identity Register, starting in 2011 or the following year. The Identity and Passport Service planned to issue 'significant numbers' of ID cards alongside British passports, but with a provision for people to opt out of having a card. The ID card was planned as mandatory only for non-EU foreign nationals coming to work in the UK, and for about 200,000 workers at airports and other sensitive places. Starting in 2010, students would be encouraged to get ID cards when they opened bank accounts. However, the new coalition government (Conservatives and Liberal-Democrats) elected in May 2010 has since announced an end to the planned ID cards.

Until now, electronic fingerprint files were used solely for delinquents and criminals. The biometric registration projects propose to extend them to all citizens, using a technology for remote-reading electronic chips (Radio Frequency Identification). In France, the Securitized Electronic National Identity project (INES) has proposed the adoption of an identity card in bank card format, divided into several distinct, impermeable 'blocs': an identity bloc, containing strictly confidential biometric data, available to the police and authorized administrations; a bloc for authenticating the card; a certified identification bloc that grants the cardholder access to certain public or private electronic procedures; an electronic signature bloc for use by electronic administrators; and, finally, a personal portfolio bloc in which each person may store complementary information such as a tax number, driving license number or the like. Impermeability between the blocs is guaranteed by cryptography. The project was originally planned to become operational by 2006, but, as a result of the vehement objections of civil liberties advocates, it was suspended by the Ministry of the Interior and 'reworked'.[11] The fact that other countries, such as Portugal, are testing an electronic ID that stores data from other cards (social security, public health service, tax status and voter registration) indicates that this is a long-term trend. The need felt by some states, such as Estonia, to maintain contact with new e-ID holders has even led the authorities to assign each person an email address valid for life.

Genetic prints are another rapidly growing biometric identification method. In 1986, the genetics expert Sir Alec John Jeffreys developed an identification technique known as Restriction Fragment Length Polymorphisms (RFLP), based on the analysis of targeted short DNA segments translated into digital codes. In 1997, a resolution of the Council of the European Union recommended the constitution of files on the basis of DNA samples. In 1995, the United Kingdom took the lead by creating a national genetic file and now hosts the largest bank of DNA profiles in the world. In 2006, it comprised no fewer than 3.3 million records, covering 5 per cent of the population. This pioneering position taken by the British scientific police prompted Interpol in 1996 to set up a working group of European experts in the field, to internationalize the process and encourage EU member countries to create laboratories, relying on the experience of the United Kingdom.[12] In 1999, the FBI joined the group. The United States had indeed begun its own pilot project in fourteen states in 1990, mainly to identify those guilty of violent crimes, an experiment it extended to every state eight years later.

At first, the UK law provided solely for the preservation of saliva samples taken from persons convicted or under indictment. Since 2001, however, the file also collects the profiles of those who are acquitted and even those not indicted,[13] to the great displeasure of Sir Alec Jeffreys, who publicly condemned this deviation. Here was proof that this type of identification procedure tends to widen its scope of enforcement and draw the net ever tighter. Since 2004, police in the UK have had the authority to take DNA samples from anyone over the age of ten who is arrested, regardless of whether they are later charged, convicted or found to be innocent. By the end of 2008, the number of ten- to eighteen-year-olds in the DNA database after being arrested was close to a million. In 2008, the European Court of Human Rights unanimously found that the UK practice of keeping indefinitely the fingerprints and DNA of people not convicted of an offence is a violation of Article 8 of the European Convention on Human Rights.

Legal frameworks everywhere have been adapted in a similar manner. In France, where the method initially concerned only those convicted of sexual and/or violent crimes, it was extended to 'suspects' of more ordinary violations by the Sarkozy 'domestic security' law in 2003, and reinforced by the 'Perben II law' in 2004, which expanded *ad infinitum* the list of offences to which the procedure applied. The law now applies to 'any individual that can be plausibly suspected of committing an offence' from among an exhaustive list including 'damage, deterioration or the threat of harm to property'. Moreover, prison sentences are lengthened for refusal to comply with police identification procedures. According to Article 706–55 of the code of penal procedure, no less than 137 types of violations can now lead to the compulsory taking and preserving of DNA samples. One example of the repressive trend of legislation: in 2006, an activist against genetically modified organisms, who had been given a one-month suspended prison sentence in 2005 for pulling up a patch of transgenic beets four years earlier, was tried in Alès for refusing to provide the gendarmes with a saliva sample. Five years after the initial crime! The Secretary General of the *Syndicat de la magistrature* (a magistrates' union) noted with irony that 'many financial offences such as insider trading, tax fraud or misuse of company property do not require DNA records'.[14]

The same discriminatory spirit of crime prevention can be noted in policies to 'fight insecurity', introduced by the authorities in certain cities run by elected officials of the right. The example par excellence is the city of Orléans, a sort of laboratory of prevention, where the installation of video cameras in 'high-risk sites' (the city centre and so-called 'problem' or 'at-risk' districts) was accompanied by a series of measures of 'public hygiene' against alcohol abuse, camping on the streets and prostitution, as well as curfews for minors and the creation of committees to warn parents and force them to 'take responsibility' for the behaviour of their children.

Weakening the principles of citizen protection

At the threshold of the 1980s, following the adoption of laws to protect individuals from abuses in data collecting in several European countries, a number of international documents in the form of agreements or recommendations set forth major principles to be followed in order to guarantee the free, balanced flow of personal information. They included the principle of *honesty*, according to which 'information should not be gathered or processed using deceptive or unlawful procedures such as telephone eavesdropping'; the principle of *finality*, by virtue of which 'the purpose justifying the creation of a file must be specified before the act is carried out, making it possible to verify the pertinence of said information and the amount of time for which it is to be preserved'; the principle of *publicity*, according to which 'the public must be able to know the list of computerized files on persons'; and the principle of *individual access*, allowing any person to 'know whether information concerning him or her is contained in a file and to have it modified or eliminated in the event of error, inaccuracy or illegal recording'.[15]

The swiftness with which intrusive procedures were voted into law in the countries of the European Union after 11 September 2001 contributed to diminishing the degree of protection guaranteed by these principles concerning the treatment and storage of data on citizens. The growing connections among administrative files, the creation of private files by companies serving as informal 'criminal records' on cheaters or bad payers, real or suspected, and the constitution of huge police files, have damaged the legal protections that had up to now served as checks on uncontrolled data-gathering. Thus, in France, a country that distinguished itself in the 1970s by adopting parliamentary measures to preserve privacy, the revised 2004 version of the Information Technology, Files and Freedom Act whittled down the authority of the National Commission on Information Technology and Freedom (see chapter 8), tending to limit it to a purely consultative role.[16]

On the pan-European police scene, the Treaty of Prüm (named for a city in western Germany), signed on 27 May 2005 by seven EU member states (Austria, Belgium, France, Germany, Luxembourg, Netherlands and Spain, and later by Finland, Italy, Portugal and Slovenia), constitutes a centrepiece, for its primary aim is to create a network of existing national databases, particularly in the area of anti-terrorism, cross-border criminality and illegal migration. The exchange of information provided for by the Treaty encompasses not only the matching of DNA data but also mutual access to fingerprint

174

and vehicle registration data. At a summit coordination meeting with his partners in January 2007, the German Minister of the Interior, Wolfgang Schäuble, provided his interpretation of the spirit of the treaty:

> Agreement was (. . .) reached on regulations concerning the exchange of data in the struggle against terrorism and regarding the movements of those engaging in violence: to prevent terrorist acts, it is thus possible to transmit personal information on individuals likely to constitute a terrorist threat. For purposes of prevention in the context of major events, the treaty permits the exchange of information on the movements of those engaging in violence such as hooligans (for example during football games or meetings of the European Council or other international summits). Thanks to the Treaty of Prüm, police cooperation has also been intensified by operational measures. Thus, the treaty authorizes various forms of joint intervention such as joint patrols, cross-border interventions to oppose threats and the possibility of transferring public authority to police agents from other contracting states. For example, police agents who provide reinforcement to another European country in order to ensure security at major events such as a European football championship or a European summit can be invested in this role with the rights and obligations of the host country.[17]

One has every right to wonder when 'demonstrators' will be included on this black list – unless they already fall into the category of hooligans, as the brutal police operations against demonstrators at summit meetings or other large-scale events 'suspected of protest' would suggest. This is not a moot question, given that one of the priority tasks of the police and intelligence services has become managing crises of public order as well as monitoring emerging protest movements. It is also attested by the severity of surveillance measures and the massive deployment of police and soldiers during the annual four-day G8 summit held in Heiligendamm in June 2007, near the northern German city of Rostock. A total of 16,000 policemen were brought in from all the regions (*Länder*) of the country; 1,100 soldiers from the Bundeswehr were placed in charge of securing the seacoast and airspace (which was sealed off over a radius of 50 kilometres surrounding the site), and overseeing a supply and transport mission; 2,000 firemen and emergency workers were also brought in. Automobile traffic was prohibited along a 21 kilometre stretch of seafront extending 11 kilometres into the Baltic Sea, with US and German warships securing the coast. The site was protected by a wire fence 12 kilometres long and 2½ metres high, at a cost of 12.5 million euros. The overall price tag for the summit was 92 million euros.

Heads of state and government brought delegations of twenty-four people, with the exception of the US delegation, which had as many as a hundred members.[18] The heavily armed security forces were nevertheless unable to prevent Greenpeace activists from penetrating the off-limits coastal area and engaging in a chase with the police. In a country once divided by a real wall, the barbed-wire fence revived some very unpleasant memories.

Current technological innovation is leading to perfecting tools for remote observation of moving crowds. After serving the Israeli army to target and eliminate numerous political leaders of Palestinian organizations, today drones are used to control and observe cities, outlying urban areas, or citizens who make use of their democratic right to engage in street protest, as shown by the 'Milipol' trade fair, devoted to the internal security of states, held in Paris in October 2007. Experiments in pairing video camera surveillance with 'intelligent' software, forming a 'rudimentary brain', are following the same trend: detection of suspect behaviour (an individual going in the wrong direction in an underground corridor, the sudden formation of a crowd on an underground platform, a vehicle stopped on a motorway emergency strip), scanning the faces of passers-by and comparing them with images in police files.

In any event, judging by the agreements concluded on the exchange of biometric files in June 2007, intra-European police cooperation is constantly developing. The ministers of the interior have indeed agreed to put their files of DNA genetic signatures and fingerprints into a network. However, because of the situation in Northern Ireland, London and Dublin refused to include in EU law the right to cross-border pursuit. The law does allow for the creation of joint investigation teams and the deployment of foreign police officers for major events. The twenty-seven member states have not yet reached a consensus on another law concerning the protection of private data communicated in a context of police and judicial cooperation; for the moment, this data is not covered by European law. There is also a divergence of opinion concerning the scope of such a measure and the conditions under which data may be transferred to another country such as the United States.[19]

Foreigners and their 'accomplices'

'Our borders are protected by electricity. A zone of lightning reigns along the perimeter of the Federation. A small, bespectacled man is seated who knows where, in front of a keyboard. He is our only soldier. All he has to do is press down on a key to crush an army of five hundred thousand men.'[20] With these words, written more than a century ago, the novelist Anatole France sketched out the future of the 'Federation of European Peoples', threatened in the year AD 2270 by an 'invasion of barbarians' from Africa and Asia. A century later, at the outer edges of Europe, in Melilla and Ceuta, along the Spanish–Moroccan border, there is a six-metre-high fence with an embedded cable network, in the form of a labyrinth, equipped with seismic detectors and watchtowers with tear-gas dispensers. Migrants from sub-Saharan Africa are shot at if they try to cross the border.

The issue of 'illegal immigration' haunts the entire Schengen Area. Laws governing the immigration and residency of foreigners have multiplied, tightening the screws on the conditions for access to the European Union. The modalities of granting visas and methods of identifying applicants have evolved accordingly, while the chances have diminished of slipping through the net of files on people who have entered or resided illegally in Europe. The definition of 'illegal immigration' has become broader: it now concerns various categories of people and channels for illegal entry and residence in the EU. In particular, it encompasses people who have entered the territory of a member state illegally, either without papers or with fake or falsified papers; people who enter with a valid visa or residence permit but overstay their visas; people whose stay, while initially legal, becomes illegal when they are hired as salaried workers; people with a valid residence permit and work permit who overstay the authorized visa period or infringe upon residence regulations in some other way. In June 2002, the European Council meeting in Seville assigned 'absolute priority' to establishing a common system of identification of data relating to visas within the Schengen Area.

This Visa Information System (VIS) is based on a centralized architecture, comprising the central information system (CS-VIS) and an interface in each member state (NI-VIS). The system's objectives include preventing and detecting threats of terrorist acts and other serious violations affecting the domestic security of the member states, facilitating the struggle against document fraud and returning undocumented people to their home country. Aside from traditional identifiers (name, sex, residence, etc.), all visas have a full-face photograph as the main biometric component, along with fingerprints and the name of the person issuing the invitation or assuming the foreigner's subsistence costs during the stay. This data will be stored for five years. The inclusion of this information was recommended by the International Civil Aviation Organization (ICAO) in its pioneering work in this area. A second agreement, concluded in May 2007 among the twenty-seven member states and the European Parliament, indicates that, starting in 2009, the European visa database will list the visas granted or refused by the 3,500 consulates in the Schengen Area. A consulate will be informed in real time of any previous requests made by a visa applicant, who will no longer be able to apply elsewhere. Some 20 million applicants per year request visas to enter the Schengen Area at the various consulates of the member states. The visa policy and the introduction of the identification system are part of the overall plan to prevent and combat illegal immigration and human trafficking. This plan, which dates from 2002 and is aimed at defining a common, integrated approach to managing migratory flows, consists of a series of measures and actions to be adopted and carried out in seven areas: not only visa policy, but also information exchange, re-admission and repatriation policy, border control, measures to be taken at border crossings, Europol and sanctions.

It was in this context that in June 2008 the European Union adopted its so-called 'return directive', defining the conditions for the deportation of illegal immigrants. Those foreigners judged likely to abscond before their case is heard are to be placed in temporary detention centres for a period not to exceed six months, but which can be extended to eighteen months if subjects do not cooperate with authorities or if documents necessary for the treatment of their case are not made available in time. Moreover, deported foreigners may not return to any EU country for five years. They may be deported to a country other than their country of origin that they have crossed to reach Europe. Human rights advocacy groups, but also several Latin American governments, publicly condemned this measure, labelling it 'the directive of shame'.

But there is more. Just as the struggle against terrorism has generated an indefinite broadening of the notions of complicity, contact and sympathizer, the 'struggle against illegal immigration' has been extended to include keeping files and monitoring those in contact with foreigners, whether they are in the country legally or illegally – in other words anyone who expresses political or personal solidarity towards them, their allies or their families. This is the spirit presiding over the creation of files intended to 'facilitate the removal of foreigners who remain on the territory illegally', in keeping with European Union policy of creating files on individuals who house foreigners or come to visit them in detention centres.

The visa policy and the overall plan of which it is a part attest to th̲ ̲ ̲ ̲ ̲ ̲ ̲ ̲ suspicion at work in the policy of generalized closing of EU borders to immigrants. Magistrates in charge of illegal immigration cases have expressed their concern and sharply criticized the increased use of new technologies. As one jurist declared:

> If we do not open certain channels allowing foreigners to immigrate legally to the European Union in parallel with our efforts to fight illegal immigration, we run the risk of being drawn into a diabolical cycle. This will force us constantly to invent and finance new stratagems at our borders and in other countries to fight illegal immigration, knowing that smugglers, traffickers and the migrants themselves are also going to come up with new ways to trick the authorities. It gives one the shivers to learn that some migrants have already mutilated their fingers to avoid having fingerprints taken or recognized.[21]

This is fertile ground for the stereotype of the immigrant as the ideal criminal. An incident that occurred in Brussels in April 2006 is symbolic in this regard. Belgian television followed the police authorities in unhesitatingly leading the public to believe that two 'North Africans' had stabbed a high school student to death to steal his MP3 in the central train station, under video surveillance. This information was refuted barely two days later, thanks to the confession (and not the video sequence) of one of the two adolescents who had committed the aggression. Both were Polish.

Terrorism, the catalyst of fear

The after-effect of the terrorist threat was to exacerbate the security obsessions and paranoid attitudes of even the most democratic governments. The ministries of the interior of the European Union member states have demonstrated a confusion of categories in defining the profile of the targets of police strategies. The focus on security experienced in all democratic countries after the September 11 attacks turned into an 'obsession with punishing', a 'dizzying over-emphasis on penal law', explains legal expert Jean Danet: 'The general movement consists in expecting criminal justice to settle everything. It is asked to provide the security controls missing from schools, families, neighbourhoods, etc. Legislators are constantly extending the penal dragnet. We are witnessing the expansion of "penalization" over time (statutes of limitations are being called into question) and space.'[22] The French law on security in everyday life, which was passed virtually unanimously in the heat of the moment in late October 2001, is a good illustration of the catalysing effect of fear generated by terrorism. It was only the beginning, however. The terms used by the French Minister of the Interior in presenting the Bill are especially significant: 'There is a before and an after September 11; our legislative arsenal could not remain unchanged after that tragedy.'[23]

Under normal circumstances, it is customary for a modification of the penal code, which by definition affects civil liberties, to be proposed by the Minister of Justice rather than the Minister of the Interior. An initial version of the Bill was presented by the government and discussed by the Parliament in April 2001, but the government strengthened it after the attacks, adding thirteen amendments intended to advance the 'struggle against terrorism' at the last minute. This late addition did not allow for genuine debate. The spectre of offences and crimes, both petty and major, conjured up by this law far exceeded the bounds of the struggle against international terrorism. For all categories of acts, the punishment was far more severe than under common law. Money laundering, complicity with a terrorist enterprise, insider trading (!), the sale of weapons and drugs, organizing illegal immigration, dodging fares in public transport, urban incivility (e.g. graffiti), gatherings to hear techno music, collective protest movements and multiple forms of revolt – all these are lumped together. The measures adopted are intrusive: searches without consent of the individual; authorization to search vehicles whether they are moving, stopped or parked on the street (it should be remembered that, in 1976, a Bill to authorize the search of vehicles in the event of a demonstration raised an outcry and was ultimately declared unconstitutional); authorization of body searches confined to private security agents in areas accessible to the public, not only in ports and airports but also stadiums, department stores, theatres, museums, etc. (measures whose enforcement clearly creates opportunities for racial profiling); and reinforcement of police powers, particularly in public housing districts, described in official terminology as 'at-risk neighbourhoods'.

Racial profiling was precisely what three teenagers were trying to escape on 27 October 2005 in one such district in Clichy-sous-Bois, on the eastern outskirts of Paris, when they took refuge in an electric power station while being chased in error by the police. Two of them were electrocuted, setting off a violent reaction – the burning of thousands of cars and several public buildings – that consumed several cities and outlying urban areas every night for more than two weeks. These riots – the most significant unrest in France since May 1968 – expressed the anger of a whole generation of children of recent immigrants, the great majority of whom had French citizenship from birth or by naturalization and yet continued to be perceived as 'North Africans' or 'blacks' and hence disqualified in advance, excluded from employment, and desperate to have their dignity recognized at last. The government's retaliation presented certain unmistakable signs. First of all, the verbal outbursts of the Minister of the Interior and future president Nicolas Sarkozy were reminiscent of the stigmatization in crowd psychology of the 'dangerous classes'. He pointedly used the word *'racaille'* – roughly equivalent to 'scum' – whose xenophobic overtones were especially significant given that Sarkozy's right-wing party sought the votes of the overtly racist National Front and equipped itself with an ad hoc legal arsenal for that purpose. Each time new measures and laws on security (and, necessarily, immigration) were introduced, the profile of the targets became clearer: any manifestation of revolt, treated as a crime, and poverty, also treated as a violation of the law. Second, the event brought about a revival of colonial legislation. On 8 November 2005, Prime Minister Dominique de Villepin decreed a state of emergency, reactivating a law dating back to 3 April 1955, adopted in the context of the Algerian War. The law's fourteen Articles had not been enforced in continental France in forty-five years. The Article actually invoked concerned cases of 'imminent peril resulting from serious violations against public order'. As for the Minister of the Interior, he seized the opportunity to talk about 'hosing down' the at-risk districts – another way of expressing the notion of 'cleaning up' (*nettoyage*), commonly used by theoreticians of counterinsurgency.

The experience acquired by the police in 'problem areas' is now influencing the choices of urban planners, who seek to circumscribe the danger, as seen for example in a measure, included in the March 2007 law on the prevention of delinquency, that addresses the renovation of outlying districts and new construction. The goal, according to the department of public security, is to 'dissuade people from action', 'block' and 'delay' malicious actions, 'diminish their effects' and facilitate police intervention. Urban development policy is taking the security dimension into account by prohibiting flat roofs from which rioters could throw projectiles or keep a lookout, burying rubbish containers to avoid fires, installing outdoor furniture that can withstand vandalism, protecting power distribution points against power failures provoked by rioters, placing concrete blocks in front of shops in danger of being rammed by cars, eliminating canopies in front of building lobbies to deter young people from gathering, facilitating the circulation of police vehicles by restricting access to pedestrian streets, avoiding hedges and walls that are too high, and so on.[24] Visibility – 'to be seen and to see from a distance'[25] – remains the key to surveillance, particularly now that it is enhanced by aerial images captured by a drone and instantaneously transmitted to the ground – a means of surveillance that has the advantage of costing less than satellites, helicopters or small planes.

This architecture of 'at-risk districts' makes reference to new frames of analysis generated by a 'sociology of order', which has been developing a typology of forms of institutional violence since the 1990s. In a book with the evocative title of *La décadence sécuritaire* (*The Decadence of Securitarianism*), two former presidents of a major magistrates' union note:

> Based on the information gathered by intelligence agents, this classification includes eight levels of violence, from Degree 1 which groups together criminal offences (theft, murder) to Degree 8, the most serious: rioting accompanied by collective confrontation against the police for three to five consecutive nights. Little by little, civilized order is no longer order that protects citizens from the violence of their neighbours or from delinquency in general but is being limited to order as defined by the police. It is from this perspective that the notion of 'lawless zone' (*zone de non-droit*) was created. The notion does not designate the demand for rights that could emanate from citizens and inhabitants when those rights no longer exist, but rather the population's behaviour towards the police. The reversal is complete.[26]

— 11 —

THE TRACEABILITY OF BODIES AND GOODS

'We're moving toward control societies that no longer operate by confining people but through continuous control and instant communication.' Gilles Deleuze wrote these words in 1990,[1] at the very moment when the mode of capital accumulation changed in both scale and nature, regarding its space-time and its ties to the state and to the societal environment. Deleuze was familiar with the writings of W. S. Burroughs on soft control and the soft machine,[2] and made good use of them. Over time, the concept of the control society, which he intuited without being able to develop it, became the locus of a multiplicity of critical approaches and intellectual explorations, whose common characteristic was the urge to understand the renewal of organizational forms of power and the forms of subjectivity associated with them. This new mode of social management is copied from the management model adopted by the post-Fordist network corporation. The socio-technical mechanisms of short-term flexible control with rapid rotation and uninterrupted flows are disseminated to all institutions. The managerial paradigm is firmly linked to new information technologies. It is rooted in the long history of organizational doctrines that shaped the paradigm of the 'functional society', culminating in the so-called information age we have been hearing about since the late 1970s. Daniel Bell, one of the very first American sociologists to formalize the concept of 'post-industrial society', brought out the connection between the information society and Saint-Simon's doctrine of industrialism, Frederick Winslow Taylor's scientific management, and the managerial concept used in reforming the US state apparatus in 1961 by Pentagon chief Robert McNamara and his advisers at the Rand Corporation.[3] Aside from this last insight, Bell was merely extrapolating from a hypothesis developed by Georges Friedmann, the sociologist of labour and the media, in his work on the genesis of the industrialization-technocracy tandem, to which we alluded at the beginning of chapter 1.

Control societies are thoroughly permeated by the 'universals of communication'. 'The most shameful moment came,' wrote Deleuze and Guattari in *What is Philosophy?*,

> when computer science, marketing, design and advertising, all the disciplines of communication, seized hold of the word concept itself and said: 'This is our concern, we are the creative ones, we are the ideas men!' Marketing has preserved the idea of a certain relationship between the concept and the event. But here the concept has become the set of product displays (historical, scientific, artistic, sexual, pragmatic) and the event has become the exhibition that sets up various displays and the 'exchange of ideas' it is supposed to promote. The only events are exhibitions, and the only concepts are products that can be sold.

If the three ages of the concept are the encyclopaedia, pedagogy and commercial professional training, 'only the second can safeguard us from falling from the heights of the first into the disaster represented by the third'.[4] Because communication and speech in these societies have been 'thoroughly permeated by money – and not by accident but by their very nature', the key thing may be to create spaces of non-communication, circuit breakers, so we can elude control.[5]

'Brands' and their communicational function have become the common denominator in defining the identity of an increasingly wide range of organizations from companies to cities, charities and official bodies.[6]

In this generalized control society, governed by the managerial model, the ability to anticipate individual behaviour, identify the probability of a specific behaviour and construct categories based on statistical frequency is the common thread among the 'styles' of marketing specialists, the 'scores' of financiers and the 'profiles' of the police. 'They are thus freeing themselves from the opposition between normal and abnormal', notes Foucault-influenced historian François Ewald. 'There are merely classes of behaviour, all of them foreseeable. The dream of a new science of humankind would be to succeed in combining Internet connections, DNA test results and certain consumer behaviours. The mystery of human nature would then be exhausted'[7] – all in the service of eminently practical aims.

The convergence of police informers

Types of machines are easily matched with each type of society – not that machines are determining, but because they express those social forms capable of generating them and using them. The old societies of sovereignty made use of simple machines – levers, pulleys, clocks; but the recent disciplinary societies equipped themselves with machines involving energy, with the passive danger of entropy and the active danger of sabotage; the societies of control operate with machines of a third type, computers, whose passive danger is jamming and whose active one is piracy or the introduction of viruses. This technological evolution must be, even more profoundly, a mutation of capitalism.[8]

So wrote Gilles Deleuze in his 'Post-scriptum on the Societies of Control', in which he called for a return to collective arrangements of which machines are only one component.

When examining societies from the standpoint of technological development, it is best to avoid dividing history into clear-cut chronological slices, for the various sediments are interwoven under the hegemony of the latest technology. The ramparts that are currently being erected in the world combine the know-how of all three ages. The meaning of this history is revealed only through lags (*décalages*), survivals, diversions, regressions and resistances. It is composed of social, political and economic realities marked by asymmetry and asynchronism. We see here once again a confirmation of the central idea according to which the prevailing mode of social regulation, to invoke openness, transparency and fluidity of flows, has by no means erased disciplinary mechanisms from the cognitive map; even places of confinement are in a state of crisis and destined to undergo continuous reform.

The new information technologies make it possible to innovate and at the same time reactivate procedures and protocols, by 'modernizing' them to suit a society henceforth perceived as 'nomad' or mobile. An obvious example is the electronic bracelet for persons convicted of a crime and considered dangerous – a remote informer emblematic of the new modes of confinement allowing for free movement. Such freedom will be severely limited, of course, the day that a tiny chip (or other so-called smart tattoo) can be implanted, burying forever the memory of shackles once locked round convicts' ankles. With the electronic bracelet, prison walls and prison guards seem to vanish, since the virtual character of intangible limits and internalized obligations suffices. But convicts who do not comply with the constraints will return to confinement. 'Lurking behind the ethereal aspect of high-tech punishment stand the watchtowers and barbed wire of

185

the ineradicable prison', writes one historian.[9] Just as the duality of components with both civilian and military applications enables the transfer of know-how from one domain to the other, the latest detection and navigation technologies have two sides: flexible control and discipline. Judging from the technological developments in the field, this will increasingly be the case. Depending on how it is applied, video surveillance itself, the symbol of Big Brother, 'either extends older forms of discipline or illustrates this new type of control, with a multitude of mixed formulas in between', note Éric Heilmann and André Vitalis on the basis of their research on video surveillance in supermarkets, banks, a high school in an outlying urban area, and various public places. However, there is one important difference between the two modes of surveillance:

> Whereas discipline requires a major effort on the part of individuals to change their natural behaviour or even their ways of being, the new type of control occurs without their knowledge, in an indirect way, and requires no participation on their part. It involves the surveillance of individuals and makes decisions about them based on a double made up of their data, traces or image.[10]

The rule of escalating technological development implies that the failure of a technology to control everything justifies the deployment of an increasingly sophisticated arsenal, without ever achieving the desired effectiveness. This is demonstrated by the race to devour individual data from every possible source, launched by the geostrategists of 'dataveillance' at the planetary level.

A flashback on credit cards

The first studies to point out the uncontrolled drift towards the use of credit cards as tools for recording and storing knowledge of buyer behaviour date back to the 1980s. One such study was carried out by a psycho-sociologist and member of a research group on technology and law at the University of Quebec in Montreal, at a time when such cards were in much greater use in North America than in Europe, ever since the release of Visa and MasterCard in the 1960s. Here is how he sounded the alarm:

> Today, credit cards constitute one of the most serious threats to fundamental rights and liberties. Insofar as they enable service companies to gather, process and disseminate increasing amounts of information on people, their behaviours, their tastes, etc. (. . .), they possess highly

186

sophisticated means for increasing control over private individuals and thereby augmenting their market share. This logic, which makes obtaining information on individuals a prerequisite for economic growth, has taken hold without any hindrance in the United States and Canada, where there are no laws protecting personal information in the private sector. This means that little by little the conditions for a generalized behavioural control, a custom-made totalitarianism, are being introduced. Commissions [in charge of protecting liberties] should be aware of the importance of the stakes if they do not wish to see their efficacy, if not their existence, called into question.[11]

The interest shown by companies in the so-called 'transactional' information contained in credit cards was only one sign among others of the changes that took place in the course of that decade in the tools used by marketing and advertising specialists to approach consumers. 'In the past five years', confided the research director at Proctor & Gamble in 1987, 'new ways of reading consumer behaviour have appeared and most are electronic; that will continue. The new technologies provide people who study consumer behaviour with a huge, rich, new database.'[12] Bar codes and optical scanning devices introduced the language of scanners and traceability (Infoscan, Behaviorscan, Scantrack, etc.) into studies on sample households or individuals. A new milestone was achieved in measuring television audiences: the 'peoplemeter', an electronic brain inserted in televisions, which records people's presence, the channel they watch, and the time they spend watching. This is done with the complicity of the TV viewer, since each member of the household signals his or her presence by pressing the identification button.

Behind the promises of 'huge, rich, new' databases, upheavals were under way in the media and advertising landscape, against a backdrop of unbridled deregulation: the formation of a global foundation for advertising networks, the avant-garde of the communication industry, along with a series of concentrations and mergers of major communication groups. At the same time, the managerial function of the 'communication' nebula was expanding. In 1988, on the basis of interviews and analysis of the strategies and legitimating discourses of the who's who of advertising networks, we described this phenomenon, which turned out to prefigure the irresistible ascension of the 'universals of communication':

To reduce the element of chance, there is an outbreak of new methods of electronic research: experiments with samples of viewers through the installation of miniature cameras in their sets; the application and conversion of military detection systems. . . What yesterday still

187

awakened democratic suspicions, because it was like the instruments of high surveillance of the private citizens, enters imperceptibly into commercial mores. The Taylors of consumption have appeared. And certain 'Doctor Nos' imagine that they will soon be able to place miniature capsules into guinea pigs to monitor facts and behaviour. Thus the absorption of the market in collective and individual life ceaselessly pushes back the limits of the intolerable![13]

When this observation is viewed alongside the warning of the Quebec researcher, it is safe to assume that other researchers attentive to the evolution of communication industries and networks must have felt the same way at that time. And yet it was only the beginning.

The systematic use of the personal data of Internet users for marketing profiling through search engines plays a large role in this regard. The amusement of providing one's data to a 'biographical' search engine or a social network site may well prevail over a reflex of caution. In the process, data on the entire age group of thirteen- to twenty-five-year-olds is collected in databases that are not necessarily legally controlled. As one lawyer, a specialist in the law of new technologies and privacy, has noted:

> The websites say they agree to comply with a certain number of rules concerning the data they gather, notably the Safe Harbour principles negotiated between the European Union and the United States. Yet no court really has the means to verify their compliance, particularly now that 'data havens' are emerging, along the lines of tax havens, where there is virtually no legislation protecting privacy.[14]

The navigator's itinerary

The multiplication of intrusive technologies has led to scenarios that even Fritz Lang would never have dared imagine when he filmed *The Thousand Eyes of Dr Mabuse*. The exponential development of the memory and calculating power of position determination instruments make legal regulation difficult. Tools for tracking the itineraries of users and consumers have now infiltrated everyday objects. They all create potential risks of violation of privacy and all provide virtual clues for electronic police surveillance, in view of the 'securitarian evolution of society', to borrow the promotional language of the security industry itself.

The 'contact-free Navigo pass', a card with a microchip fitted with a small radio frequency identification (RFID) emitter, introduced in the Paris region by the regional transport authority RATP, is a perfect example of these challenges. It was originally a Europe-wide project for remote ticketing, involving Italian, Portuguese, Belgian and French transport operators. The project was named Calypso, after the Greek nymph in Homer's *Odyssey* who succeeded in keeping Ulysses a prisoner on her island for ten years! Following an experimental phase of about four years when the card was reserved for young people, it was made available to the general public in the metropolitan Paris area in 2005. Within two years, nearly 2 million passengers had opted for the transport pass. The chip contains all the information relative to the subscription as well as the cardholder (name, address, photograph, travel) and an antenna that communicates with the validator. A terminal at the entrance to all modes of public transport (metro, regional express train, bus, tramway) reads the pass even if it is in a handbag or jacket pocket. The project includes eventually installing Navigo passes on mobile phones, which would then serve as transport tickets. This system would function regardless of whether the phone is in use, switched off or running on a low battery. Such a method has already been introduced in Italy and Japan. In the long run, the Navigo pass is expected to mark the end of tickets and magnetic payment – in short, the elimination of any alternative.

As in the project for a secure electronic national identity card (INES), the personal data contained in the chip can be read without contact during automated control procedures, which raises the issue of the confidentiality of data relating to individual travel. To guarantee privacy, the National Commission on Information Technology and Freedom (CNIL; see chapter 8) recommended that such data 'be used in a form that makes it possible to identify users only for the purpose of combating fraud and during the time needed to detect fraud, not to exceed two consecutive days'. There is no need to lapse into paranoia to imagine the uses that could be made of centralized data on individuals' itineraries. For example, it offers the possibility of 'cross-checking different groups of people travelling to different demonstration meeting places to detect the most rebellious ones', or so observed the jury of the seventh annual Big Brother Awards, which nominated the RATP in 2007 for the 'Orwell Prize for a whole body of work'. The policy adopted by British authorities, recently faced with attacks and planned attacks in public transport, merely confirms such doubts about the weakness of regulatory safeguards.

Again, as in the case of the electronic national identity card, the Navigo project not only claims to reduce fraud but also to enhance user comfort by 'making life easier'. In this instance, 'making life easier' refers to the speed of the operation, which is four times faster than using an ordinary magnetized ticket. All technologies that endanger the privacy of citizens need this type of supporting discourse. The GIXEL, a professional organization of the 'industries of interconnection, components and electronic sub-systems', says as much in its 'Blue Paper' (*Livre bleu*), addressed to its public and private clients:

> Security is very often experienced in our democratic societies as a violation of individual liberties. It is therefore necessary to persuade people to accept the technologies used, among them, biometrics, video surveillance and identity checks. Several methods will have to be developed by public authorities and manufacturers to ensure the acceptance of biometrics. They will have to be accompanied by an effort to show conviviality, to be attentive to people, and to point out the technology's more attractive functions. This education begins in nursery schools where the children use the technology to enter and leave the school and have lunch at the school restaurant; the parents use it to identify themselves when they come to pick up the children.[15]

In November 2005, a group of teenagers protested the commonplace use of biometric techniques in everyday life at a high school in Gif-sur-Yvette, 30 kilometres south-west of Paris and just minutes away from the Saclay high-tech nuclear complex. Disguised as clowns, they destroyed two biometric terminals, provided free of charge by the manufacturer in a pilot programme to control the flow of students at the school self-service cafeteria. The terminals had been installed at the beginning of the school year without waiting for an authorization from the CNIL – in other words, illegally. Following a complaint by the high school principal, three of the young people were found guilty by the magistrate's court of destruction of public property. The students were supported by the League of Human Rights, which took the opportunity to denounce the ever-increasing use of surveillance systems encouraged by the research institutes and high-tech industries of the Saclay complex.

'Smart labels': the temptation to excess

What might formerly have passed for science fiction is now technologically within reach. The underlying political and social implications of microchip applications, like those of other sensitive innovations such as genetically modified organisms and nanotechnologies, have now been revealed. Embedded in manufactured products, microchip technology naturally meets the demand for tracking the life of objects, from the production chain to the consumer (manufacturing site, transport, inspection, etc.). It provides valuable aid in the struggle against counterfeiting and the management of health and food risks, but it is also fraught with potential threats to privacy as an instrument for deciphering buyers' behaviour, sometimes without their knowledge, as well as customer traffic, as a means of targeting them individually. This use of microchips has occasioned much fantasizing on the part of major distribution suppliers and trade names as well as marketing and advertising professionals.

In June 2006, the CNIL presented the facts of the case: 'Due to their massive dissemination, the individual nature and invisibility of the identifiers of branded objects and the risk of individual profiling, the CNIL considers that RFIDs are "personal identifiers" in the sense defined in the Information Technology, Files and Freedom Law.' According to this regulatory body, the solution would consist in neutralizing the chip once the object is purchased.

The European Commission appeared to be convinced of the importance of what was at stake. In 2006, an exploratory public debate on RFIDs was organized for a group of manufacturers, major distributors, consumer associations and governments; an online 'citizens' forum' was also opened for three months. There was growing awareness of the need to supervise this technology and change existing regulations to ensure better protection of personal data and privacy. The target date was March 2007, when a major meeting was to be held on the topic in Brussels. The Commission called upon the Auto-ID Lab of the Massachusetts Institute of Technology to convene specialists from around the world. This laboratory was the hub of a research project involving six centres (two in the United States and one each in China, Japan, Europe and Australia) supported by roughly a hundred sponsors, including the five largest distributors. A schedule was adopted and a group of interested parties was set up to advise and assist the Commission in drafting a proposal in 2008 for a European policy on RFID applications. At the March meeting, however, the Commissioner for Information Society and the Media, in charge of the project, played down the dangers pointed out a year earlier by the CNIL. Subsequently, the European Commission sought above all to focus on 'strengthening the presence of EU firms in the radio frequency ID label market' and clearly 'did not intend to remain on the sidelines of a lucrative technology with a market enjoying 60% growth worldwide', and announced it was 'seeing to it that Europe would eliminate the impediments to the huge potential of RFID technology'.[16] The figures were staggering: by 2010, an estimated 1 trillion everyday objects would be affected by the use of chips.

191

The commissioner also emphasized the central role, in the European Union's strategy, of generating public awareness about the advantages of RFID. According to 61 per cent of the participants in the online forum, the information made available to the public on the stakes of RFID was 'inadequate'. What the Commissioner avoided pointing out, however, was that half of those same Internet users thought the regulations should be changed, and two thirds thought the technology should include a system to deactivate the electronic chip, of whom 61 per cent thought this should be done automatically when the product is sold; 46 per cent preferred that the chip be removable; and 40 per cent wanted to limit the radius of the sensors as much as possible. Finally, only 14 per cent indicated they trusted the industry to regulate itself and comply voluntarily with the relevant principles of good conduct. A journalist from *Le Monde* commented three weeks before the meeting in Brussels:

> Even if it emanates from a ridiculously low sample (2190 opinions), this list of solutions undoubtedly provides a glimpse of the range of regulatory measures that could accompany RFID in its dazzling development in the future, but the issue is still far from being resolved and it is the voice of the lobbies that will now be heard – manufacturers, associations and researchers.[17]

And which researchers? The primary objective of the studies produced by the world's most reputable research centres remains basically to test the chip's reliability and its economic and social acceptability – not to mention the fact that the globalization of the everyday use of such technologies reflects the US notion of privacy, rather than European principles of protection of private life. As for critical studies showing that the incorporation of RFID into daily life is not neutral, but rather corresponds to a particular project of society, they are few and far between. Their scarcity reflects the legitimacy acquired by the ultra-liberal view of the sovereign consumer, acting on free will in a free world and convinced that he or she is navigating in cyberspace without constraint.

The implications of embedding chips in manufactured products is merely the visible part of the iceberg of research on consumer behaviour, given that electronic networking with consumers is the core concern of major brands, advertisers and operators. The appearance in 2005 of the first advertisements that were interactive with mobile phones was another sign of this. Countless full-scale tests have already been carried out to connect Internet users with targeted advertising according to the location where they may be found, and in which they

192

agree to have their movements monitored in real time.[18] Other experiments involve riddling supermarket shelves with chips or recognition software, using strategically placed cameras to detect customers' expressions, gestures and actions in relation to a given product, and thus glean ideas on repackaging or store reorganization.[19] Hypermarkets feel pressured by the innovations of online commerce. 'The Internet is accustoming consumers to never having to wait and being able to make immediate selections on the basis of exhaustive information. They will soon find it intolerable not to find these functions in a department store. The new technologies are pushing sales outlets to redefine themselves,' explains the chairman of Laser, a subsidiary of Galeries Lafayette, a large Paris department store.[20]

The proliferation of this type of digital technology goes hand in hand with the increasingly favourable reception accorded to the new approaches to the consumer proposed by neuromarketing. In the 1980s, the anthropological and micro-sociological approach known in France as 'ethnographic marketing' opened up new avenues in contradiction with the usual theories explaining consumer and user behaviour.[21] Ethnographic marketing called into question the basic unit, i.e., the individual, in dominant disciplines such as the psychology of motivation, opinions and attitudes, but also the basic postulate of rational choice through access to information in neoclassical economics, as well as the methodological individualism of such great importance in macro-sociology. Today, advertising and marketing are connecting with the neurosciences in the hope of locating the areas of the brain to be stimulated according to brand objectives. They hope more generally to resolve the mystery of the consumer who remains, in spite of everything, an elusive subject.

In the early days of industrial society, the pioneers of cranioscopy and brain dissections, seeking to localize human inclinations, paved the way by using society's outcasts in prisons, hospitals and orphanages as objects for experimentation. Today, the engineering of consent in so-called hypermodern society has chosen in turn to make the sale of 'available human brain time'[22] for the manufacture of audiences the indispensable condition of its mode of mass control.

Towards genetic population management?

'The three most agonizing questions are those involving the subtle shift from checking identity to checking behaviour, the interconnection of data, and the gathering of data without the knowledge of the people

193

concerned.'[23] It was in these terms that the French CCNE (National Consultative Committee on Ethics for Life and Health Sciences) justified examining the issue of 'biometrics, identifying data and human rights' in France, and announcing its views on the subject in late April 2007. This independent authority, created in 1983 to 'render opinions on the ethical problems and societal questions raised by the progress of knowledge in biology, medicine and health', pointed out the risks of an unchecked 'biometricization', notably in its opinion number 98, entitled 'Biometrics, identifying data and human rights'.

Noting the supremacy acquired by biometrics over other identification measures, as a result of the rise of obsessive security concerns provoked by terrorist attacks among other causes, the CCNE examined the arsenal of measurable indicators used by these techniques and the quasi-infallibility attributed to them. These parameters aim not only to 'describe individuals, but also to define them, know who they are, what they do, what they consume'. The committee on ethics illustrated the danger of 'dehumanization' with the example of a recent European project connected to the sixth European framework programme for research and technological development (<www.humabio-eu.org>). The goal of the project is 'to study new physiological biometric parameters (recordings of electroencephalograms, electrocardiograms and electro-oculograms) by combining them among themselves and with classical identifying data to obtain highly efficient identification systems, and recording these characteristics using new wireless sensors, at the risk of obtaining them without the person's knowledge'. The project, the CCNE observed:

> appears worrying to us because it also seeks to use these physiological parameters to check the absence of alcohol or drug consumption or the recent sleep deprivation of workers who perform tasks such as transporting money, piloting an aeroplane or handling hazardous products, not just when they begin their tasks but over longer periods of time. The safety objective of this approach would be inconceivable, of course, without the consent of the parties involved and the agreement of company doctors, but above all, it must be weighed against the seriousness of the intrusion into the sphere of personal life. This risk of instrumentalization of human beings for security purposes is a concern for occupational medicine, where doctors may be tempted to transfer their relationship with workers to masses of parametric data, just as a medical practice that privileges images and figures runs the risk of dehumanizing medicine.[24]

The CCNE highlighted discrimination against certain categories of the population as one of the main worrisome trends in the use of police files. Not only did it express reservations about extending the list of offences that could entail taking genetic prints; it also took a position on the period of their preservation, which in France was forty years for convicted offenders and twenty-five years in the other cases, and, in the United Kingdom, a century. In the eyes of the committee, this is tantamount to 'preservation without limits, without controls, without any possibility of requesting removal by the interested party', which is contrary to the principles of statutory limits and amnesty. It is as if the whole point was to produce 'an accumulation or storing of data 'for all practical purposes' that would allow discriminatory searches of stored data, practices of exclusion or grouping together for ambiguous purposes', such as 'identifying ethnic minorities or political diversion'.[25] According to the CCNE, mixing public and private data represents a major risk, and no mixing should be permitted: 'Comparing administrative databases with health records could lead to serious discrimination in the area of insurance or employment, particularly at the time of hiring. This seems all the more likely in view of the current systematic use of electronic search engines by employers and recruiters.' Finally, the widespread use of new morphological identification procedures 'could obviously lead to stigmatizing certain individuals such as those with a disability, and to excluding those who do not easily fit measurable criteria'.[26]

The opinion of the committee on ethics is also a warning against the commonly accepted distinction between 'coding' and 'non-coding' areas of the human genome. This idea is peddled, for example, in a handbook, written by an Interpol working group, that aims to 'raise the awareness' of the general public concerning the safeguards introduced by the police and the courts to avoid uses of DNA samples that do not respect human rights. In this document, one reads, for example: 'All DNA systems referred to in forensic analysis focus on the non-coding areas of the genome. This means that these systems do not include information about physical or psychological characteristics, diseases or disposition to diseases.'[27] However, the committee emphasizes that 'the basis for this distinction may be inaccurate and in all likelihood the non-coding areas contain a wealth of diverse information', even if the genetic prints used today by the police and the courts 'concern only sexual markers and theoretically non-coding sequences'.[28]

The call for ethical vigilance in the face of the new normative tools of the securitarian order takes on its full significance when it refers to the deeper logics at work in contemporary democratic regimes. The development of parametric systems and devices to classify

195

human beings is also the product of a model of society, politics and economics whose coherence depends on placing individuals increasingly in competition with one another. Such a society is incapable of managing differences; the dogma of performance, efficiency and effectiveness becomes a neo-Darwinian criterion of selection, separating the strong from the weak, at the expense of a project of society in which the collective interest and ties between individuals are the main guarantors of innovation and social and technical imagination.

With the excessive use of biometrics, the old demon of eugenic formatting has resurfaced in modern form, as attested by the report on behavioural problems among children and adolescents published in 2005 by the French National Institute of Health and Medical Research (Inserm).[29] In the report, experts define the symptoms of pathological behaviour in children (physical aggression, negativity and hyperactivity, reflected in the refusal to obey, kicking or biting schoolmates or not waiting for one's turn). On the basis of these findings, they recommended screening and even treatment, starting in kindergarten, of such early signs of social deviance. Through this preventive operation against precocious 'delinquency', the monitoring of children turns into a 'pedagogy of tracking', as witnessed by the introduction in kindergarten classes of a 'behaviour assessment record' that will follow children like a police record throughout their school life'.[30] The report, heavily influenced by Anglo-American socio-biology, was shelved in the wake of the outcry from psychiatrists and pedagogues. Yet the underlying thesis that certain behaviours are innate surfaced again indirectly during the 2007 French presidential campaign, when the candidate of the 'unbridled Right' created a stir by claiming the existence of genetic predispositions to paedophilia and, among some young people, to suicide.[31] It was a perfectly intentional verbal slip.

The problem posed here is hardly new, even though the instruments for exploring and analysing the human brain have changed. Today, as in the past, the security–insecurity dialectic pushes governments to look for biological indicators of the dangerousness of the individual. In a series of policy sectors including penal policy, health care, education, and immigration, the securitarian management of populations through medical and biological expertise, obsessed with evaluation, is becoming increasingly prevalent. The danger lies in sacrificing the citizen-subject to a behavioural model in which the individual is measurable, calculable, and subservient to the norm. The corollary of the rise of the 'ideology of expertise', warns psychoanalyst Elisabeth Roudinesco, is the 'risk of transforming practitioners of the psyche into security agents'.[32]

EPILOGUE

A basic impasse of all control machines is this: Control needs time in which to exercise control. Because control also needs opposition or acquiescence; otherwise, it ceases to be control [. . ..] All control systems try to make control as tight as possible, but at the same time, if they succeeded completely there would be nothing left to control [. . .] When there is no more opposition, control becomes a meaningless proposition. It is highly questionable whether a human organism could survive complete control. There would be nothing there. No persons there. *Life is will* (motivation) and the workers would no longer be alive, perhaps literally.

William S. Burroughs, The Limits of Control (1975)

He who thus domineers over you has only two eyes, only two hands, only one body, no more than is possessed by the least man among the infinite numbers dwelling in your cities; he has indeed nothing more than the power that you confer upon him to destroy you. Where has he acquired enough eyes to spy upon you, if you do not provide them yourselves? How can he have so many arms to beat you with, if he does not borrow them from you? The feet that trample down your cities, where does he get them if they are not your own? How does he have any power over you except through you? How would he dare assail you if he had no cooperation from you? What could he do to you if you yourselves did not connive with the thief who plunders you, if you were not accomplices of the murderer who kills you, if you were not traitors to yourselves? . . . Resolve to serve no more, and you are at once freed.

Étienne de la Boétie, Discourse of Voluntary Servitude (1576)

When Gilles Deleuze proposed the concept of 'control societies' in 1990, the socio-political configuration was already different from that of the 1970s when Foucault undertook his archaeology of the security society as an emanation of liberal society. On the eve of the new millennium, this configuration again underwent a major metamorphosis. Security turned into a security obsession. Global society revealed its totalizing dimension, interfering in every area of collective and individual life. Control societies, organized according to a managerial mode, are still in place, bolstered by the imperatives of financial capital. Autonomy, creativity, responsiveness and adaptability have become the cardinal components of the new regime of truth. Its reverse side consists of management targets and a culture of results, the intensification of labour, motivation under constraint or voluntary servitude, social precariousness, and a propensity to impose guilt on wage workers by causing them to internalize work objectives. Such self-constraint combines with new systems of full-time remote surveillance based on the inquisitorial power of information technology. A new mode of governing society by tracking is now emerging, in which everyone who circulates is liable to be under surveillance. What has changed in the last decade is that control societies are now coupled with suspicion societies. These are structured to protect themselves against 'insurgents', a term that belies the history of hatred implicit in the language of counterinsurgency doctrines. While the term is still common in English and in other Latin languages, it is no longer used in French.

This exception sheds light on the rule. Terrorist attacks have distilled their effects. Grey, hostile areas of insecurity and instability have become more extensive, playing a parasitical role in the global economy. The ultraliberal project for a new world order through the use of information technology has shifted from strategies of soft power to war without mercy as 'just war', in defiance of established international law and the very idea of civilization. The logic of integrating individual societies into a globalized whole, which post-Cold War euphoria repressed with much help from myths such as the 'end of history', has now revealed itself openly. It can only be achieved through strategies of force and constraint. The illusion of the decomposition of the nation-state faded at the same time as the belief in the inexorable end of the logic of empire, to the benefit of private actors whose capacity to become autonomous would increase. The so-called global war has worked as an accelerator of trends. It is now clear that several parallel developments have suddenly revealed their interconnections and convergences, pointing to a new configuration of power. Integration and interoperability are the passwords for reducing vulnerability and anticipating risk, uncertainty and global threats. Ties have become established or reinforced between industry, the state, the army and the police; between civilians and the military, internal and external (in)security, homeland territory and the space of transnational networks; between economic and socio-political logics, merging control over bodies with control over hearts and minds, thus confronting democratic governments with the culmination of a historical process begun long ago. It is under the economic regime of a liberalism given over to commodified reason that the strategy of surveillance guided by the reason of state first became embedded and continues to be embedded today.

Yet, as Williams Burroughs reminds us in the epigraph above, control is never complete. For 'Life is will'. In the face of the inability of unbridled, discriminating and life-destroying capitalism to fulfil its promises of a new universalism, the winds of rebellion have again begun to blow in the early twenty-first century, after more than a decade of waning social mobilization and critical thinking about the stakes of power. We have witnessed revolts of despair, riots, uprisings, peaceful and violent protests at the polls and in the streets at the local, national and planetary level. Counter-fires were lit; they have been flickering and hesitant, but nevertheless sufficient to disturb the globalizing project that instituted itself too quickly as the unsurpassable horizon. As these responses became more visible, the propensity to criminalize them increased. The decision of the G7 to convert its annual meetings into barricaded camps, taken at the Genoa Summit, two months before the September 11 attacks, was symptomatic. The decision was made as the forces of order violently repressed global justice movement demonstrators in the streets when they protested against the pretension of the rich countries to dictate the affairs of the planet.

From the standpoint of the evolution of democracy, while there is some debate on the singular problem of the new control systems, it has yet to be massively appropriated by the citizenry. Any attempts to take up this challenge usually have to go against the current. In 2004, restrictions were placed on the scope of the Information Technology, Files and Freedom Act, which was originally passed in France in 1978 through the efforts of grassroots organizations and set an example at the international level. The change went unnoticed, according to the few groups that protested against it. The French National Consultative Committee on Ethics (CCNE) noted:

> Because of the paradox that has arisen between the protection of private life and violations of privacy we are witnessing a sort of confiscation of freedom by consent. In a hidden manner, in the name of the security

paradigm, our society is becoming accustomed to the use of these bio-metric markers and everyone in the end accepts, even somewhat indif-ferently, the idea of being identified, observed, detected and tracked.[1]

As François Ewald notes, in this context in which security manage-ment has become a question of techniques, Thomas Jefferson's words are once again relevant: 'Those who sacrifice freedom for safety deserve neither.'[2] At the level of collective mentalities, a type of habituation has occurred; it has widened the threshold of tolerance and led many people to consent, sometimes without even realizing it, to significant losses of privacy and fundamental rights. This is happening not only with regard to surveillance and identification techniques, but also the instruments used by the media-advertising complex to measure and capture individual lifestyles. Instrumentalist views of information, communication and culture continue to perme-ate even the most democratic and progressive sectors of society. The call by Deleuze and Guattari for a return to the 'age of pedagogy' is especially pertinent today, at a time when the culture of the 'Network of networks' is cultivating a Promethean belief in the advent of an era of automatic access to knowledge as well as resistance, which has become second nature to Internet users. This is the perverse effect of the Internet's encyclopaedic supply of knowledge. However, technol-ogies, even interactive ones, are not inherently democratic. Only their mode of organization and use by society can cause them to further a project of insurgency against the established rules. The excitement of surfing in cyberspace cannot overshadow the fact that individualistic behaviours are the foundation of the Net and that its role in creating a culture of the public sphere is by no means a given; it is a matter of social construction.

Most of the initiatives to combat the imbalances caused by the security order are taken by unions of democratic magistrates, lawyers and jurists, human rights organizations, civil liberties groups atten-tive to the effects of the computerization of society, Internet activists, independent media collectives, critical media observers, and groups that denounce the negative implications of biometrics and nano-technologies for freedoms. Fortunately, these themes are becoming more widely shared thanks to the diversification of the international public space since the start of the new millennium. Examples of this trend include the creation of international networks for study and research on the tension between security and the loss of freedoms, such as the multidisciplinary network Liberty and Security; the rise of multinational activist networks such as Indymedia, the International

Campaign Against Mass Surveillance (ICAMS) and the Campaign for the Right to Communication in the Information Society (CRIS); the mobilization of social and professional actors at world summit meetings on the information society, such as those in Geneva in 2003 and Tunis in 2005, and the debates leading to the adoption of the Convention on the Protection and Promotion of the Diversity of Cultural Expression by the UNESCO General Assembly in 2005. This new, heterogeneous configuration of groups has expressed itself with a united voice while acknowledging their differences. Structural issues have been raised regarding the segregationist nature of the project for a 'New World Information Order' via the global information super-highway, announced with great pomp by the G7 in 1995. Reflection has begun among jurists about communication rights which, by guaranteeing freedom, access, diversity and active participation in the public sphere, would protect citizens against reasons of state and the concentration of the media, information and culture industries. The displacement of the debate on what was originally framed as the 'digital divide', towards what explains it, i.e., the socioeconomic divide, has helped to reveal what the security-based view of networks had obscured from the outset.

Governments are resisting recognition of these new citizen-actors. They are refusing to broaden the composition of bodies (when they exist) responsible for ensuring a balance between advances in information technology and protection of the right to privacy and freedom, or to allocate the means these bodies need to fulfil their mission of public mediation. Yet the choice is clear: either there will be a qualitative leap in citizen participation in the management of society, or we will move towards an increasingly authoritarian exercise of power and a negation of rights.

A threefold conclusion has gradually imposed itself to give meaning to the imperative of democratic vigilance regarding the mechanisms and apparatuses of intrusion. First of all, so-called post-industrial or 'immaterial' capitalism, by promoting structures of subjectivation and the production of knowledge, culture and social networks for commercial ends, has opened up a new kind of struggle at once cultural, social and economic. Second, it is important to grasp the problem from both ends of the chain, in daily life as well as in the structure of our society, from a local as well as a global point of view. The critique of the security order will only become intelligible when the founding dogmas of the new information order's hegemonic project are challenged: unilateral governance of the Network, the logic of private appropriation or patrimonialization of information, science

201

and knowledge by the dominant entities of the global economy, the exclusive power of market actors to define technical norms. Finally, one way of wresting the issue of the 'security culture' from the vision of police statistics is to include the right to security among the social rights necessary to make security possible: the right to work, education, housing, health care and communication – rights in whose absence there can be no human dignity.

NOTES

1 SURVEILLANCE: DELINQUENCY AS A POLITICAL OBSERVATORY

1 J. Bentham, 'Panopticon', in M. Bozovic (ed.), *The Panopticon Writings* (London: Verso, 1995), pp. 11–12.
2 R. Evans, 'Bentham's Panopticon. An Incident in the Social History of Architecture', *Architectural Association Quarterly* 3/2 (1971): 21–37.
3 M. Foucault, *Surveiller et punir. Naissance de la prison* (Paris: Gallimard, 1975), p. 203; available in English as *Discipline and Punish: The Birth of the Prison*, trans. A. Sheridan (London: Penguin, 1979).
4 N. Elias, *La Civilisation des moeurs* (Paris: Calmann-Levy, 1973 [1939]), p. 271; available in English as *The Civilizing Process: The History of Manners and State Formation and Civilization*, trans. E. Jephcott (Oxford: Blackwell, 1994).
5 N. Elias, *La Dynamique de l'Occident* (Paris: Press Pocket, 1975 [1939]), pp. 309–10; available in English as *The Civilizing Process: The History of Manners and State Formation and Civilization*, trans. E. Jephcott (Oxford: Blackwell, 1994).
6 M. Foucault, *Naissance de la biopolitique* (Paris: Gallimard/Seuil, 2004); available in English as *The Birth of Biopolitics*, trans. G. Burchell (London: Palgrave Macmillan, 2008).
7 M. Foucault, *Sécurité, territoire, population* (Paris: Gallimard/Seuil, 2004), p. 77; available in English as *Security, Territory, Population*, trans. G. Burchell (London: Palgrave Macmillan, 2007).
8 A. Mattelart, *The Invention of Communication*, trans. S. Emanuel (Minneapolis/London: University of Minnesota Press, 1996); *Histoire de l'utopie planétaire. De la cité prophétique à la société globale* (Paris: La Découverte, 1999).
9 G. Friedmann, 'Les technocrates et la civilisation technicienne', in G. Gurvitch, *Industrialisation et technocratie* (Paris: Armand Colin, 1949), pp. 44–5.
10 G. Lanteri-Laura, *Histoire de la phrénologie* (Paris: PUF, 1970).
11 R. Töpffer, *Oeuvres complètes*, éditions du Centenaire (under the direction of P. Cailler and H. Darel) (Geneva: Skira, 1943–5).
12 G. Lanteri-Laura, *Histoire de la phrénologie*, op. cit., p. 235.

13 A. Quételet, *Sur l'homme et le développement de ses facultés ou essai de physique sociale* (Paris: Bachelier, 1835), 2 vols.

14 G. Canguilhem, *Le Normal et le Pathologique* (Paris: PUF, 5th edn), pp. 182–3; available in English as *The Normal and the Pathological*, trans. C. R. Fawcett (New York: Zone Books, 1991).

15 Ibid., p. 175.

16 Cf., for example, Y. Levin and A. Lindesmith, 'English Ecology and Criminology of the Past Century', in G. A. Theodorson (dir.), *Studies in Human Ecology* (Evanston, IL: Row, Peterson and Co., 1961), p. 14.

17 A. Desrosières, *La politique des grands nombres, Histoire de la raison statistique* (Paris: La Découverte, 1993), p. 99; available in English as *The Politics of Large Numbers. A History of Statistical Reasoning*, trans. C. Naish (Cambridge, MA: Harvard University Press, 2002).

18 Cf. the 'Assurances' entry in the *Grand dictionnaire universel* (1865), vol. 1, p. 819.

19 F. Ewald, *l'État-providence* (Paris: Fayard, 1986).

20 A. Quételet, *Anthropométrie ou mesure des différentes facultés de l'homme* (Brussels: Muquardt, 1871).

21 M. De Ryckere, 'Le signalement anthropométrique', in *Actes du troisième Congrès international d'anthropologie criminelle*, August 1892 (Brussels: F. Hayez, 1893), p. 97.

22 A. Bertillon, *La photographie judiciaire* (Paris: Gauthier-Villars, 1890).

23 A. Bertillon. *Anthropological Descriptions: New Methods of Determining Individual Identity*. Conference given at the International Penitentiary Congress in Rome, 22 November 1885 (France: Administrative Printing, Melun, 1887).

24 F. Galton, *Finger-Prints Directories* (London: Macmillan, 1895), p. XIII.

25 A. d'Arsonval, et. al., *Compte-rendu des séances de l'Académie des sciences*, t. CXLV (Paris: Académie des sciences, 1 July 1907), p. 29.

26 F. L. Herbette, 'Address of Mr. Herbette', *Anthropological Descriptions: New Method of Determining Individual Identity*. Conference given at the International Penitentiary Congress in Rome, 22 November, 1885 (France: Administrative Printing, Melun, 1887), p. 28.

27 *Actes du troisième Congrès international d'anthropologie criminelle*, August 1892 (Brussels: F. Hayez, 1893), p. 481.

28 J. Vucetich, *Proyecto de ley de registro general de identificación* (La Plata, Buenos Aires: Universidad nacional de la Plata, 1929).

29 L. Reyna Almandos, 'Métodos de identificación judicial. La dactiloscopia y la defensa social', *Revista Ciencias Sociales* (La Plata, Buenos Aires: 1911), p. 10.

30 Ibid.

31 L. Reyna Almandos, *Dactiloscopia argentina. Su historia e influencia en la legislación* (La Plata: Universidad nacional de La Plata, 1932), p. 148.

32 C. Saunders and N. Southey, *A Dictionary of South African History* (Capetown/Johannesburg: David Philip, 1998), p. 130.

2 PUNISHING: THE APPREHENDED MULTITUDE

1 C. Lombroso, *L'Homme criminel, étude anthropologique et médicale* (Paris: Alcan, 1887), p. 231; Italian 1st edn: C. Lombroso, *L'Uomo deliquente*

(Turin: Fratelli Bocca, 1876); available in English as *Criminal Man*, trans. M. Gibson and N. Hahn Rafter (Durham, NC: Duke University Press, 2006).

2 *Actes du troisième Congrès d'anthropologie criminelle*, Brussels (August 1892) (Brussels: F. Hayez, 1893), p. 124.
3 G. Tarde, *La Criminalité comparée* (Paris: Alcan, 1886), pp. 36–7.
4 *Actes du troisième Congrès d'anthropologie criminelle*, op. cit., pp. 9–10.
5 C. Lombroso and R. Lasch, 'Le délit politique', *Actes du premier Congrès international d'anthropologie criminelle*, Rome, November 1885 (Turin: Fratelli Bocca, 1887), p. 38.
6 G. Tarde, 'Les crimes des foules', *Actes du troisième Congrès d'anthropologie criminelle*, op. cit., p. 73.
7 S. Sighele, *La Foule criminelle. Essai de psychologie collective* (Paris: Alcan, 1901, 2nd edn), p. 68.
8 Ibid., p. 22.
9 Ibid., p. 21.
10 G. Le Bon, *Lois psychologiques de l'évolution des peuples* (Paris: Alcan, 1894), pp. 55–6.
11 Ibid., p. 141.
12 R. A. Nye, *The Origins of Crowd Psychology: Gustave Le Bon and the Crisis of Mass Democracy in the Third Republic* (London: Sage, 1975).
13 G. Le Bon, *Lois psychologiques de l'évolution des peuples*, op. cit., p. 14.
14 G. Le Bon, *Psychologie des foules* (1895) (Paris: PUF, 1988, 6th edn), p. 17; available in English as *The Crowd: A Study of the Popular Mind* (Dunwoody, GA: Norman S. Berg, 1977).
15 J. Van Ginneken, *Crowds, Psychology and Politics 1871–1899* (Cambridge: Cambridge University Press, 1992).
16 S. Sighele, *La Foule criminelle. Essai de psychologie collective* (Paris: Alcan, 1901, 2nd edn), pp. 241 and 248.
17 S. Sighele, *Littérature et criminalité* (Paris: Giard et Brière, 1908), pp. 116 and 183.
18 G. Tarde, *Les Lois de l'imitation* (Paris: Alcan, 1890).
19 G. Trade, 'Les crimes des foules', op. cit., p.74.
20 Ibid., p. 82.
21 Ibid., p. 74.
22 *Actes du troisième Congrès d'anthropologie criminelle*, op. cit., p. 379.
23 Ibid., pp. 381–2.
24 G. Tarde, 'La criminalité et les phénomènes économiques', *Congrès international d'anthropologie criminelle, Compte rendu des travaux de la cinquième session* (Amsterdam, 1901), p. 203.
25 G. Tarde, *L'Opinion et la foule* (Paris: Alcan, 1901), p. 2.

3 MANAGING MASS SOCIETY: THE LESSONS OF TOTAL WAR

1 Quoted in A. Ryan, 'Russell en guerre contre la guerre', in P. Soulez (dir.), *Les Philosophes et la guerre de 14* (Paris: Presses universitaires de Vincennes, 1988), p. 157.
2 E. Jünger, *L'État universel. La mobilisation totale* (Paris: Gallimard, 1990), p. 109.

3 H. Lasswell, *Propaganda Technique in the World War* (New York: Alfred Knopf Inc., 1927), p. 14.
4 H. Lasswell, *Propaganda Technique in the World War*, op. cit.
5 W. Lippmann, *Public Opinion* (London: G. Allen and Unwin, 1922), p. 394.
6 Ibid., p. 378.
7 H. Lasswell, *Propaganda Technique in the World War*, op. cit., p. 222.
8 H. Lasswell, 'The Structure and Function of Communication in Society', in L. Bryson (ed.), *The Communication of Ideas* (New York: Harper, 1948).
9 E. Bernays, *Propaganda* (New York: Ig Publishing, 2004 [1928]), p. 37.
10 Ibid., p. 73.
11 J. Dewey, *Reconstruction in Philosophy* (New York: Henry Holt, 1920; 1950), p. 160.
12 S. Ewen, *Captains of Consciousness: Advertising and the Social Roots of the Consumer Society* (New York: McGraw-Hill, 1976), p. 22.
13 J. Aronson, *The Press and the Cold War* (New York: The Bobbs-Merrill Co., 1970).
14 J.-F. Rauger, 'Quand D.W. Griffith s'emparait de la Révolution française', *Le Monde* (5 July 2006), p. 26.
15 A. Rabinbach, *The Human Motor, Energy Fatigue, and the Origins of Modernity* (New York: Basic Books, 1990).
16 See the glossary of the Canadian Government Office of Translation Services on 'Les valeurs et l'éthique du management' (<www.translationbureau. gc.ca>).
17 C. S. Maier, 'Between Taylorism and Technocracy: European Ideologies and the Vision of Industrial Productivity in the 1920s', *The Journal of Contemporary History* 5/2 (1970): 27–61.
18 Quoted in G. Friedmann, 'Les technocrates et la civilisation technicienne', in G. Gurvitch, *Industrialisation et technocratie* (Paris: Armand Colin, 1949), p. 51.
19 A. Gramsci, 'Americanism and Fordism' (1929), in Q. Hoare and G. Nowell Smith (ed.), *Selection from the Prison Notebooks* (London: Lawrence and Wishart, 1973), pp. 277–318.
20 E. Zamyatin, *The Islanders*, trans. T. S. Berczynski (Ann Arbor, MI: Trilogy Publisher, 1978).
21 E. Zamyatin, *We*, trans. M. Ginsburg (New York: Viking Press, 1972).
22 A. Huxley, *Brave New World* (New York: Harper Perennial, reprint edn, 1998; K. Boye, *Kallocaïn* (Stockholm: Albert Bonniers Forlag AB, 1940); available in English as *Kallocain*, trans. G. Lannestock (Madison, WI: University of Wisconsin Press, 1966); G. Orwell, *Nineteen Eighty-Four* (London: Penguin (in association with Secker and Warbug), 1989).
23 In H. Kumata and W. Schramm, 'Propaganda Theory of the German Nazis', in W. E. Daugherty and M. Janowitz (eds), *A Psychological Warfare Casebook* (Baltimore, MD: Johns Hopkins University Press, 1958), p. 48.
24 G. G. Bruntz, 'Allied Propaganda and the Collapse of German Morale in 1918', in W. E. Daugherty and M. Janowitz (eds), *A Psychological Warfare Casebook*, op. cit., p. 105.
25 A. Hitler, *Mein Kampf* (New York: Reynal & Hitchcock, 1939).
26 M. Kitchen, *The Silent Dictatorship: The Politics of the German High Command under Hindenburg and Ludendorff 1916–1918* (New York: Holmes & Meier, 1976).

27 E. Ludendorff, *Der Totale Krieg* (Munchen, 1934), p. 10; available in English as *The Nation at War* (London: Hutchinson, 1936).
28 C. von Clausewitz, *On War*, trans. M. Howard and P. Paret (ed.) (New York: Everyman's Library, Alfred A. Knopf, 1993), pp. 731, 733, and 77.
29 W. Benjamin, 'Théories du fascisme allemand', *Interférences* 1 (1981): 30; available in English as 'Theories of German Fascism', trans. J. Wikoff and U. Zimmerman, in A. Kaes, M. Jay and E. Dimendberg (eds), *The Weimar Republic Sourcebook* (Berkeley, CA: University of California Press, 1994).
30 Ibid., p. 34.
31 Ibid., pp. 26–8.
32 E. Jünger, *L'État universel. La mobilisation totale*, op. cit., pp. 110–11.
33 C. Schmitt, *Die Diktatur* (Munich: Duncker & Humboldt, 1928).
34 Cf. G. Agamben, *State of Exception* (Chicago, IL: University of Chicago Press, 2005).
35 N. J. Spykman, *America's Strategy in World Politics. The United States and the Balance of Power* (New York: Harcourt, Brace & World Inc., 1942), p. 38.

4 THE COLD WAR AND THE RELIGION OF NATIONAL SECURITY

1 Cf. A. M. Schlesinger, *The Imperial Presidency* (New York: Houghton Mifflin, 1973; 2004), pp. 333–76.
2 J. Comblin, *Le Pouvoir militaire en Amérique latine. L'idéologie de la sécurité nationale* (Paris: Jean-Pierre Delarge, 1977), p. 80.
3 D. Reynolds, 'The European Dimension of the Cold War', in M. P. Leffler and D. S. Painter (eds), *Origins of the Cold War, An International History* (London: Routledge, 1994), p. 132.
4 G. Orwell, *Nineteen Eighty-Four* (London: Penguin (in association with Secker & Warburg Ltd), 1989), p. 322.
5 J. Schumpeter, quoted in A. M. Schlesinger, *The Imperial Presidency*, op. cit., p. 184.
6 Quoted in M. Dyer, *The Weapon on the Wall: Rethinking Psychological Warfare* (Baltimore, MD: Johns Hopkins Press, 1959), p. 25.
7 US Senate, *US Senate Foreign and Military Intelligence. Book I, Final Report of the Select Committee to Study Government Operations with Respect to Intelligence Activities* (Washington, DC: US Government Printing, 26 April, 1976), p. 9.
8 J. W. Fulbright, *Old Myths and New Realities* (New York: Vintage Books, 1964), p. 7. Cf. also J. W. Fulbright, *The Pentagon Propaganda Machine* (New York: Vintage Books, 1971).
9 R. Borosage, 'The Making of the National Security State', in L. D. Rodberg and D. Shearer (eds), *The Pentagon Watchers* (New York: Doubleday Anchor, 1970), p. 10.
10 P. Crowl, 'Alfred Thayer Mahan: The Naval Historian', in P. Paret, *Makers of Modern Strategy, From Machiavelli to the Nuclear Age* (Princeton, NJ: Princeton University Press, 1986), p. 468.
11 M. P. Leffler, 'National Security and US Foreign Policy', in M. P. Leffler and D. S. Painter (eds), *Origins of the Cold War*, op. cit., pp. 19–20.

12 B. H. Williams, 'The Importance of Research and Development to National Security', *Military Review* 30 (February 1950): 11.
13 A. Mattelart, *The Information Society. An Introduction*, trans. J. A. Cohen and S. G. Taponier (London: Sage, 2003).
14 OECD, *Allocation des Resources dans le domaine de l'informatique et des télécommunications* (Part 3, basic report) (Paris, 1975).
15 US Senate, *US Senate Foreign and Military Intelligence. Book I, Final Report of the Select Committee to Study Government Operations with Respect to Intelligence Activities*, op. cit., p. 42.
16 Ibid., p. 21.
17 Cf. S. Senese, 'Report on the Doctrine of National Security', presented at The Bertrand Russell Tribunal, Rome, January, 1976, published in *LARU Working Papers* 16 (Toronto, June 1976): 64–97.
18 US Senate, *US Senate Foreign and Military Intelligence*, op. cit., pp. 11–12.
19 A. Mattelart, *Multinational Corporations & the Control of Culture*, trans. M. Chanan (Sussex: Harvester Press, 1979).
20 W. E. Daugherty, 'Changing Concepts', in W. E. Daugherty and M. Janowitz (eds), *A Psychological Warfare Casebook, Operations Research Office* (Baltimore, MD: Johns Hopkins University Press, for Operations Research Office, Johns Hopkins University: 1958), p. 13.
21 J. W. Riley and W. Schramm, *The Reds Take a City: The Communist Occupation of Seoul with Eyewitness Accounts* (New Brunswick, NJ: Rutgers University Press, 1951).
22 M. Dyer, *The Weapon on the Wall: Rethinking Psychological Warfare*, op. cit., p. 58.
23 P. L. Lazarsfeld, 'The Prognosis for International Communications Research', *Public Opinion Quarterly* 16 (1953): 490.
24 US Senate, *USIA Appropriations Authorization, Fiscal Year 1973, Hearing before the Committee on Foreign Relations, United States Senate, March 20–21 and 28, 1972* (Washington, DC: US Government Printing Office, 1972).
25 D. Lerner, *Sykewar: Psychological Warfare against Germany. D-Day to VE-Day* (New York: George W. Stewart, Publisher, Inc., 1949).
26 D. Lerner, *The Passing of Traditional Society: Modernizing the Middle East* (New York: Free Press, 1958).
27 D. Lerner and R. Richardson, 'Swords and Ploughshares: The Turkish Army as a Modernizing Force', *World Politics* 13 (October 1960): 19–44.

5 'CIVIC ACTION' OR THE REAPPROPRIATION OF THE NATIONAL SECURITY DOCTRINE

1 R. Nixon, *The Real War* (New York: Simon and Schuster, 1980).
2 R. A. Moore, 'Toward a Definition of Military Nationbuilding', *Military Review* 53 (July 1973): 34–48.
3 Cf. L. Pye, *Politics, Personality and Nation Building* (New Haven, CT: Yale University Press, 1962); D. Wilson, 'Nationbuilding and Revolutionary War', in K. W. Deutsch and W. J. Foltz, *Nationbuilding* (New York: Atherton Press, 1962); available at: <www.rand.org/pubs/papers/2005/P2624.pdf>.
4 Quoted in E. Campos Coelho, *Em busca de identidade: o exército e a politica na sociedade brasileira* (Rio de Janeiro: Forense-Universitaria, 1976), p. 5.

5   A. Joxe, 'Globalisation et violence: divergences entre cultures stratégiques européennes et américaines', in J. Liberman, *Démythifier l'universalité des valeurs américaines* (Paris: Parangon, 2004), pp. 83–4.

6   J. Comblin, *Le Pouvoir militaire en Amérique latine. L'idéologie de la sécurité nationale* (Paris: Jean-Pierre Delarge, 1977), p. 58.

7   A. Stepan, *The Military in Politics: Changing Patterns in Brazil* (Princeton, NJ: Princeton University Press, 1971).

8   Escola Superior de Guerra (ESG), *Aspectos da doutrina da Escola superior de Guerra e suas bases teoricas* (Rio de Janeiro: Departamento de estudos, 1978), p. 4.

9   General Meira Mattos, *Brasil, geopolitica e destino* (Rio de Janeiro: José Olympio, 1975), p. 60.

10 General A. Golbery do Couto e Silva, *Geopolítica do Brasil* (Rio de Janeiro: José Olympio, 1967, 2nd edn), pp. 137–8.

11 A. Mattelart and H. Schmucler, *Communication & Information Technologies: Freedom of Choice for Latin America?*, trans. D. Buxton (Norwood, NJ: Ablex, 1985).

12 P. Virilio, 'La guerre pure', *Critique* 341 (October 1975): 1098–1103.

13 General A. Golbery do Couto e Silva, *Geopolítica do Brasil*, op. cit., 1967, p. 14.

14 E. Campos Coelho, *Em busca de identidade: o exército e a política na sociedade brasileira*, op. cit., p. 175.

15 Published originally as *Le Carnaval des images*, 1987.

16 Mattelart M. and Mattelart A., *The Carnival of Images; Brazilian Television Fiction*, trans. D. Buxton (New York/Westport/London: Bergin and Garvey (an imprint of Greenwood), 1990), p. 31.

17 Ibid., p.27. [This quote was slightly edited for clarity. – translators' note.]

18 B. Brecht, 'Art et politique', *Sur le Réalisme* (Paris: L'Arche, 1970); available in English as *On Art & Politics*, ed. and trans. S. Giles and T. S. Kuhnn (London: Methuen Drama, 2003).

19 A. Mattelart, 'Un fascisme créole en quête d'idéologues', *Le Monde diplomatique* (July 1974).

20 A. Pinochet, *Geopolítica* (Santiago, Chile: Andrés Bello), 1974.

21 P. Baraona, A. Pinochet et. al., *Fuerza armadas y seguridad nacional* (Santiago, Chile: Ediciones Portada, 1973).

22 M. Rodriguez, 'La experiencia política chilena y las Actas constitucionales', *Mensaje* 254 (November 1976): 559.

23 R. Nixon, *The Real War*, op. cit., p. 35.

24 T. Moulian, *El consumo me consume* (Santiago, Chile: LOM, 1999), p. 48.

25 Présidence de la République, *Livre blanc sur la défense et la sécurité nationale* (Paris: La Documentation française, 2008).

6 COUNTERINSURGENCY, THE CROSSROADS OF EXPEDITIONARY FORCES

1   Cf. W. J. Pomeroy, *Guerrilla and Counter Guerrilla Warfare* (New York: International Publishers, 1964).

2   R. Clutterbuck, *Terrorism in an Unstable World* (London: Routledge, 1994), pp. 125–6.

3   C. Saunders and N. Southey, *A Dictionary of South African History* (Capetown: David Philip, 1998), p. 49.

4   Cf. F. Kitson, *Low Intensity Operations: Subversion, Insurgency, Peace-Keeping* (London: Faber and Faber, 1971).

5   Colonel J. Némo, 'La guerre dans le milieu social', *Revue de la défense nationale* XII (May 1956): 605–24. By the same author: 'La guerre dans la foule', *Revue de la défense nationale* XII (June 1956). In English: Colonel Némo, 'The Place of Guerrilla Action in War' (digested from *Revue Militaire Générale*, January 1957), in 'Foreign Military Digests', *Military Review* 37 (November 1957): 99–107; available at: <http://calldp.leavenworth.army.mil/eng_mr/2001060515583052/1957/NOV/digests.pdf>.

6   S. Chakotin, *The Rape of the Masses: The Psychology of Totalitarian Political Propaganda* (London: Routledge & Sons, 1940).

7   M.-M. Robin, *Escadrons de la mort, l'École française* (Paris: La Découverte, 2004), p. 72.

8   R. Trinquier, *La Guerre moderne* (Paris: La Table ronde, 1961), pp. 45–6.

9   Ibid., p. 7.

10   Ibid., p. 56.

11   Ibid., p. 39.

12   H. Marrou, 'La torture, une honte. . .', *Le Monde* (5 April 1956); reprinted in *Le Monde* 2/150 (30 December 2005). See also P. Vidal-Naquet, *La Torture sous la République* (Paris: Maspero, 1972).

13   R. Trinquier, *La Guerre moderne*, op. cit., p. 81.

14   Ibid., p. 83.

15   Lieutenant-Colonel D. A. Starry, 'La guerre révolutionnaire', *Military Review* 47 (February 1967): 68.

16   G. A. Kelly, 'Revolutionary War and Psychological Action', *Military Review* 40 (October 1960): 4–10.

17   G. A. Kelly, 'Footnotes on Revolutionary War', *Military Review* 42 (September 1962): 31–9. See also W. Darnell-Jacobs, 'Wars of Liberation', *Military Review* 42 (July 1962): 45–52.

18   G. A. Kelly, 'Footnotes on Revolutionary War', op. cit.

19   Quoted in M. Klare, *War without End: American Planning for the Next Vietnam* (New York: Vintage Books, 1972), p. 44.

20   R. Clutterbuck, *Terrorism in an Unstable World* (London: Routledge, 1994), pp. 125–6.

21   S. T. Hosmer and S. O. Crane, *Counterinsurgency: A Symposium April 16–20* (Santa Monica, CA: Rand Corporation, November 1962 (R-412-ARPA)).

22   D. Galula, *Pacification in Algeria 1956–1958* (Santa Monica, CA: Rand Corporation, 1963 (RM-3878-ARPA)). By the same author: *Counterinsurgency Warfare: Theory and Practice* (New York: Praeger, 1964).

23   R. Trinquier, *Modern Warfare: A French View of Counterinsurgency* (New York: Praeger, 1964).

24   D. Galula, *Pacification in Algeria*, op. cit., pp. 64–5.

25   M. Klare, *War Without End*, op. cit., pp. 264–6.

26   US Senate, *USIA Appropriation Authorization, Fiscal Year 1973. Hearing before the Committee on Foreign Relations. United States Senate, March 20–21 and 28, 1972* (Washington, DC: US Government Printing Office, 1972), pp. 54–5.

27 G. Selser, *Espionaje en América Latina, el Pentágono y las técnicas sociológicas* (Buenos Aires: Ediciones Iguazu, 1966); I.L. Horowitz (ed.), *The Rise and Fall of Project Camelot* (Cambridge, MA: MIT Press, 1967).
28 M. Gordon et. al., *Cocon-Counterconspiracy (Politica). The Development of a Simulation of Internal National Conflict under Revolutionary Conflict Conditions* (Cambridge, MA: ABT Associates Inc., November 1965). Read also 'The 'Politica' Game', *Berkeley Barb* (14–20 September 1973): 2 and 8.
29 See A. Mattelart, 'The Mass Media and the "Mass Line" of the Bourgeoisie' in *Mass Media, Ideologies and the Revolutionary Movement*, trans. M. Coad (Brighton: Harvester Press, 1980), pp. 147–85. This strategy of the 'mass line' of the forces opposing the government of President Salvador Allende is at the centre of the documentary film *La Spirale* (145 min., 1976), which we made with Chris Marker. The English version of the film (*The Spiral*, 1976) was translated by Susan Sontag and narrated by Donald Sutherland.
30 R. E. Osgood, *Limited War Revisited* (Boulder, CO: Westview Press, 1979), p. 45. This quotation is taken from M. Klare, 'La contre-insurrection, doctrine américaine', *Le Monde diplomatique* (April 1981).
31 B. Hoffman, 'Forward to the New Edition', in D. Galula, *Pacification in Algeria,* op. cit., pp. III and IV.
32 Ibid., pp. V and VI.
33 R. Trinquier, *La Guerre moderne*, op. cit., pp. 38–9.
34 J. Mayer, 'Whatever It Takes: the Politics of the Man Behind "24"', *The New Yorker* (19 February 2007); available at: <htttp://www.newyorker.com/reporting/2007/02/19/070219fa_fact_mayer>, p. 2.
35 Ibid., p. 8.
36 J. Littell, *Les Bienveillantes* (Paris: Gallimard, 2006); English version: *The Kindly Ones*, translated by Charlotte Mandell (New York: HarperCollins, 2009).
37 T. Wieder, 'Une rencontre à l'École normale supérieure autour des *Bienveillantes* de Jonathan Littell', *Le Monde des Livres* (27 April 2007).
38 P. Pachet, 'La pensée de la torture', *Encyclopedia Universalis* (1993).

7 THE INTERNATIONALIZATION OF TORTURE

1 The Staff of the Inter-American Defense College, 'The Inter-American Defense College', *Military Review* 50 (April 1970): 20–7.
2 D. C. Schuffstall, 'Ninth Conference of American Armies', *Military Review* 50 (April 1970): 88–93.
3 M. Klare, *War without End. American Planning for the Next Vietnam* (New York: Vintage Books, 1972), p. 178.
4 USARSA, 'US Army School of the Americas', *Military Review* 50 (April 1970): 94–100.
5 Statistics issued by the US Southern Command. Cf. N. Stein, 'US Army School for Scoundrels', *NACLA's Latin America & Empire Report* VIII/3 (March 1974): 24.
6 F. Rivas Sánchez and E. Reimann Weigert, *Las Fuerzas armadas de Chile: un caso de penetración imperialista* (Mexico City: Ediciones 75, 1976), p. 44.
7 Ibid., pp. 41–3.

8   E. Jelin, *Los Trabajos de la memoria* (Buenos Aires/Madrid: Siglo XXI, 2002), pp. 102–3.

9   US Senate, *Hearing before the Subcommittee to Investigate Problems Connected with Refugees and Escapees of the Committee on the Judiciary, United States Senate, 93rd Congress, July 28* (Washington, DC: US Government Printing Office, 1974), p. 175.

10 S. Calloni, *Los Años del Lobo. Operación Cóndor* (Buenos Aires: Ediciones Continente, 1999). See also: J. Dinges, *The Condor Years: How Pinochet and His Allies Brought Terrorism to Three Continents* (New York: The New Press, 2004).

11 L. Nadel and H. Weiner, 'Would You Sell a Computer to Hitler?', *Computer Decisions* 9/2 (February 1977): 22–6.

12 AID 'Document: AID Police Plan for 1971–1972', *NACLA (North American Congress on Latin America) Newsletter* V/4 (July–August 1971): 12.

13 US Senate, 'US Policies and Programs in Brazil', *Hearings before the Subcommittee on Western Hemisphere Affairs, Committee on Foreign Relations, (4–5, 11 May, 1971)* (Washington, DC: US Government Printing Office, 1971).

14 P. Labreveux, 'Argentine. Trois officiers généraux français mettent en garde le chef de l'État contre les "méthodes peu conformes aux traditions militaires"', *Le Monde* (26 August 1977).

15 R. Trinquier, *La Guerra moderna* (Buenos Aires: Editorial Rioplatense, 1963). By the same author: *Guerra, subversión, revolución* (Buenos Aires: Editorial Rioplatense, 1975).

16 Regarding the direct involvement of French military experts in the history of the Argentine and other Latin American dictatorships, see the investigation of the protagonists carried out by Marie-Monique Robin in *Escadrons de la mort, l'École française* (Paris: La Découverte, 2004). A documentary by the same title, also by Marie-Monique Robin, is available on DVD; it includes numerous exclusive first-hand accounts, sometimes filmed using a hidden camera.

17 M. Orsolini, *La Crisis del Ejército* (Buenos Aires: Ediciones Arayu, 1964), pp. 52–3 (quoted in M.-M. Robin, *Escadrons de la mort*, op. cit., p. 217).

18 G. Arriagada Herrera, 'Seguridad nacional y política, *Mensaje* 254 (November 1976; Santiago, Chile).

19 See the issue of *Cultures & Conflits* (1994) 13–14, devoted to 'Disparitions'; Amnesty International, *Les 'Disparus'. Rapport sur une nouvelle technique de répression* (Paris: Seuil, 1981); CONADEP, *Nunca Más. Informe de la Comisión nacional sobre la desaparición de personas* (Buenos Aires: Eudeba, 1984).

20 P. Calveiro, *Poder y desaparición. Los campos de concentración en Argentina* (Buenos Aires: Colihue, 1998).

21 A. Garcia-Castro, 'Por un análisis político de la desaparición forzada', in N. Richard (ed.), *Políticas y estéticas de la memoria* (Santiago, Chile: Editorial Cuarto propio, 2000). Read also A. Garcia-Castro, *La Mort lente des disparus au Chili sous la négociation civils-militaires (1973–2002)* (Paris: Maisonneuve et Larose, 2002).

22 A. Mattelart, 'Notes on the Ideology of the Military State', in A. Mattelart and S. Siegelaub (eds), *Communication and Class Struggle, An Anthology in 2 Volumes* (New York: International General Editions, 1979), vol. 1, pp. 423–5.

23 T. Roland, *La Fabuleuse histoire de la Coupe du monde* (Paris: La Martinière, 1998), p. 204.

24 Cf. the publications of the Lelio Basso International Foundation (*Fondazione internazionale Lelio Basso*), named for the Italian senator who promoted the initiative of the Russell Tribunal II; especially the issue of the journal *Fondazione* 2/3 (2005) on 'La Tortura Oggi'.

25 Cf. M. Keck and K. Sikkink, *Activists Beyond Borders: Advocacy Networks in International Politics* (Ithaca, NY: Cornell University Press, 1998).

26 E. Jelin, *Los Trabajos de la memoria*, op. cit., p. 2. See also E. Jelin and S. Kaufman, 'Layers of Memories. Twenty Years after in Argentina', in T. G. Ashplant et. al. (eds), *The Politics of War Memory and Commemoration* (London: Routledge, 2000), pp. 89–110.

27 C. Feld, 'La télévision comme scène de la mémoire de la dictature en Argentine. Une étude sur les récits et les représentations de la disparition forcée des personnes', a doctoral thesis in information and communication sciences, under the direction of A. Mattelart, presented and defended on 17 May 2004 (Université de Paris VIII-Vincennes à Saint-Denis), p. 94. By the same author, read *Del Estrado a la pantalla: Las imágenes del juicio a los ex-comandantes en Argentina* (Buenos Aires/Madrid: Siglo XXI Editores, 2002).

28 See the report published by the Agencia latinoamericana de información (ALAI): 'Militarización-Bases-Guerra', *América Latina en movimiento* (Quito January 2007): 416–17.

29 See A. Pairone, 'Vuelven éjercitos a las calles de América Latina', *Reforma* (Mexico) (10 September 2007). For an exhaustive review of public policies in the area of security, see FLACSO (Facultad latinoamericana de ciencias sociales), *Reporte del sector Seguridad de América latina y el Caribe* (Santiago, Chile, 2007).

8 THE NEW DOMESTIC ORDER

1 E. Morin, 'Pour une sociologie de la crise', *Communications* 12 (1968): 11, 13.

2 Z. Brzezinski, 'Introductory Note', in M. Crozier et al., *The Crisis of Democracy* (New York: New York University Press, 1975), p. 3.

3 M. Crozier, S. P. Huntington and J. Watanuki, *The Crisis of Democracy: Report on the Governability of Democracies to the Trilateral Commission* (New York: New York University Press, 1975), p. 8.

4 Ibid., pp. 6–7.

5 Ibid., pp. 98–9 and 115.

6 Ibid., p. 182.

7 R. Nixon, *The Real War* (New York: Simon and Schuster, 1980), p. 260.

8 S. Nora and A. Minc, *L'Informatisaton de la société* (Paris: La Documentation française, 1978), p. 115; available in English as *The Computerization of Society*, Intro. by D. Bell (Cambridge, MA: MIT Press, 1980).

9 Ibid., pp. 123 and 125.

10 Ibid., p. 60.

11 Commission nationale de l'informatique et des libertés (CNIL), *Rapport* (Paris: La Documentation française, 1975), p. 7.

12 J.-P. Faivret and J.-L. Missika, 'Informatique et libertés', *Les Temps modernes* (October 1977): 375.
13 A. Vitalis, *Informatique, pouvoir et libertés* (Paris: Économica, 1988, 2nd edn).
14 CNIL, *Rapport*, op. cit., p. 56.
15 Ibid., p. 38.
16 B. Le Gendre, 'Le premier rapport de la Commission Informatique et Libertés,' *Le Monde* (10 December 1980), p. 11.
17 Government of Sweden, *The Vulnerability of the Computerized Society* (Stockholm, 1978); A. Madec, *Les Flux transfrontières de données* (Paris: La Documentation française, 1982).
18 M. Pagès, M. Bonetti, V. de Gaulejac and D. Descendre, *L'Emprise de l'organisation* (Paris: PUF, 1979).
19 Université de Vincennes, *Le Nouvel Ordre intérieur* (Paris: Alain Moreau, 1980).
20 IBM, 'IBM Papers', *Berkeley Barb* (22–8 November 1975). For a more extensive extract from this document, cf. A. Mattelart, *Multinational Corporations and the Control of Culture*, trans. M. Chanan (Brighton: Harvester Press, 1979), pp. 289–90.
21 C. Marighela, *For the Liberation of Brazil*, trans. J. Butt and R. Sheed, with an introduction by Richard Gott (Harmondsworth: Penguin, 1971).
22 Cf., for example, B. M. Jenkins, *Terrorism Works – Sometimes* (Santa Monica, CA: Rand Corporation, 1974); R. Clutterbuck, *Living with Terrorism* (London: Faber and Faber, 1975).
23 Erich Fried, *100 Gedichte ohne Vaterland* (Berlin: Wagenbach, 1978); available in English as *100 Poems Without a Country*, trans. S. Hood (London: Calder Publications Ltd, 1987).
24 *Le Monde diplomatique* ('Dossier Justice') (January 1978); *Actes. Cahiers d'action juridique* (special issue 'L'Europe de la répression ou l'insécurité d'État') (spring 1978); A. and M. Mattelart, *De l'usage des médias en temps de crise* (Paris: Alain Moreau, 1979); Université de Vincennes, *Le Nouvel Ordre intérieur*, op. cit.
25 A. Sanguinetti, 'La menace intérieure: l'armée contre le peuple', *Non! Repères pour le socialisme* (April–May 1981) 6: 33 and 41.
26 The Consitutional Council (*Conseil Constitutionnel*) rules on whether proposed statutes conform with the Constitution, after they have been voted by Parliament and before they are signed into law by the President of the Republic.
27 P. Lascoumes et. al., 'L'Europe de la répression ou l'insécurité d'État', *Actes* (spring 1978): 8.
28 W. Laqueur, *The Age of Terrorism* (Boston, MA: Little, Brown & Co., 1987).
29 P. Schlesinger, G. Murdock and P. Elliott, *Televising Terrorism: Political Violence in Popular Culture* (London: Comedia, 1983), p. 166.
30 G. Soulier, 'Le terrorisme et l'évolution des droits et libertés en Europe', in M.-B. Tahon and A. Corten (eds), *L'Italie: le philosophe et le gendarme, Actes du colloque de Montréal* (Montreal: VLB éditeur, 1986), p. 340. This volume contains the presentations given in a conference held in November 1984 at the University of Quebec at Montréal (UQAM), and includes several papers related to this debate, notably on the introduction through legislation

of the concept of 'national security' in the 1980s, in connection with immigration policy in Canada. Ten years earlier Canada had adopted a 'war measures act to meet the challenge of virtual and apprehended insurrection'.

31 P. Lascoumes et. al., 'La répression en Irlande et la Commission des droits de l'homme', *Actes (Supplément)* 17 (spring 1978): 48.
32 R. Clutterbuck, *Terrorism in an Unstable World* (London: Routledge, 1994), p. 65.
33 R. Boure, *Les Interdictions professionnelles en Allemagne fédérale* (Paris: Maspero, 1978).
34 Université de Vincennes, *Le Nouvel Ordre intérieur*, op. cit., p. 264.
35 G. Soulier, 'Le terrorisme et l'évolution des droits et libertés en Europe', op. cit., p. 233.
36 P. Lascousmes et. al., 'L'Europe de la répression ou l'insécurité d'État, op. cit.
37 A. and M. Mattelart, *Rethinking Media Theory*, trans. M. Urquidi and J. A. Cohen (Minneapolis, MN: University of Minnesota Press, 1992), p. 150 (French edn published in 1986).
38 F. J. Hinkelammert, 'La política del mercado total. Su teologización y nuestra respuesta', *Pasos* (San José, Costa Rica), pp. 2, 3. By the same author, see *The Ideological Weapons of Death: A Theological Critique* (Maryknoll, NY: Orbis Books, 1986).
39 M. Novak and J. W. Cooper (eds.), *The Corporation: A Theological Inquiry*, (Washington, DC: American Enterprise Institute, 1981), p. 203.
40 I. Wallerstein, 'Le capitalisme touche à sa fin', *Le Monde (Supplément)* (12–13 October 2008): VIII. For a short version of this interview in English, see: <www.monthlyreview.org/mrzine/wallerstein161008.html>.

9 WAR WITHOUT END: THE TECHNO-SECURITY PARADIGM

1 J. Arquilla and D. Ronfeldt, *The Emergence of Noopolitik: Toward an American Information Strategy* (Santa Monica, CA: Rand Corp., 1999).
2 C. Swett, *Strategic Assessment: The Internet* (Washington, DC: Department of Defense, 1995).
3 D. Campbell, *Interception Capabilities 2000* (European Parliament, 1999); see: <http://www.nrc.nl/W2/Lab/Echelon/interccapabilities2000.html>.
4 BBC News (25 July 2005).
5 Available at: <www.cdi.org//friendlyversion/printversion.cfm?document ID=1729>.
6 'Rushing off a Cliff', *New York Times* editorial (28 September 2006).
7 D. Hughes, 'Net-Centric War's Focus Should be Counterterrorism', *Aviation Week and Space Technology* (16 December 2002): 55.
8 'Editorial', *Aviation Week and Space Technology* (21 October 2002): 74.
9 J. Poindexter, *Overview of the Information Awareness Office* (Anaheim, CA: DARPATech 2002 Conference, 2 August 2002).
10 ICAMS (International Campaign Against Mass Surveillance), *The Emergence of a Global Infrastructure for Mass Registration and Surveillance* (April 2005); available at:<www.i-cams.org/ICAMS1.pdf>.
11 Y. Eudes, 'Enquête: la guerre en privé', *Le Monde* (5 April 2007): 22–4.
12 *Les Cahiers de la compétitivité: les enjeux de la sécurité*, Supplement published by *Le Monde* (11 October 2007): I–III.

13 L. Mampaey, 'Restructurations, déreglementation et profits dans l'industrie de l'armement', *Le Monde diplomatique* (October 2006): 10. See also L. Mampaey and C. Serfati, 'Les groupes de l'armement et les marchés financiers: vers une convention 'guerre sans limites'?', in F. Chesnais (ed.), *La Finance mondialisée* (Paris: La Découverte, 2004); available at: <http://www.grip.org/bdg/g1067.html>.

14 E. Alterman, 'Il paraît que les médias américains sont de gauche', *Le Monde diplomatique* (March 2003); available at: <http://www.monde-diplomatique.fr/. . ./ALTERMAN/9978>.

15 E. Alterman, 'George W. Bush on the Press (and on Democracy)', in *The World Political Forum, Media between Citizens and Power* (Taranto, Italy: Chimienti Editore, 2006), pp. 79–86.

16 F. Fukuyama, 'Une incapacité à reconnaître la réalité', entretien avec D. Vernet, *Le Monde* (14–15 January 2007): 14. See also: J. S. Nye, Jr, 'The Decline of America's Soft Power', *Foreign Affairs* 83/3 (May–June 2004): 16–20.

17 The Stanley Foundation/Institute for Near East & Gulf Military Analysis, *Open Media and Transitioning Societies in the Arab Middle East. Implications for U.S. Security Policy* (2006), p. 5; available at: <www.Stanley-foundation.org>. See also M. Lynch, *Voices of the New Arab Public: Iraq, al Jazeera, and Middle East Politics Today* (New York: Columbia University Press, 2007).

18 Ibid., p. 27.

19 N. Mineta, 'Homeland Security & Defense Conferences', *Aviation Week and Space Technology* (4 March 2002): S.1.

20 Cf. A. Mattelart, 'Qui contrôle les concepts?', *Le Monde diplomatique* (July 2007); available at <http://www.monde-diplomatique.fr/2007/08/MATTELART/15008>.

21 Department of Defense, *Information Operations Roadmap* (30 October 2003), pp. 6, 13.

22 In W. B. Scott, 'Milspace Comes of Age in Fighting Terror', *Aviation Week and Space Technology* (8 April 2002): 78.

23 ICAMS (International Campaign Against Mass Surveillance), 'The Emergence of a Global Infrastructure For Mass Registration and Surveillance: 10 Signposts', 2005. Available at: <http://www.i-cams.org/Surveillance_intro.html>.

24 See Chapter 7.

25 C. Johnson, *Nemesis: The Last Days of the American Republic* (New York: Metropolitan Books, 2006).

26 F. Williams, *The Right to Know* (London: Longman, 1969).

27 Cf. S. Cypel, *Les Emmurés. La société israélienne dans l'impasse* (Paris: La Découverte, 2006); E. Weizman and R. Segal (dir.), *Une occupation civile. La politique de l'architecture israélienne* (Besançon: Editions de l'Imprimeur, 2004).

28 D. Rodman, 'Israel's National Security Doctrine: An Introductory Overview', *MERIA – Middle East Review of International Affairs* 5/3 (September 2001); available at: <www.biu.ac.il/SOC/besa/meria/journal/2001/issue3/jv5n3a6.html>.

29 D. A. Fulghum and R. Wall, 'Israel Refocuses on Urban Warfare', *Aviation Weekly and Space Technology* (13 May 2002): 24–6; 'Israel Pursues High

Tech Despite War Cost', *Aviation Weekly and Space Technology* (24 June 2002): 78–80 .

30 Cf. the website: <www.suspectdetection.com/about/html>.

31 M. Bôle-Richard, 'En Israel, la Cour suprême justifie les assassinats ciblés', *Le Monde* (16 December 2006): 4.

32 D. Grossman, 'Writing in the Dark', *New York Times Magazine* (13 May 2007); available at: <http://www.nytimes.com/2007/05/13/magazine/13Israel-t.html>.

10 THE EUROPEAN POLICE AREA

1 The Europol Convention, available at: <http://www.europol.europa.eu/index.asp?page=legalconv#ARTICLE%202>.

2 J.-C. Paye, *Vers un État policier en Belgique?* (Brussels: EPO/Revue Nouvelle, 2000), pp. 136–7. For a critical discussion, see also: V. Mitsilegas, 'The coherence of the adopted measures, during the last years by the EU with regard to organized crime' (20 November 2006), available at: <http://www.libertysecurity.org/auteur420.html>.

3 J.-C. Paye, op. cit., p. 145.

4 P. Busquin (European Commissioner in charge of research/European Commission), 'Vers un programme de promotion de la sécurité européenne par la recherche et la technologie' (3 February 2004), available at: <http://www.grip.org/bdg/pdf/g412.pdf>.

5 See the website of the group for research and information on peace and security (GRIP): <www.grip.org>.

6 C. Serfati, *Impérialisme et militarisme. Actualité du XXIᵉ siècle* (Lausanne: Page Deux Éditions, 2004).

7 T. Ferenczi, 'Droits de l'Homme: les États en accusation', *Le Monde* (30 November 2007): 2.

8 D. Murakami-Wood (ed.), *A Report on the Surveillance Society* (September 2006), available at: <http://www.ico.gov.uksurveillance_society_full_report_2006.pdf>.

9 P. Jamet, 'L'État veut-il tuer Internet en France?', *Le Monde* (21 April 2007): 23.

10 P. Gélie, 'Washington veut imposer des visas à tous les Européens', *Le Figaro* (2–3 June 2007): 3.

11 M. Mentré, 'INES, les libertés publiques et individuelles en danger', *La lettre Axiales* 54 (3rd quarter, 2005): 3–4; P. Piazza, 'Les résistances au projet INES', *Cultures et Conflits* 64 (winter 2006): 65–76.

12 W. Schuller, L. Fereday and R. Scheithauer (eds), *Interpol Handbook on DNA Data Exchange and Practice. Recommendations from the Interpol DNA Monitoring Expert Group* (Lyon, France: International Criminal Police Organization, 2001), 1st edn.

13 A. Jeffreys, 'Privacy Fears over DNA Database' (*BBC News* (interview), 12 September 2002).

14 M. Van Renterghem, 'Enquête: la tentation du fichage génétique de masse', *Le Monde* (26 September 2006): 26–7.

15 See the report 'Les flux transfrontières de données', *Problèmes politiques et sociaux* 406 (January 1981): 36.

16 M. Marzouki, 'La loi informatique et libertés de 1978 à 2004: du scandale pour les libertés à une culture de la sécurité', CNIL Conference 'Informatique: servitudes ou libertés?' (Paris, 7–8 November 2005). See: <http://www. polytic.lip6.fr/article.php3?id_article=95>.

17 Wolfgang Schäuble (Federal Minister of the Interior), 'Les ministres de l'intérieur soutiennent l'initiative de mise en réseau des bases de données policières à l'échelle européenne en vue d'une poursuite efficace des crimes', Présidence du Conseil (17 January 2007).

18 Figures published in *Le Monde* (6 June 2007): 4.

19 'Les polices de l'Union européenne mettent en commun leurs fichiers biométriques', *Le Monde* with AFP (13 June 2007); available at: <http:// combatsdroitshomme.blog.lemonde.fr/>.

20 A. France (1905), *Sur la pierre blanche* (Paris/Geneva: Ressources, 1979 (reprint)), p. 307.

21 P. de Bruycker, 'Jusqu'où contrôler l'immigration?', interview by C. Simon, *Le Monde* (24–5 September 2006): 18.

22 J. Danet, 'La justice face à l'obsession de punir', interview with N. Guibert, *Le Monde* (29–30 April 2007): 13.

23 Daniel Vaillant, quoted in *Le Monde* (1 November 2001); available at: <http://www.assemblee-nationale.fr/dg/dg3297.asp>.

24 See: < www.lemonde.fr/. . ./01/26/ violences-urbaines-la-police-s-empare-de-la-renovation-des-quartiers_1003974_0.html>.

25 E. Chalumeau, *Guide des études de sûreté et de sécurité publique* (Paris: La Documentation française, 2007).

26 G. Sainati and U. Schalchli, *La Décadence sécuritaire* (Paris: La Fabrique, 2007), pp. 79–80.

11 THE TRACEABILITY OF BODIES AND GOODS

1 G. Deleuze, 'Control and Becoming', *Negotiations: 1972–1990*, trans. and ed. M. Joughin (New York: Columbia University Press, 1995), p. 174. This conversation with T. Negri is also available at: <www.generation-online. org>.

2 W. S. Burroughs, *The Soft Machine* (New York: Grove Press, 1961); *The Limits of Control*, 1975, see: <http://limitedcontrol.posterous.com/ the-limits-of-control-by-willi>; *The Adding Machine: Selected Essays* (New York: Seaver Books, 1985).

3 D. Bell, *The Coming of Post-Industrial Society: A Venture in Social Forecasting* (New York: Basic Books, 1973), p. 357.

4 G. Deleuze and F. Guattari, *What is Philosophy?*, trans. G. Burchell and H. Tomlinson and (New York: Columbia University Press, 1994), pp. 10 and 12.

5 G. Deleuze, 'Control and Becoming' (Gilles Deleuze in conversation with Toni Negri), in *Negotiations 1972–1990*, trans. M. Joughin (New York: Columbia University Press, 1997), p. 176; originally published in *Futur Antérieur* (1990) 1. See also: <http://www.generation-online.org/p/fpdeleuze3.htm>.

6 A. Mons, *La Métaphore sociale* (Paris: PUF, 1992).

7 F. Ewald, 'Voici venue l'ère du contrôle généralisé', *Enjeux, Les Echos* (1 February 2008): 84–5.

8   See G. Deleuze, 'Post-scriptum on the Societies of Control', in *Negotiations 1972–1990*, op. cit., pp. 177–82. See also: <http://libcom.org/library/postscript-on-the-societies-of-control-gilles-deleuze>.
9   O. Razac, 'Bracelet électronique mobile: les barreaux à la cheville', *Libération* (22 March 2007): 17.
10 E. Heilmann and A. Vitalis, *Nouvelles technologies, Nouvelles regulations? Rapport de recherches*, Programme Pirvilles CNRS/IHESI (Université Louis-Pasteur de Strasbourg/Université de Bordeaux-III, May 1996), p. 78.
11 J.-P. Lemasson, 'Les cartes de paiement. La privatisation de la vie privée'; *TIS-Technologies de l'information et Société* 1/1 (1989): 109–19.
12 Quoted in A. Mattelart, *Advertising International: The Privatization of Public Space*, trans. M. Chanan (London: Routledge, 1991), p. 152; French edn published in 1989.
13 Ibid., pp. 158–9. See also the report on audience measurement in INA, *Dossiers de l'audiovisuel* 22 (Paris: INA/La Documentation française, 1988).
14 V. Dufief, 'Une mutation qui gomme la frontière entre vie privée et vie publique', Dossier, *Le Monde* (*Economie*) (27 November 2007): III.
15 See the website of the Big Brother Awards France: <http://bigbrotherwards.eu.org/Livre-Bleu-du-Gixel-les-BBA-republient-la.html>.
16 See the website: <www.lespasseurs.com/dotclear/index,php/2007/03/16/1572> and <ec.europa.eu/information_society/policy/rfid>.
17 A. Reverchon, 'Les 'etiquettes intelligentes' inquiètent les consommateurs', *Le Monde* (*Économie*) (27 February 2007): IV.
18 L. Girard, 'La pub s'incruste dans nos neurones', *Le Monde* (2 May 2006): 19.
19 C. Calla and S. Lauer, 'Achetez, vous êtes surveillé', *Le Monde* (3–4 February 2007): 18.
20 Ibid.
21 Cf. M. Douglas and B. Isherwood, *The World of Goods: Towards an Anthropology of Consumption* (London: Routledge, 1979); J. Sherry (dir.), *Contemporary Marketing and Consumer Behaviour: An Anthropological Sourcebook* (London: Sage, 1995).
22 This was the expression used by the chairman of the French private television channel TF-1, Patrick LeLay, when he declared in July 2004 that the aim of his channel was to sell 'available human brain time' to Coca-Cola.
23 CCNE, 'Biométrie, données identifiantes et droits de l'homme', *Avis* 98 (26 April 2007): 4. See: <www.ccne-ethique.fr>.
24 Ibid., p. 5.
25 Ibid., p. 13.
26 Ibid., p. 6.
27 W. Schuller, L. Fereday, and R. Scheithauer (eds), *Interpol Handbook on DNA Data Exchange and Practice* (Lyon, France: International Criminal Police Organization, 2001, 1st edn), p. 40.
28 CCNE, 'Biométrie, données identifantes et droits de l'homme', op. cit., p. 6.
29 Expertise Collective Inserm, *Troubles des conduites chez l'enfant et l'adolescent* (Paris: Inserm, 2005).
30 A. Sauvage and O. Sauvage-Déprez, 'Maternelles sous contrôle; le fichage des enfants', in G. Neyrand (ed.), *Faut-il avoir peur de nos enfants? Politiques sécuritaires et enfance* (Paris: La Découverte, 2006), pp. 49–50.

31 In an interview with M. Onfray in *Philosophie Magazine*, April 2007, Nicolas Sarkozy stated: 'I am inclined, for my part, to think that people are born paedophiles and that, by the way, it is a problem that we do not know how to treat this pathology. There are 1,200 or 1,300 young people who commit suicide in France every year and it is not because their parents did not care for them properly, but because, genetically, they had a weakness, they suffered from a prior condition. [. . .] Circumstances do not explain everything; innate tendencies play a huge part.'

32 E. Roudinesco, 'Les 'psy' face à l'idéologie de l'expertise', *Le Monde* (19 January 2008): 22.

EPILOGUE

1 CCNE, "Biométrie, données identifiantes et droits de l'homme", *Avis* 98 (26 April 2007): 17; available at: <www.ccne-ethique.fr>.

2 Ewald F., "Voici venue l'ère du contrôle généralisé", *Enjeux-Les Echos* (1 February 2008): 84–5.

GENERAL BIBLIOGRAPHY BY TOPIC

English translations of works in French or in other languages (when they exist) are indicated after the original.

ACTION ON PUBLIC OPINION

Aronson, J. (1970), *The Press and the Cold War* (New York: The Bobbs-Merrill Co.).

Bernays, E. (2004 [1928]), *Propaganda* (New York: Ig Publishing).

Breton, P. (1997), *La Parole manipulée* (Paris: La Découverte).

Chakotin, S. (1940), *The Rape of the Masses: The Psychology of Totalitarian Political Propaganda* (New York: Alliance/London: Routledge).

Chomsky, N. (1996), *Class Warfare: Interviews with David Barsamian* (New York: Continuum).

Daugherty, W. E. and Janowitz, M. (eds) (1958), *A Psychological Warfare Casebook* (Baltimore, MD: Johns Hopkins University Press, for Operations Research Office, Johns Hopkins University).

Dennis, E. (ed.) (1991), *The Media at War: The Press and the Persian Gulf Conflict* (New York: Columbia University/Gannett Foundation).

Dyer, M. (1959), *The Weapon on the Wall: Rethinking Psychological Warfare* (Baltimore, MD: Johns Hopkins University Press).

Edelman, M. (2001), *The Politics of Misinformation* (Cambridge: Cambridge University Press).

Ellul, J. (1973), *Propagandas*, trans K. Kellen and J. Lerner (New York: Vintage).

Ewen, S. (1976), *Captains of Consciousness: Advertising and the Social Roots of the Consumer Society* (New York: McGraw-Hill).

Fulbright, J. W. (1971), *The Pentagon Propaganda Machine* (New York: Vintage Books).

Herman, E. S. and Chomsky, N. (1988), *Manufacturing Consent: The Political Economy of the Mass Media* (New York: Pantheon Books).

Lasswell, H. (1927), *Propaganda Technique in the World War* (New York: Alfred Knopf Inc.).

Lazarsfeld, P. L. (1952), 'The Prognosis for International Communication Research', *Public Opinion Quarterly* 16: 481–90.
Lerner, D. (1949), *Sykewar: Psychological Warfare against Germany. D-Day to VE-Day* (New York: George W. Stewart, Publisher, Inc.).
Lerner, D. (1958), *The Passing of Traditional Society: Modernizing the Middle East* (New York: Free Press).
Lippmann, W. (1922), *Public Opinion* (London: G. Allen and Unwin).
Lynch, M. (2007), *Voices of the New Arab Public: Iraq, al Jazeera, and Middle East Politics Today* (New York: Columbia University Press).
Mattelart, A. and Mattelart, M. (1990), *The Carnival of Images: Brazilian Television Fiction* (1987), trans. D. Buxton (New York/Westport/London: Bergin and Garvey (an imprint of Greenwood)).
Mattelart, A. and Mattelart, M. (1992), *Rethinking Media Theory* (1986), trans. M. Urquidi and J. A. Cohen (Minneapolis, MN: University of Minnesota Press).
Ramonet, I. (1998), *La tyrannie de la communication* (Paris: Galilée).
Riley, J. W. and Schramm, W. (1951), *The Reds Take a City: The Communist Occupation of Seoul with Eyewitness Accounts* (New Brunswick, NJ: Rutgers University Press).
Schiller, H. (1973), *The Mind Managers* (Boston, MA: Beacon Press).
Stanley Foundation/Institute for Near East & Gulf Military Analysis (2006), *Open Media and Transitioning Societies in the Arab Middle East. Implications for US Security Policy*, available at: <www. Stanleyfoundation.org>.
Virilio, P. (2000), *Strategy of Deception*, trans. C. Turner (London: Verso).

BIOTYPOLOGIES

Canguilhem, G. (1991), *The Normal and the Pathological*, trans. C. R. Fawcett (New York: Zone Books).
Desrosières, A. (2002 [1993]), *The Politics of Large Numbers: A History of Statistical Reasoning*, trans. C. Naish (Cambridge, MA: Harvard University Press).
Dumont, M. (1984), 'Le succès mondain d'une fausse science: la physiognomonie de Johann Kaspar Lavater', *Actes de la recherche en sciences sociales* 54: 2–30.
Ewald, F. (1986), *L'État-providence* (Paris: Fayard).
Harcourt, B. E. (2006), *Against Prediction: Profiling, Policing, and Punishing in an Actuarial Age* (Chicago, IL: Chicago University Press).
Lanteri-Laura, G. (1970), *Histoire de la phrénologie* (Paris: PUF).
Levin, Y. and Lindesmith, A. (1961), 'English Ecology and Criminology of the Past Century', in G. A. Theodorson (ed.), *Studies in Human Ecology* (Evanston, IL: Row, Peterson and Co.), pp. 14–21.
Lombroso, C. (2006 [1876]), *Criminal Man*, trans. M. Gibson and N. Hahn Rafter (Durham, NC: Duke University Press).
Quételet, A. (1835), *Sur l'homme et le développement de ses facultés ou essai de physique sociale* (Paris: Bachelier), 2 vols.
Quételet, A. (1871), *Anthropométrie ou mesure des différentes facultés de l'homme* (Brussels: Muquardt).

CONTROL SOCIETY

Beniger, J. R. (1986), *The Control Revolution: Technological and Economic Origins of the Information Society* (Cambridge, MA: Harvard University Press).

Boetie, E. (de La) (1942 [1576]), *Discourse on Voluntary Servitude*, trans. H. Kurz (New York: Columbia University Press).

Burroughs, W. S. (1961), *The Soft Machine* (New York: Grove Press).

Burroughs W. S. (1975), *The Limits of Control*, available at: <http://limitedcontrol.posterous.com/the-limits-of-control-by-willi>.

Burroughs, W. S. (1985), *The Adding Machine: Selected Essays* (New York: Seaver Books).

Deleuze, G. and Guattari, F. (1994), *What is Philosophy?*, trans. G. Burchell and H. Tomlinson (New York: Columbia University Press).

Deleuze, G. and Parnet, C. (2007), *Dialogues II*, trans. H. Tomlinson (Chicago, IL: Chicago University Press).

Foucault, M. (2007), *Security, Territory, Population*, trans. G. Burchell (London: Palgrave Macmillan).

Foucault, M. (2008), *The Birth of Biopolitics*, trans. G. Burchell (London: Palgrave Macmillan).

Hardt, M. (1998) 'The Global Sociology of Control', *Discourse* 20/3: 177–92.

Heller, T. (ed.) (2006), 'Dossier: Organisation, dispositif, sujet', *Études de communication* 28: 3–155.

Laufer, R. and Paradeise, C. (1982), *Le Prince bureaucrate. Machiavel au pays du marketing*, (Paris: Flammarion).

Mattelart, A. (1991), *Advertising International: The Privatization of Public Space* (1989), trans M. Chanan (London: Routledge).

Pagès, M., Bonetti, M., De Gaulejac, V. and Descendre, D. (1979), *L'Emprise de l'organisation* (Paris: PUF).

Sauvage, A. and Sauvage-Deprez, O. (2006), 'Maternelles sous contrôle: le fichage des enfants', in Gérard Neyrand (ed.), *Faut-il avoir peur de nos enfants? Politiques sécuritaires et enfance* (Paris: La Découverte), pp. 49–50.

COUNTERINSURGENCY

Arquilla, J. and Ronfeldt, D. (2002), *Networks and Netwar: The Future of Terror, Crime and Militancy* (Santa Monica, CA: Rand Corporation).

Clutterbuck, R. (1994), *Terrorism in an Unstable World* (London: Routledge).

Galula, D. (1963), *Pacification in Algeria 1956–1958* (Santa Monica, CA: Rand Corporation; new edn, 2006).

Horowitz, I. L., (ed.), (1967), *The Rise and Fall of Project Camelot* (Cambridge, MA: MIT Press).

Kitson, F. (1971), *Low Intensity Operations: Subversion Insurgency, Peace Keeping* (London: Faber and Faber).

Klare, T. M. (1972), *War without End: American Planning for the Next Vietnam* (New York: Vintage Books).

Némo, J. (1956), 'La guerre dans le milieu social', *Revue de défense nationale* XII (May): 605–24.

Némo J. (1957), 'The Place of Guerrilla Action in War', *Military Review* 37

(November): 99–107; available at: <http://calldp.leavenworth.army.mil/eng_mr/2001060515583052/1957/NOV/digests. pdf >.

Osgood, R. E. (1979), *Limited War Revisited* (Boulder, CO: Westview Press).

Pomeroy, W. J. (1964) *Guerrilla and Counter Guerrilla Warfare* (New York: International Publishers).

Robin, M.-M. (2004), *Escadrons de la mort, l'École française* (Paris: La Découverte}.

Selser, G. (1966), *Espionaje en América Latina, el Pentágono y las técnicas sociológicas* (Buenos Aires: Ediciones Iguazú).

Trinquier, R. (1964), *Modern Warfare: A French View of Counterinsurgency* (1961) (New York: Praeger).

CRISIS

Balandier, G. (1988), *Le Désordre. Éloge du mouvement* (Paris: Fayard).

Beck, U. (2002) 'The Terrorist Threat: World Risk Society Revisited', *Theory, Culture & Society* 19/4: 39–55.

Crozier, M., Huntington, S. P. and Watanuki, J. (1975), *The Crisis of Democracy: Report on the Governability of Democracies to the Trilateral Commission* (New York: New York University Press).

Ewald, F. (2002) 'The Return of Descartes' Malicious Demon: An Outline of a Philosophy of Precaution', in T. Baker and J. Simon (eds.), *Embracing Risk: The Changing Culture of Insurance and Responsibility* (Chicago, IL: University of Chicago Press).

Government of Sweden (1978) *The Vulnerability of the Computerized Society* (Stockholm).

Lagadec, P. (1988), *États d'urgence. Défaillances technologiques et déstabilisation sociale* (Paris: Seuil).

Mattelart, M. (1986), *Women, Media, Crisis: Femininity and Disorder* (London: Comedia).

Montana, P. J. and Roukis, G. S. (eds) (1983), *Managing Terrorism: Strategies for the Corporate Executive* (Westport, CT: Quorum Books).

Morin, E. (ed.) (1968), 'Dossier: Mai 1968. La Prise de parole', *Communications* 12: 2–179.

Raboy, M. and Dagenais, B. (eds) (1992), *Media, Crisis and Democracy* (London: Sage).

Schiller, H. (1984), *Information and the Crisis Economy* (Norwood, NJ: Ablex).

Tiryakian, E. A. (ed.) (1984), *The Global Crisis: Sociological Analyses and Responses* (Leiden: E.J. Brill).

CROWD PSYCHOLOGY

Freud, S. (1955 [1921]), 'Group Psychology and the Analysis of the Ego', *The Complete Psychological Works of Sigmund Freud*, trans. J. Strachey with A. Freud (London: Hogarth Press), vol. 18.

Le Bon, G. (1894), *Lois psychologiques de l'évolution des peuples* (Paris: Alcan).

Le Bon, G. (1977 [1895]), *The Crowd: A Study of the Popular Mind* (Dunwoody, GA: Norman S. Berg).
Lombroso, C. and Laschi, R. (1887), 'Le délit politique', *Actes du premier congrès international d'anthropologie criminelle (Biologie et sociologie) Rome, novembre 1885* (Torino: Fratelli Bocca).
Nye, R. A. (1975), *The Origins of Crowd Psychology: Gustave Le Bon and the Crisis of Mass Democracy in the Third Republic* (London: Sage).
Sighele, S. (1901), *La Foule criminelle. Essai de psychologie collective* (Paris: Alcan, 2nd edn).
Tarde, G. (1890), *Les Lois de l'imitation* (Paris: Alcan).
Tarde, G. (1893), 'Les crimes des foules', *Actes du troisième Congrès d'anthropologie criminelle, Bruxelles, août 1892* (Brussels: F. Hayez).
Tarde, G. (1901), *L'Opinion et la foule* (Paris: Alcan).
Van Ginneken, J. (1992), *Crowds, Psychology and Politics 1871–1899* (Cambridge: Cambridge University Press).

DYSTOPIAS

Boye, K. (1966 [1940]), *Kallocain*, trans. G. Lannestock (Madison, WI: University of Wisconsin Press).
Huxley, A. (1998 [1932]), *Brave New World* (New York: Harper Perennial).
Kafka, F. (2006 [1925]), *The Trial*, trans. D. Wyllie (South Australia: University of Adelaide Library (ebooks@Adelaide)).
Orwell, G. (1989 [1949]), *Nineteen Eighty-Four* (London: Penguin).
Zamyatin, Y. (1972 [1920]), *We*, trans. M. Ginsburg (New York: Viking Press).

EMPIRE

ALAI (Agencia Latinoamericana de Información) (2007), 'Militarización-Bases-Guerra. Propuestas sociales', Quito, *América Latina en movimiento*, nn. 416–17.
Arquilla, J. and Ronfeldt, D. (1999), *The Emergence of Noopolitik: Toward an American Information Strategy* (Santa Monica, CA: Rand Corp.).
Brzezinski, Z. (1969), *Between Two Ages. America's Role in the Technetronic Era* (New York: Viking Press).
Hardt, M. and Negri, A. (2000), *Empire* (Cambridge, MA: Harvard University Press).
Johnson, C. (2006), *Nemesis: The Last Days of the American Republic* (New York: Metropolitan Books).
Julien, C. (1968), *L'Empire américain* (Paris: Grasset).
Klare, M. T. (2001), *Resource Wars: The New Landscape of Global Conflict* (New York: Henry Holt and Co.).
Liberman, J. (ed.) (2004), *Démythifier l'universalité des valeurs américaines* (Paris: Parangon).
Mattelart, A. (1979), *Multinational Corporations & the Control of Culture*, trans. M. Chanan (Brighton: Harvester Press).
Mumford, L. (1974), *The Pentagon of Power* (New York: Harcourt, Brace and Janovich).

Nye, J. S. Jr (1990), *Bound to Lead: The Changing Nature of American Power* (New York: Basic Books).

Paret, P. (ed.) (1986), *Makers of Modern Strategy: From Machiavelli to the Nuclear Age* (Princeton, NJ: Princeton University Press).

Serfati, C. (2004), *Impérialisme et militarisme. Actualité du XXIᵉ siècle* (Lausanne: Éditions Page Deux).

Spykman, N. J. (1942), *America's Strategy in World Politics: The United States and the Balance of Power* (New York: Harcourt, Brace & World Inc.).

EXCEPTION

Agamben, G. (2005), *State of Exception*, trans. K. Attell (Chicago, IL: University of Chicago Press).

Benjamin, W. (1994), 'Theories of German Fascism', trans. J. Wikoff and U. Zimmerman, in A. Kaes, M. Jay and E. Dimendberg (eds) (1994), *The Weimar Republic Sourcebook* (Berkeley, CA: University of California Press).

Danet, J. (2006), *Justice pénale, le tournant* (Paris: Gallimard).

Jünger, E. (1980), *Der Weltstaat. Die Totale Mobilmachung* (Stuttgart: Ernst Klett Verlag).

Kitchen, M. (1976), *The Silent Dictatorship: The Politics of the German High Command under Hindenburg and Ludendorff, 1916–1918* (New York: Holmes & Meier/London: Croom Helm).

Ludendorff, E. (1936), *The Nation at War* (London: Hutchinson).

Monod, J. C. (2007), *Penser l'ennemi, affronter l'exception. Réflexions critiques sur l'actualité de Carl Schmitt* (Paris: La Découverte).

Paye, J.-C. (2004), *La Fin de l'État de droit. La lutte antiterroriste: de l'état d'exception à la dictature* (Paris: La Dispute).

FORCED DISAPPEARANCES AND TORTURE

Algeri, V. (ed.) (2005), 'La Tortura oggi nel mondo', *Fondazione internazionale Lelio Basso* XI 2–3: 3–31; available at: <www.internazionaleleliobasso.it/. . ./ Fondazione_2-3_05.pdf>.

Ashplant, T. G. et al. (eds) (2000), *The Politics of War Memory and Commemoration* (London: Routledge).

Bigo, D. (ed.) (1994), 'Dossier: Les disparitions', *Cultures et Conflits* 13–14; available at: <http://conflits.revues.org/index58.html>.

Caloni, S. (1999), *Los Años del Lobo. Operación Condor* (Buenos Aires: Ediciones Continente).

Calveiro, P. (1998), *Poder y desaparición. Los campos de concentración en Argentina* (Buenos Aires: Colihue).

Dinges, J. (2004), *The Condor Years: How Pinochet and His Allies Brought Terrorism to Three Continents* (New York: The New Press).

Feld, C. (2002), *Del Estrado a la pantalla: Las imágenes del juicio a los ex-comandantes en Argentina* (Buenos Aires/Madrid: Siglo XXI Editores).

Garcia Castro, A. (2002), *La Mort lente des disparus au Chili sous la négociation civils-militaires (1973–2002)* (Paris: Maisonneuve-Larose).

Garcia Castro, A. (2006), '"Qu'il nous soit permis d'écrire avant de disparaître",

Argentine, 1976–2006', *Cultures et Conflits* 62; available at: <http://conflits. revues.org/pdf/2071>.

Jelin, E. (2002), *Los Trabajos de la memoria* (Buenos Aires/Madrid: Siglo XXI Editores).

Pachet, P. (1993), 'La pensée de la torture', *Encyclopaedia Universalis* ('Organum'), vol. 17.

Rivas Sánchez, F. and Reimann Weigert, E. (1976), *Las Fuerzas armadas de Chile: Un caso de penetración imperialista* (Mexico City: Ediciones 75).

Robin, M.-M. (2004), *Escadrons de la mort, l'École française* (Paris: La Découverte).

Trinquier, R. (1964 [1961]), *Modern Warfare: A French View of Counterinsurgency* (New York: Praeger).

Vidal-Naquet, P. (1972), *La Torture sous la République* (Paris: Maspero).

IDENTIFICATION

Alberganti, M. (2007), *Sous l'œil des puces. La RFID et la démocratie* (Paris: Actes Sud).

Bertillon, A. (1887), *Anthropological Descriptions: New Method of Determining Individual Identity. Conference given at the International Penitentiary Congress at Rome, 22 November 1885* (Melun, France: Administrative Printing).

Bertillon, A. (1890), *La Photographie judiciaire* (Paris: Gauthier-Villars).

Bigo, D. (ed.) (2001), 'Dossier: Défense et identités: un contexte de sécurité global', *Cultures et Conflits* 44; available at: <http://conflits.revues.org/ index37.html>.

Caplan, J. and Torpey, J. (eds) (2001), *Documenting Individual Identity: The Development of State Practices since the French Revolution* (Princeton, NJ: Princeton University Press).

CCNE (2007), 'Biométrie, données identifiantes et droits de l'homme', *Avis* 98 (26 April); available at: <www.ccne-ethique.fr>.

Ceyhan, A. (ed.) (2006), 'Dossier: 'Identifier et surveiller'', *Cultures et Conflits* 64; available at: <http://conflits.revues.org/index2123.html>.

Piazza, P. (2004), *Histoire de la carte nationale d'identité* (Paris: Odile Jacob).

Reyna Almandos, L. (1932), *Dactiloscopia argentina. Su historia e influencia en la legislación* (La Plata: Universidad nacional de La Plata).

Schuller, W., Fereday, L. and Scheithauer, R. (ed.) (2001), *Interpol Handbook on DNA Data Exchange and Practice. Recommendations from the Interpol DNA Monitoring Expert Group* (Lyon, France: International Criminal Police Organization, 1st edn).

Vigier, P. and Faure, A. (eds) (1987), *Maintien de l'ordre et polices en France et en Europe au XIXᵉ siècle* (Paris: Créaphis).

Vucetich, J. (1929), *Proyecto de ley de registro general de identificación* (La Plata: Universidad nacional de La Plata).

INFORMATION TECHNOLOGY AND FREEDOM

Juffé, M. (ed.) (2001), 'Dossier: La communication entre libéralisme et démocratie', *Terminal* 84: 3–180.

Madec, A. (1982), *Les Flux transfrontières de données* (Paris: La Documentation française).

Mattelart, A. and Schmucler, H. (1985), *Communication and Information Technologies: Freedom of Choice for Latin America?*, trans. D. Buxton (Norwood, NJ: Ablex).

Miège, B. (ed.) (2000), 'Dossier: Questionner la société de l'information', *Réseaux* 101: 9–38.

Nora, S. and Minc, A. (1980), *The Computerization of Society*, Introduction by D. Bell (Cambridge, MA: MIT Press).

Rodotà, S. (1999), *La Démocratie électronique* (Rennes: Éditions Apogée).

Virilio, P. (2005), *The Information Bomb*, trans. C. Turner (London: Verso).

Vitalis, A. (1988), *Informatique, pouvoir et libertés* (Paris: Économica, 2nd edn).

NATIONAL SECURITY

Aronson, J. (1970), *The Press and the Cold War* (New York: The Bobbs-Merrill Co.).

Blanquart, P., Valier, A., Vasthy, D. (eds) (1974), 'Dossier: L'enjeu latino-américain après le coup de Santiago', *Politique aujourd'hui* 1–2 (January–February): 1–144.

Comblin, J. (1977), *Le Pouvoir militaire en Amérique latine. L'idéologie de la sécurité nationale* (Paris: J.-P. Delarge/ Editions universitaires).

Deutsch, K. W. and Foltz, W. J. (1962), *Nationbuilding* (New York: Atherton Press).

Golbery do Couto e Silva (1967), *Geopolítica do Brasil* (Rio de Janeiro, José Olympio, 2nd edn).

Hinkelammert, F. J. (1981), *Las Armas ideológicas de la muerte* (San José,Costa Rica: DEI (Departamento Ecuménico de Investigaciones), 2nd edn).

Leffler, M. P. and Painter, D. S. (eds) (1994), *Origins of the Cold War: An International History* (London: Routledge).

McNamara, R. S. (1968), *The Essence of Security* (New York: Harper & Row).

Mauro, Marini R. et al. (1975), 'Dossier: Chili', *Les Temps Modernes* XXX 342: 618–846.

Meyer, J. (ed.) (1977) 'Dossier: L'Amérique latine', *Critique* xxxiii, 363–4: 705–875.

Pye, L. (1962), *Politics, Personality, and Nation Building* (New Haven, CT: Yale University Press).

Rodberg, L. S. and Shearer, D. (eds) (1970), *The Pentagon Watchers* (New York: Doubleday Anchor).

US Senate (1975), *Foreign and Military Intelligence. Book I, Final Report of the Select Committee to Study Governmental Operations with Respect to Intelligence Activities, April 26, 1976* (Washington, DC: US Government Printing).

Virilio, P. (1983), *Pure War* (New York: Semiotexte).

NETWORK GLOBALIZATION

Arquilla, J. and Ronfeldt, D. (2001), *Networks and Netwars: The Future of Terror, Crime and Militancy* (Santa Monica, CA: Rand Corp.).

Campbell, D. (2001), *Surveillance électronique planétaire* (Paris: Allia).
Castells, M. (1996–7), *The Information Age: Economy, Society and Culture*. 3 vols (Malden, MA/ Oxford: Blackwell).
Chesnais, F. (ed.) (2004), *La Finance mondialisée* (Paris: La Découverte).
Freitag, M. and Pineault, É. (eds) (1999), *Le Monde enchaîné* (Montréal: Éditions Nota Bene).
Kleck, V. (2007), *Numérique et Cie. Sociétés en réseaux et gouvernance* (Paris: Éditions Charles Léopold Meyer).
Mattelart, A. (1999), *Histoire de l'utopie planétaire, De la cité prophétique à la société globale* (Paris: La Découverte).
Mattelart, A. (2000), *Networking the World 1794–2000*, trans. L. Carrey-Libbrecht and J. A. Cohen (Minneapolis, MN: University of Minnesota Press).
Mattelart, A. (2003), *The Information Society: An Introduction*, trans S. Taponier and J. A. Cohen (London: Sage).
Mattelart, T. (ed.) (2002), *La Mondialisation des médias contre la censure* (Paris/ Brussels: INA/De Boeck).
Mattelart, A. and Tremblay, G. (eds) (2003), *Globalisme et pluralisme. Communication, démocratie et globalisation* (Québec: Presses de l'Université Laval).
Musso, P. (1997), *Télécommunications et philosophie des réseaux. La postérité paradoxale de Saint-Simon* (Paris: PUF).
Schiller, D. (1999), *Digital Capitalism: Networking the Global Market System* (Cambridge, MA: MIT Press).

NEW DOMESTIC ORDER

Boure, R. (1978), *Les Interdictions professionnelles en Allemagne fédérale* (Paris: Maspero).
Clutterbuck, R. (1975), *Living with Terrorism* (London: Faber and Faber).
Julien, C. (ed.) (1979), 'Dossier: Le nouvel ordre intérieur ', *Le Monde diplomatique* (March) XXVI 300: 5–10.
Lascoumes, P. (ed.) (1978), 'Dossier: L'Europe de la répression ou l'insécurité d'état', *Actes* 17 (spring): 2–64.
Laqueur, W. (1987), *The Age of Terrorism* (Boston, MA: Little, Brown and Co.).
Schlesinger, P., Murdock, G. and Elliott, P. (1983), *Televising Terrorism: Political Violence in Popular Culture* (London: Comedia).
Soulier, G. (1986), 'Le terrorisme et l'évolution des droits et libertés en Europe', in M.-B. Tahon and A. Corten (eds), *L'Italie: le philosophe et le gendarme, Actes du Colloque de Montréal* (Montréal: VLB éditeur).
Université de Vincennes (1980), *Le Nouvel Ordre intérieur* (Paris: Alain Moreau).

RESISTANCE

ACLU (American Civil Liberties Union) (2004), *The Surveillance-Industrial Complex: How the American Government is Conscripting Businesses and*

Individuals in the Construction of a Surveillance Society, written by Jay Stanley (New York: ACLU); available at: <http://www.aclu.org/SafeandFree>.

Balibar, E. (2003), *We, the People of Europe: Reflections on Transnational Citizenship* (Princeton, NJ: Princeton University Press).

Bigo, D. and Walker, R. B. J. (2006), 'Liberté et sécurité en Europe: enjeux contemporains', *Cultures et Conflits* 61; available at: <http://conflits.revues.org/index2040.html>.

C.A.S.E. Collective (2006), 'Critical Approach to Security in Europe: A Networked Manifesto', *Security Dialogue* 37/4: 443–87.

Chandler, A. D. Jr and Mazlish, B. (eds) (2005), *Leviathans: Multinational Corporations and the New Global History* (Cambridge: Cambridge University Press).

Granjon, F. (ed.) (2007), 'Dossier: Société de l'information. Faut-il avoir peur des médias?', *Contretemps* 18 (February): 12–98.

ICAMS (International Campaign Against Mass Surveillance) (2006), *Développement d'un vaste système de fichage et de surveillance à grande échelle*, available at: <http://www.i-cams.org/About_ICAMS.html>.

Keck, M. and Sikkink, K. (1998), *Activists Beyond Borders: Advocacy Networks in International Politics* (Ithaca, NY: Cornell University Press).

Maler, H. and Schwartz, A. (Acrimed) (2006), *Médias en campagne. Retour sur le referendum de 2005* (Paris: Syllepse).

MARCUSE (Mouvement autonome de réflexion critique à l'usage des survivants de l'économie) (2004), *De la Misère humaine en milieu publicitaire. Comment le monde se meurt de notre mode de vie* (Paris: La Découverte).

Mattelart, A. (2007) *Diversité culturelle et mondialisation* (Paris: La Découverte, 2nd edn).

Piazza, P. (2006), 'Les résistances au projet INES', *Cultures et Conflits* 64: 65–76.

Vitalis, A. and Proulx, S. (eds) (1999), *Vers une citoyenneté simulée. Médias, réseaux et communication* (Rennes: Apogée).

SECRET

Authier, M. and Thonon, M. (1982), *Secret et sécurité* (Paris: Centre de recherche/université Paris-VIII, Service de la prospective et études économiques (SPES), Direction générale des télécommunications).

Canetti, E. (1962), *Crowd and Power*, trans. C. Stewart (New York: Viking Press).

Deleuze, G. and Guattari, F. (2004), *A Thousand Plateaus*, trans. B. Massumi (New York: Continuum).

Moynihan, D. P. (1998) *Secrecy: The American Experience* (New Haven, CT: Yale University Press).

Nixon, R. (1990), *The Real War* (New York: Simon and Schuster); 1st edn, 1980.

Simmel, G., (1906) 'The Sociology of Secrecy and of Secret Societies', *American Journal of Sociology* 11 (The Mead Project); available at: <http://www.brocku.ca/MeadProject/Simmel/Simmel_1906.html>.

US Senate (1972), *USIA Appropriations Authorization, Fiscal Year 1973, Hearing before the Committee on Foreign Relations, March 20–21 and 28, 1972* (Washington, DC: US Government Printing).

SURVEILLANCE SOCIETY

Bentham, J. (1995), *Panopticon, in* M. Bozovic (ed.), *The Panopticon Writings* (London: Verso).

Elias, N. (1994 [1939]), *The Civilizing Process: The History of Manners and State Formation and Civilization*, trans. E. Jephcott (Oxford: Blackwell).

Evans, R. (1971), 'Bentham's Panopticon: An Incident in the Social History of Architecture', *Architectural Association Quarterly* III/2: 21–37.

Foucault, M. (1979 [1975]), *Discipline and Punish: The Birth of the Prison*, trans A. Sheridan (London: Penguin).

Higgs, E. (2001), 'The Rise of the Information State: The Development of Central State Surveillance of the Citizen in England, 1500–2000', *The Journal of Historical Sociology* 14 (June): 175–97.

Lyon, D. (1994), *The Electronic Eye: The Rise of Surveillance Society* (Minneapolis, MN: University of Minnesota Press).

Lyon, D. (2007), *Surveillance Studies. An Overview* (Cambridge: Polity).

Mattelart, A. (1996 [1994]), *The Invention of Communication*, trans. S. Emanuel (Minneapolis, MN: University of Minnesota Press).

Murakami-Wood, D. (ed.) (2006), *A Report on the Surveillance Society* (September); available at: <http://www.ico...uksurveillance_society_full_report_2006.pdf> and at: <http://www.dataprotection.ie/viewdoc.asp?DpcOD=386

Sainati, G. and Schalchli, U. (2007), *La Décadence sécuritaire* (Paris: La Fabrique).

Wacquant, L. (2002), *Prisons of Poverty* (Minneapolis, MN: University of Minnesota Press).

TECHNOCRACY

Bell, D. (1973), *The Coming of Post-Industrial Society: A Venture in Social Forecasting* (New York: Basic Books); new edn, 1999.

Chandler, Jr. A. D. (1977), *The Visible Hand: The Managerial Revolution in American Business* (Cambridge, MA: The Belknap Press of Harvard University Press).

Gramsci, A. (1973 [1929]), 'Americanism and Fordism', in Q. Hoare and G. Nowell Smith (eds), *Selections from the Prison Notebooks of Antonio Gramsci* (London: Lawrence and Wishart), pp. 277–318.

Maier, C. S. (1970), 'Between Taylorism and Technocracy: European Ideologies and the Vision of Industrial Productivity in the 1920s', *The Journal of Contemporary History* 5/2: 27–61.

Friedmann, G. (1949) 'Les technocrates et la civilisation technicienne', in G. Gurvitch (ed.), *Industrialisation et technocratie* (Paris: Armand Colin), pp. 41–62.

Rabinbach, A. (1990), *The Human Motor. Energy, Fatigue, and the Origins of Modernity* (New York: Basic Books).

Robins, K. and Webster, F. (1999), *Times of Technoculture: From the Information Society to Virtual Life* (London: Routledge).

Yates, J. A. (1989). *Control through Communication: The Rise of System in American Management* (Baltimore, MD: Johns Hopkins University Press).

231

GENERAL BIBLIOGRAPHY BY TOPIC

A FEW WEBSITES

INFORMATION SOCIETY

Campaign for Communication Rights in Information Society (CRIS): <http://www.crisinfo.org>.
Droits et libertés face à l'informatisation de la société (DELIS): <http://delis.sgdg.org>.
Electronic Privacy Information Center (EPIC): <http://www.epic.org>.
World Summit of Information Society (WSIS): <http://www.itu.int/wsis>.

SURVEILLANCE SOCIETY

Challenge, interdisciplinary research network: <http://www.libertysecurity.org>.
International Campaign Against Mass Surveillance (ICAMS): <http://www.i-cams.org/About_ICAMS.html>.
<http://www.sciencescitoyennes.org>
<www.statewatch.org>

MEDIA AND INDEPENDENT MEDIA CRITIQUES

<http://www.disinfo.com>
<http://www.freepress.org>
<http://www.indymedia.org>

INDEX